VERY LIKE A WHALE

VERY LIKE A WHALE

The Assessment of Writing Programs

EDWARD M. WHITE
NORBERT ELLIOT
IRVIN PECKHAM

UTAH STATE UNIVERSITY PRESS
Logan

© 2015 by the University Press of Colorado
Published by Utah State University Press

An imprint of University Press of Colorado
5589 Arapahoe Avenue, Suite 206C
Boulder, Colorado 80303

 The University Press of Colorado is a proud member of
The Association of American University Presses.

The University Press of Colorado is a cooperative publishing enterprise supported,
in part, by Adams State University, Colorado State University, Fort Lewis College,
Metropolitan State University of Denver, Regis University, University of Colorado,
University of Northern Colorado, Utah State University, and Western State Colorado
University.

The paper used in this publication meets the minimum requirements of the American
National Standard for Information Sciences—Permanence of Paper for Printed Library
Materials. ANSI Z39.48–1992

ISBN: 978-0-87421-985-2 (paperback)
ISBN: 978-0-87421-986-9 (ebook)

Library of Congress Cataloging-in-Publication Data

White, Edward M. (Edward Michael), 1933–
  Very like a whale : the assessment of writing programs / Edward M. White, Norbert
Elliot, Irvin Peckham.
    pages cm
  ISBN 978-0-87421-985-2 (paperback) — ISBN 978-0-87421-986-9 (ebook)
1. English language—Rhetoric—Study and teaching (Higher)—Evaluation.
2. Academic writing—Study and teaching (Higher)—Evaluation. 3. Report writing—
Study and teaching (Higher)—Evaluation. I. Elliot, Norbert. II. Peckham, Irvin. III.
Title.
  PE1404.W484 2015
  808'.0420711—dc23
                              2014025859

Cover photograph © Nick Stubbs / Shutterstock.

CONTENTS

VERY LIKE A WHALE

INTRODUCTION

On July 26, 1602, a play entitled *The Revenge of Hamlet Prince [of] Denmark* was entered in the Stationers' Register by the printer James Roberts. The play was printed in 1604, most probably from the author's own manuscript. The existence of an unauthorized text published in 1603 written by "William Shake-speare" gives a clue to the first performance of the play in 1601. That text's reference to children's acting companies, then in great popularity, also provides some evidence for the play's completion by mid-1601, with performance soon following (Edwards 1985).

The series of tenuous claims about the date of completion and performance of *Hamlet* are accompanied by nuanced arguments about the meaning of the play. In the eighteenth century, Samuel Johnson despised the "useless and wanton cruelty" Hamlet shows toward Ophelia, daughter of the digressive Polonius and young woman in waiting to be the wife of the Denmark's tragic prince (Furness 1877, 145). In the nineteenth century, Samuel Taylor Coleridge found in Hamlet someone who, although he knows Uncle Claudius has murdered his father and married his mother by the end of the first act, is incapable of revenge. Four acts and two scenes worth of contemplation by Hamlet on being and not being preceding the murder of Claudius led Coleridge to characterize Hamlet as a character of "great, enormous intellectual activity, and a consequent proportionate aversion to real action" (155). For William Hazlitt, Hamlet's thoughts are "as real as our own thoughts. . . . It is *we* who are Hamlet" (155).

In the twentieth century, Oxford University's A. C. Bradley (1949) published *Shakespearean Tragedy,* thus beginning a new tradition of literary studies: authoritative analysis by men employed in newly created departments of English to tackle the job of professional criticism.

Under the direction of literary scholars throughout the twentieth century, attention turned from historical criticism to formalism, from psychoanalysis to poststructuralism, as various forms of criticism emerged. In the twenty-first century, other voices guide us, such as Margaret Litvin (2011) and her analysis of *Hamlet* as an Arab political text embodying a global kaleidoscope of frustration and hope. There is also the singular

DOI: 10.7330/9780874219869.c000

voice of the great Longinian critic Harold Bloom (2011). Reminding us that we turn to literature to learn lessons of our better selves, Bloom finds that Hamlet's consciousness "turns even more inward, away from credences and into the labyrinth of questionings" (87). For the Sterling Professor of Humanities at Yale University, celebration of the sublime serves as the "supreme aesthetic virtue," one associated with "a certain affective and cognitive response" (16). And so it is, for Bloom, that Hamlet's soliloquies are masterpieces of Shakespeare the thinker.

The three authors of the book you are about to read earned doctorates in literature in departments of English at Harvard University (White), the University of Tennessee (Elliot), and the University of California, San Diego (Peckham). The voices they hear are similar to those heard by Bloom. With AARP cards embedded firmly in their wallets, the three seniors, formally educated in literary studies, selected a passage from *Hamlet* for the title of this book. Here, they follow Bloom in believing that the Age of Resentment is limited in its ability to advance our thinking and that attention to the particular—in both its familiarity and sublimity—is a good way, in Bloom's words, to transport and elevate readers (Bloom 2011, 16). From act 3, scene 2, here is the passage from which we take our cue:

> *HAMLET*. Do you see yonder cloud that's almost in shape of a camel?
>
> *POLONIUS*. By t'mass, and 'tis like a camel indeed.
>
> *HAMLET*. Methinks it is like a weasel.
>
> *POLONIUS*. It is backed like a weasel.
>
> *HAMLET*. Or like a whale?
>
> *POLONIUS*. Very like a whale. (Edwards 1985 3. 2. 340–45)

Everything is best understood in context. By this point in the play, Hamlet has returned from his studies in Wittenberg to find chaos unleashed in his home; has met the Ghost of his dead father; and has witnessed his uncle's guilty behavior. Later in the scene, Hamlet will kill Polonius mistakenly, believing he is Claudius hidden behind a curtain in his mother's private apartment. The brief scene between Hamlet and Polonius occurs at a turning point in the play, one in which past and future swirl into that labyrinth of questions.

There is surely some sycophancy in the exchange between archetypal Western intellectual and court bumbler, as Phillip Edwards (1985) points out in his edition of the play. But there is also both transience and indeterminacy. "A cloud is whatever you think it to be," Edwards writes," and, like the authenticity of the Ghost, one's view of it changes all the time" (180).

Complexity and contingency, irony and indeterminacy—the perfect passage indeed for a book about action that must be taken in uncertain times, in which claims are tenuous and logic nuanced, in which language must be fluid to encompass new ideas.

OUR AUDIENCE

The topic of this book is the assessment of writing programs in postsecondary American education. This is a book written for those who design, redesign, and assess writing programs. It is for teachers of writing and writing researchers, those we have often found to be one and the same person. By centralizing the writing program as integral to the fulfillment of an institution's mission, ours is a book written to end the too-often terrible isolation and disenfranchisement of individuals and the programs in which they serve (Dryer 2008; Micciche 2002). Written with the firm belief that writing program administrators are among the most important people on any campus, we will present new models, strategies, and language that will continue to empower our profession through the unique lens of writing program assessment. Inevitably, we will be dealing from time to time with the vexed issue of writing assessment, but that is a somewhat different topic, now dealt with in the many recent books and articles we will reference in the following five chapters. The assessment of student writing may be and usually is part of a program assessment, but only a piece of the puzzle. As a distinct genre, we define writing program assessment as the process of documenting and reflecting on the impact of the program's coordinated efforts. As a proposed innovation, we believe this assessment is best done by those who share and contribute to the program.

Because a new era of assessment has begun, we believe that new conceptualizations—shown in the thirteen figures and seventeen tables we present throughout the book and the new vocabulary we use in our glossary—are needed. As a service to our profession, this book seeks to make clear and available recent and important concepts associated with assessment to those in the profession of rhetoric and composition/writing studies. In the chapters that follow, we provide strategies that will allow readers to gather information about the relative success of a writing program in achieving its identified program goals. Ever attentive to audience, we firmly believe writing programs must provide valid evidence that the program is serving students, instructors, administrators, alumni, accreditors, and policymakers.

Lofty aims indeed. How to get such dreamy stuff in play for the deliberation that will surely follow as you read this book?

Imagine running into the three authors, alone or together, between sessions at the annual meeting of the Conference on College Composition and Communication. Or, perhaps, at dinner after a summer meeting of the Council of Writing Program Administrators. Or over late-night coffee and drinks after a winter meeting of the Modern Language Association. Here we find the most immediate audience and tone for our book: chatting with colleagues and students. Let's imagine just such a conversation:

> *YOU.* So, how are you three? I hear you have a new book on writing assessment.
>
> *US.* Men of our age flock together; we are birds of a feather, as the old proverb says. At our meetings the tale is common: We cannot eat. We cannot drink. The pleasures of youth and love are fled away. There was a good time once, but now that is gone, and life is no longer life.
>
> *YOU.* Sounds dreadful.
>
> *US.* Not really. It's just amusing to recollect the enduring wisdom of *The Republic*. But, to your observation that we have a new book on writing assessment, we do not. We have a new book on writing program assessment.
>
> *YOU.* What's the difference?
>
> *US.* Writing assessment is an event—something undertaken at a particular time for a particular purpose. Writing program assessment is a longitudinal process of accountability—of documenting all the efforts a writing program undertakes to create important consequences for its many constituencies.
>
> *YOU.* Be specific.
>
> *US.* A writing assessment episode produces student scores. A writing program assessment uses those scores and many other sources of evidence to demonstrate how the program serves its community.
>
> *YOU.* More specific.
>
> *US.* A writing assessment episode may be documented in a table of scores, disaggregated according to important student populations, including mean, standard deviation, and range. Assessment of a writing program certainly includes such tables; however, the assessment might also include evidence such as a table in which the salary and benefits of those who work in the program are compared to data from the American Association of University Professors annual report on the economic status of the profession.
>
> *YOU.* Big difference. So, this new book is about justice?

US. It is about the kinds of evidence needed to argue for a variety of aims, justice included. As ethics goes, our position is more deonto-logical than not.

YOU. What's with the vocabulary? First, there were the statistical terms. Now, there are the philosophical ones. Why not just speak simply?

US. We are speaking as clearly as we can to try to capture the complex concepts involved with writing program assessment. But we cannot always speak simply because the cultural, social, and economic cir-cumstances surrounding writing programs are not simple. We must embrace fluidity.

YOU. Example?

US. When we teach and assess writing, we are imagining a certain embodiment of writing. A long history of measurement tells us the best way of talking about such an embodiment is to refer to the con-struct of writing. Once that vocabulary is in place, we can then talk about how the construct is modeled for students and measured in research regarding their performance. We can then use that knowl-edge to improve the program and those it serves.

YOU. And what is your evidence that any of this is going to work? Isn't this all just the trademark of positivism?

US. Accountability always works. The more we communicate what we do, the better for all of us. That communication can take place in many ways, and some of those ways are going to be empirical.

YOU. We'll be the judge of that.

US. Thus shall we live dear to one another.

Any tendency toward querulousness will be overcome, we promise, by the good-natured banter of such conversation and the sincere desire to advance new ways of thinking about writing program assessment.

OUR FIELD

When the three authors were in school, the field we now belong to did not exist. Setting out with a bit of reflection about our field will help us map out the voyage.

The successful efforts of the Visibility Project, begun by the Consortium of Doctoral Programs in Rhetoric and Composition in 2004, led to a presence for our field in the National Research Council's taxonomy of research disciplines and the Classification of Instructional Programs (CIP). In the former, the term *rhetoric and composition* designates a single phrase for our field. More comprehensive is the series of terms used in the CIP, so we provide them here and will return to them from time to time in the book:

- 23.13 rhetoric and composition/writing studies;
  - ○ 23.1301 writing, general;
  - ○ 23.1302 creative writing;
  - ○ 23.1303 professional, technical, business, and scientific writing;
  - ○ 23.1304 rhetoric and composition;
  - ○ 23.1399 rhetoric and composition/writing studies, other

Classified as part of CIP code 23—English language and literature/letters—the new code (23.13) was parallel with literature (23.14) and established for us a room of our own. In their description of what Louise Wetherbee Phelps and John M. Ackerman term the "epideictic moment of 2010," the 23.13 series was approved for coding within the CIP system and is now firmly in place. Here practitioners can express "dynamic multiple identities," Phelps and Ackerman write, "capturing the variance and differentiation of the field as represented in its instructional programs, both general and specialized" (Phelps and Ackerman 2010, 200). There is even a code for "other" that will allow the field to emerge as changes occur in the curricular environment, advances are made in research and theory, and multidisciplinary collaborations arise. When we use the term *our field* in this book, it is to these CIP codes—and all they contain—that we proudly refer.

Within the curriculum of the institutions of the Consortium of Doctoral Programs in Rhetoric and Composition, students of seminars with titles such as Research Methods in Rhetoric and Composition—with their emphasis on empirical methods—surely constitute an audience for our book. But, at present, that audience is small, and it is our hope that the ideas advanced in this book will encourage all degree programs in rhetoric and composition/writing studies to require courses in quantitative and qualitative empirical methods. Because assessment is a field related to so many others in both research and theoretical developments, readers may also be found within these fields of study included in the CIP: applied linguistics (16.0105); business administration and management (25.0201); cognitive psychology and psycholinguistics (42.2701); computer and information sciences (11.0101); educational assessment, testing, and measurement (13.0604); and psychometrics and quantitative psychology (42.1901). In addition, academic administrators interested in integrating writing programs—often one of the most accountable instructional programs on campus—into the accreditation processes of degree programs and institutions themselves will find this book helpful. Administrators will find that investment in a writing program is one of the best investments they will ever make.

OUR ORIENTATION

Important advances in research and theory have taken place since the publication of *Evaluating College Writing Programs* by Witte and Faigley (1983) and Edward White's (1989) *Developing Successful College Writing Programs.* In a review of books about writing program administrators, Shirley Rose (2012) notes the significance of understanding writing program administration as a unique field. Specifically identified in CIP 23.1304, the field of writing program administration advances as it extends its influences, develops its history, and prepares its practitioners, just as Rose suggests. The conclusion of Rose's review is particularly important: "We fail in meeting our responsibilities to our graduate students in rhetoric and composition studies if they finish their degrees without coming to an understanding—whether it be through WPA [writing program administrator] course work, internships, or apprenticeships—that much of their work in the field will be managerial, either in formal WPA positions or in informal managerial positions as teachers in writing programs and/or writing researchers" (229). Our orientation in this book is aligned with that position: we meet our responsibilities to all key stakeholders—advisory boards, administration, faculty, parents, professional organizations, students, and the public—if we ensure that writing programs embrace research and management as equal and interdependent, a position taken in the integrative approach of *A Rhetoric for Writing Program Administrators* (Malenczyk 2013). We hope readers will discover that the main purpose of this book—to advance the concept of writing program assessment as a unique genre in which constructs are modeled for students within unique institutional ecologies—will help a wide range of audiences meet those responsibilities.

Our experience with writing program assessment convinces us that it needs to be an expansive and inclusive effort, one based in the local campus environment yet designed for comparative reporting. Such assessment encompasses documentation, including representation of student work, acknowledgment that students learn about writing in many ways within and beyond the curriculum, awareness of the digital context within which we all now function, and attention to the diverse audiences that will read and respond to the information writing program administrators produce. We therefore advance a powerful genre of research using methods and methodologies best begun and refined locally, with the results reported in formats that allow collaboration and accountability to be built within and among campuses.

Writing the foreword for Stephen P. Witte and Lester Faigley's volume thirty years ago, Lee Odell (1983) began with the realization that "it becomes clear that we may no longer assume that evaluating student writing is the same thing as evaluating a composition program" (ix). He then proceeded to pose questions as relevant now as they were then: What do we need to find out when we evaluate a writing program? How do we determine whether a program is all it should be? Indeed, do we, in fact, have a writing program? If we do, how stable will it prove over time? Is the program to have any long-term influence on students' writing?

To answer these questions, and some of our own, we designed our book to be informed by the lessons of history, case study, best practice, evidence-based inquiry, and theory.

What, we ask, does the history of program assessment and writing assessment tell us about current practice? In chapter 1, we trace historical trends and conceptual developments in writing program assessment and the larger related field of program assessment. To document the symphonic efforts of the writing program, we offer a model of the ingredients of a contemporary writing program, a model that extends from preenrollment through graduate-school and workplace preparation. So that the writing program remains in resonance with regional and other programmatic assessment, thus leveraging its stability over time, we position an institution's writing program as a distinct genre dedicated to modeling writing constructs—that is, the concepts of writing used by our profession—within a distinct, local environment. Figure 1.1 depicts the new era of assessment that has now begun.

In chapter 2 we address lessons learned from collective case studies of two writing programs. In a frank examination that finds that neither program is really what it should be, we are able to use these lessons from the field to establish categories of evidence—what we need to find out—as we assess our own writing programs. In establishing an assessment system that will produce categories of validity evidence, this chapter emphasizes the importance of writing program design. Two essential elements—construct modeling and construct span—are shown in Figure 2.3 and Figure 2.4.

Informed by historical and case-study analysis, we turn in chapter 3 to a best-practice approach for anticipating evidential categories, gathering validity evidence, and mapping construct models to individual classroom tasks. Because student performance remains of paramount importance to all who prepare and review assessment results, we propose a trait-based model of assessment—Phase 2 ePortfolio assessment—as a vehicle that expresses the many ways the institution models the writing construct. As a planned expression of local agency, Phase 2 ePortfolio Assessment allows writing to be collected and evaluated across time and circumstance so evidence of the long-term influence of the writing program can be gathered. While we have focused on assessment of the writing construct because it is at the center of writing program assessment, a brief look at Table 3.3 reveals the many sources of evidence integral to program assessment. A look at Figures 3.1 and 3.2 shows how the sources of evidence can be used to improve the writing program in the process of assessing it.

Are there key measurement concepts, we wondered, that are helpful in writing program assessment? In chapter 4, we present a series of empirical reporting guidelines we believe are essential to those engaged in evidence-based research involving writing programs. Ranging from quantitative descriptive statistics to qualitative content analysis, these reporting practices allow in-depth knowledge about a specific program and yield comparative information about other programs similar to it. These practices are shown in Figure 4.1.

In chapter 5, we present our conceptual overall model, termed Design for Assessment (DFA) and depicted in Figure 5.1. Designed to capture evidence from the writing program's many activities, DFA establishes assessment aims—from consequence to communication—to assure that, in advance, those responsible for the writing program anticipate evidence collection and widespread participation as part of the assessment cycle.

In advance. That phrase suggests one of two key concepts driving our vision of writing program assessment. The first is that those responsible for writing program design anticipate accountability demands and work to address them in the design of the program itself. External evaluators from regional accreditation agencies such as the Middle States Commission on Higher Education and program accreditation agencies such as the Accreditation Board for Engineering and Technology are a permanent part of postsecondary education for the foreseeable future. Yet there is no mandate that the occasion for an external evaluation—the limited time a visiting team spends on campus and its brief analysis—should be the only reporting that matters for an institution. Local reports to administrators, later refined and delivered at conferences and published in journals, provide an excellent guide to external evaluators when they arrive on campus. As such, this book is offered to support all those involved in the difficult and complex work of designing, and redesigning, writing programs. The second key concept, related to the first, is that we firmly believe in the importance of localism. What we seek in this volume is a way for writing program administrators to signify to all stakeholders that the institution's writing program recognizes its wide responsibilities and has taken the time to apply the best knowledge from our field for the benefit of the individual student. As we will demonstrate time and again, value dualisms and value hierarchies—such as the needless disjuncture between constructivism and positivism that so often interrupts important assessment research—need not prevent us from comparing and contrasting our unique programs with those of others to help students and increase knowledge. Isolationism is the logical outcome of separation; resonance within the field is the hallmark of community, which does not disallow the special circumstances of local contexts and traditions.

OUR THANKS

More than most books, this one required years of cooperation among its three authors and constant forbearance from our families. Special thanks to Volney White, Frances Ward, and the memory of Sarah Peckham. We are grateful to Michael Spooner, editor at Utah State University Press, for his steady encouragement and generosity with shifting deadlines. Our colleagues at the press were magnificent. From manuscript to production, the book was expertly prepared under the guidance of Laura Furney, managing editor. Final figures and tables were prepared by editorial assistant Karli Fish. The evocative cover was designed by Daniel Pratt, production manager. The manuscript was expertly edited by composition scholar Kami Day. We are especially thankful to Danielle Judka, an NJIT undergraduate student of extraordinary design talent majoring in electrical and computer engineering technology, who prepared all the original figures. Advance readers of the manuscript helped us with our many revisions: Tara Alvarez, Brent Bridgeman, William Condon, Nancy Coppola, Andrew Klobucar, Mya Poe, and an anonymous publisher's reviewer. The magnitude of our professional debts to scholars in writing studies and educational measurement is evident in our references; we are well aware that we stood on the shoulders of many.

A NOTE BEFORE BEGINNING

In *Going North Thinking West: The Intersections of Social Class, Critical Thinking, and Politicized Writing Instruction,* Irvin Peckham (2010a) stresses the need for deeply contextualized understanding as part of writing instruction. Pedagogical emphasis on the vague concept of critical thinking and the remorseless pursuit of persuasion combine to present barriers, unwitting though they may be, to diverse groups of students. Such stratification may, in turn, limit their abilities to work meaningfully with language. For Peckham, as for his coauthors in the book you are about to read, there is no such thing as "just writing"—that derogatory phrase suggesting that the pursuit of competency in many genres of writing is merely a working-class notion of literacy (Linkon, Peckham, and Lanier-Nabors 2004; Unruh 2012).

How to begin? As teachers, Peckham (2010a) tells us, we should investigate our students' "literacy skills and goals, honor them, and work with them to help them improve their skills and reach their goals, even though their goals may be quite different from the ones teachers had in mind" (101). At the same time, we need to assist them, and evaluate their progress, toward goals they may not have or may not be able to articulate at the start of their studies. If we approach this task with the sensitivity and professionalism it demands, both the curriculum and its assessment become much more complicated than they have seemed to be in the past. Perhaps some of our colleagues will see this work as a departure from the humanistic enterprise, but we see it rather as an expansion of it. The questions we provide at the end of each chapter reveal our dedication to the sense of inquiry that is the very essence of the humanities.

That is a pretty good place to start—with an eye on the pragmatic and a willingness to honor context. Here is a cloud we can watch take shape.

1

TRENDS

The national investment in composition instruction remains huge, despite recent budget cuts throughout the educational system. At the high-school level, we can count 358,136 students taking the advanced placement examination in English language and composition (College Board 2013, Table 9), the better-prepared tip of a population concerned with entry-level college writing. The National Center for Education Statistics (2012; Hussar and Bailey 2008, Fig. C) reports that total enrollment in degree-granting institutions increased 23 percent from 1992 to 2006. Between 2006 and 2017, a period of only eleven years, enrollment is projected to top at least 19.4 million students, almost all of whom will be enrolled at some level in college writing courses.

Such growth is accompanied by new challenges. Citing a 300 percent rise in average tuition during the past three decades, an average bachelor's degree debt of more than $29,400, and a graduation rate of only 58 percent for a four-year degree within six years, the Department of Education has launched federal initiatives to ensure quality in postsecondary institutions (White House 2013). Of special interest is the emerging Postsecondary Institution Ratings System (PIRS) that will be used to produce individual college scorecards linked to student financial-aid levels. Students attending colleges with higher ratings could, for instance, be eligible for larger Pell Grants and favorable rates on student loans. The opposite would be true for students at colleges with lower ratings (National Association of Student Financial Aid Administrators 2014).

In light of such developments, it is both reasonable and responsible for administrators and public officials to inquire into the effectiveness of the writing instruction programs in which students are enrolled, particularly at two crucial transfer points: between high school and college, and between graduation and career development. For over fifty years, composition researchers and assessment specialists have been attempting to provide reliable evidence—beyond the felt experience of

DOI: 10.7330/9780874219869.c001

teachers—that composition instruction leads to valuable categories of student improvement, including evidence that students are better writers. But the results have been infrequently laudable, often mixed, and sometimes disappointing.

WRITING PROGRAM ASSESSMENT: A DISCOURAGING HISTORY

Among the many reasons for this complex situation, perhaps the most important is the difficulty of defining writing and the objectives of writing instruction at the transfer points we have described. This complexity is deepened when assessment is understood as integral to the daily administration of writing programs and is made even more complex when program assessment is understood as a form of research. Even our leaders seem to be at a loss. For Rose and Weiser (1999), writing program research is taken to be "theoretically-informed, systematic, principled inquiry for the purpose of developing, sustaining, and leading a sound yet dynamic writing program" (ix). For Douglas Hesse (2012), that definition is an Aristotelian act of structuralism. Writing program research, he believes, most benefits by attention to the acts, purposes, and audiences of the programs themselves. Like Polonius echoing Hamlet's sarcasm, different observers see different things in shadowy shapes.

What we might call the *definition problem* is all the more significant because writing has been so simply defined. In 1963, Albert K. Kitzhaber measured writing performance by elaborate error count, thereby defining good writing as correct writing, a construct few would defend today Kitzhaber (1963). The Braddock, Lloyd-Jones, and Schoer (1963) study defined writing research in terms of limited empirical methodologies, thereby ruling out characteristics of writing not readily measurable. When some writing programs developed as separate entities from the English departments within which they customarily resided (marked by the founding of the Council of Writing Program Administrators [CWPA] in 1976), researchers began anew to define what such programs were seeking to attain beyond measures emphasizing knowledge of conventions. A team of researchers led by Michael Scriven (1981) produced twenty separate technical reports in a Carnegie Foundation-funded attempt to document the outcomes of the (then) Bay Area Writing Project from 1976 to 1979; the findings were inconclusive, though the revised volume provided what the authors called a "handbook" for those doing further research on the topic. The Fund for the Improvement of Post-Secondary Education funded a study culminating in an important volume in 1983 by Stephen Witte and Lester Faigley that focused primarily on a more expansive vision of what a college writing program could accomplish and found the usual empirical study inadequate because the assessment objectives were unclear: "We have suggested that the complexity of writing programs has done much to limit the development of adequate evaluative procedures and methods. Yet the sheer complexity of the thing evaluated is not the only reason the art of writing program evaluation remains in its infancy" (Witte and Faigley 1983, 66).

At the same time, a project led by Edward White and funded by the National Institute of Education employed empirical methods in a five-year effort to determine the writing program features most correlated with effective student writing. Published in a final report (White and Polin 1986), the results presented findings of interest but contained predominately descriptive information about the kinds of writing instruction then most in use. Although research—most notably the meta-analysis by Hillocks (1986) and the taxonomy by Stephen North (1987)—also appeared in the mid-1980s, the frustrating variety of definitions of good writing continued. And, as expected, equally absent were reports of convincing research on writing programs. Recent studies have expanded knowledge of program assessment by attempting to articulate the objectives of writing across the curriculum (Bazerman et al. 2005; Yancey and Huot 1997) and writing in the disciplines (Neff and Whithaus 2008; Poe, Lerner, and Craig 2010). Such specificity has yielded enormous benefits for the design of programmatic assessment, with recent scholarship focusing on the assessment of writing centers through attention to key elements of locally based assessment, including alignment of the program with institutional mission, establishing meaningful outcomes, and communicating assessment results (Schendel and Macauley 2012).

Yet we are not alone in our struggle. Interwoven with dissatisfaction about the inability of our field to come to terms with the success of its own instructional programs is a century's worth of similar expressions of doubt in the nation's educational system itself—especially its ability to produce reform through educational research (Lagemann 2000). If we seek a hallmark document, we could do no better than Edwin C. Broome's (1903) *A Historical and Critical Discussion of College Admission Requirements*. Analyzing admissions practices at Harvard, Yale, Princeton, Columbia, the University of Michigan, and Cornell, he cited "evils resulting from diversity in admissions requirements" (128). With its origin in 1887 and its aim to lessen such evils through standardization, the Middle States Association of Colleges and Schools Commission on Higher Education, along with other regional accreditation agencies, appeared to be part of the solution until the century's end. By 1991 the commission itself was under criticism from the federal government as it became increasingly apparent that standard gauge systemization was not the answer to valid assessment (Harcleroad 1980; Tedesco 1999). A proposed House bill to reauthorize the Higher Education Act of 1992 argued that state agencies should replace private accrediting groups such as Middle States, thus becoming the primary reviewers of institutions receiving Title IV funding (Parsons 1997). When the dust settled and the act was reauthorized, it was clear that the regional agencies would have to achieve new levels of accountability themselves if they were to continue to exist. The six regional accreditation agencies— Middle States, the New England Association of Colleges and Schools, the Commission on Institutions of Higher Education, the North Central Association of Colleges and Schools Higher Learning Commission, the Northwest Commission on Colleges and Universities, the Southern Association of Colleges and Schools Commission on Colleges, and the Western Association of Colleges and Schools Accrediting Commission of Senior Colleges and Universities—would now, by law, have to conduct reviews of institutions where the student-loan default rates exceeded 25 percent. Specific areas of institutional review were required. Writing program evaluation did not stand alone but was one element in the overall dissatisfaction with program accountability. If accountability were to be taken as a demonstration of accepted responsibility and wise resource use, the accreditation community would now be required to take a fresh look at its educational quality assurance system (Astin and Antonio 2012; Price et al. 2008).

Within the writing community, this fresh look took dramatic form on the active listserv associated with the WPA. In response to a query on the list in 1996, White suggested that it may have become time to articulate a consensus on the objectives of the first-year composition course. The overwhelming response to this proposal led to the formation of an outcomes group in 1997, which then led to multiple drafts (with about 240 colleagues taking part in 1998) of an *Outcomes Statement* approved by the WPA Executive Committee (at last giving this ad hoc volunteer group some formal standing). The *Outcomes Statement* was then published in *WPA: Writing Program Administration* (Outcomes Group 1999) and *College English* (Harrington et al. 2001), and became the focus of *The Outcomes Book* (Harrington et al. 2005). The widespread impact of the *Outcomes Statement* became clear in that book, and its continuing influence remains apparent in *The WPA Outcomes Statement: A Decade Later* (Behm et al. 2012). In 2014 the *Outcomes Statement* was updated to reflect changes in the field and current practices in first-year writing (Dryer et al. 2014).While an entry-level writing course is by itself only part of a college writing program—an argument we will make time and again—the ability to articulate a consensus on outcomes for the transition between high school and college became a major step in writing program assessment.

Further developments ensued. In 2011, the CWPA, in collaboration with the National Council of Teachers of English (NCTE) and the National Writing Project (NWP), issued the *Framework for Success in Postsecondary Writing* (CWPA, NCTE, and NWP 2011; O'Neill et al. 2012). While the *WPA Outcomes Statement* defined what was expected at the end of entry-level college composition, the *Framework for Success* focused on a broadened concept of writing ability so students could reach the intended outcomes. Alert to the ways that the *Framework for Success* could support kindergarten through twelfth-grade teachers, its authors added "habits of mind" as ways of approaching learning that would foster student success across disciplinary boundaries by means of attention to intrapersonal and interpersonal domains: curiosity, openness, engagement, creativity, persistence, responsibility, flexibility, and metacognition. These habits of mind, in turn, would be developed through reading, writing, and critical analysis experiences of the *Outcomes Statement*. The *Framework* has indeed generated some controversy, in part because the habits of mind—those intrapersonal and interpersonal domains— are more challenging to measure than the clarity of the cognitive domain expressed in the *Outcomes Statement*. In its insistence that questions such as What is writing? and How should we assess writing development? be answered, the *Framework* asks us to consider the writing construct in all its complexity.

While the *Outcomes Statement* has by no means brought the first-year composition course almost universally required in American colleges and universities into conformity (Isaacs and Knight 2012), it has provided a set of objectives and definitions that seem to apply widely enough to the course to suggest to textbook publishers a more outcomes-based approach to the field. Recent research by Emily J. Isaacs (2014) of 106 American Association of State Colleges and Universities Institutions reveals that 68 percent of writing program administrators conducted formal review of student writing in light of outcomes or objectives. To address such assessment needs, many publishers now link textbook features to the *Outcomes Statement*. One publisher—McGraw-Hill—has published a popular text whose theoretical underpinnings are directly related to the statement. The team of editors for the McGraw-Hill Guide used the statement as a framework for the book while at the same time using modern theories about writing as reflection (Brady and Schreiber 2013; Fox, White, and Tian 2014; Giles 2010; Inoue and Richmond, forthcoming; Smith and Yancey 2000; Yancey 1998) to foster assessment as part of the course (Kelly-Riley and Elliot 2014). Other publishers have followed this lead. As we write, most new textbooks for introductory writing courses include references or chapters citing the *Outcomes Statement*. The combination of portfolio-based writing assessment and outcomes-based curriculum derived from a national consensus document represents something new in the world of composition programs: a consensus model of the writing construct.

The history of writing program evaluation and its intersection with the history of accreditation in general suggests that a new era in writing program assessment is at hand. While we present both the risks and benefits of the Age of Accountability, our brief history of writing program assessment—which is not intended to be encyclopedic and which someone must surely write—suggests that informed, programmatic practices are rapidly becoming the order of the day. Developed locally, these practices can yield great benefits for specific institutional sites. Perhaps the best place to begin a programmatic approach to assessment is, as we have suggested above, with attention to definitions.

WRITING PROGRAMS: AN INTEGRATED FRAMEWORK

Many members of the public, as well as some in the university community, mistakenly believe that one or two courses in writing constitute an entire writing program capable of helping students to achieve the writing ability they—and future employers or graduate teachers—expect of college graduates. Among writing professionals, this is satirically referred to as *inoculation theory*—the metaphor stemming from the theory of McGuire and Papageorgis (1961) that resistance to harmful practices can be enhanced by exposure. In this metaphor, writing courses required early in the undergraduate curriculum serve as a polio shot, forever inoculating the student against future infections of comma faults, citation errors, faulty logic, and inadequate critical thinking. A moment's reflection is time enough for anyone who has done much writing, or has paid much attention to longitudinal research (Fishman 2012; Haswell 2000), to remember that the development of writing ability is a slow and laborious process that is, for many, a lifetime's work. While the entry-level composition class is an important part of every student's college learning, if it stands alone in the curriculum it becomes one more requirement students seek to "get out of the way" so they can get to more important matters, such as the requirements for their major course of study. One major practical incentive to maintaining writing-across-the-curriculum programs and writing-in-the-disciplines programs is to relieve that isolation of the first-year writing course and to increase opportunities for knowledge transfer (Holdstein 2014).

What has long been needed is an approach to writing program assessment that advances strategically planned integration instead of focusing on isolated assessment events. *The Program Evaluation Standards* (Yarbrough et al. 2011) provides a good definition of a program as "much more than just activities" (xxiii). Defined in detail, a program is a set of activities that uses managed resources to achieve specified, documentable outcomes (xxiv). Extending this definition to writing programs, we see that many universities have developed writing programs that contain all or most of the following components:

- a defined construct model that is used as the basis for the writing program;
- preenrollment assessment and placement to identify just-qualified students through tests, evaluation of transfer-course work, or directed student self-placement;
- required writing courses, often including basic writing for poorly prepared students and honors classes for well-prepared students;
- a writing center, where students seeking help with their writing can find tutors and other support services, directed by a writing center professional;
- a writing-across-the-curriculum (WAC) in-service program for faculty, with a WAC coordinator offering a range of support activities;
- writing intensive course requirements, usually designated and offered by departments or schools of the student's major discipline and overseen by a campus faculty committee committed to writing in the disciplines (WID);
- graduation writing requirements, which may include writing-proficiency examinations, portfolios, or capstone courses emphasizing writing in the major;
- writing requirements for entry into graduate programs, such as examinations, statements of purpose, or portfolios;
- thesis and dissertation requirements for graduate degrees;
- a writing program administrator (WPA) with graduate degrees in rhetoric and composition who speaks for writing on campus and has overall administrative responsibility for the entire writing program;
- a plan for sustainable financial support, with particular attention to salary and benefits (American Association of University Professors 2014);

- an articulated research agenda and program of research so the many composition pedagogies identified by Tate et al. (2013)—from basic writing through new media—can inform and be informed by research conducted within the program (Anson 2008); and

- an overall strategic plan for the program that establishes its mission, priorities, objectives, strategies, targets, metrics, accountability, and impact (Bryson 2011; Quinn 1980; Schendel and Macauley 2012; Smith 2011).

A WPA census of 814 respondents representing 734 four-year colleges and universities reveals that 57 percent of those institutions have a WAC program and writing requirement beyond the first year (Fralix and Gladstein 2014). While far from universal, programmatic approaches to writing instruction and assessment throughout the curriculum are growing. Louder than any mission statement, a writing program containing all or most of these components beyond first-year writing asserts that writing matters. Attention to these writing program components as they are examined through the process of validation justifies the claims of Rose and Weiser (1999, 2002) that writing program assessment is a field of research and a site for theorization and responds to the call by Hesse (2012) for attention to conceptual mapping at local institutions.

VALIDATION: AN EVIDENTIAL PROCESS

Assessment in our field refers to activities that provide information about the degree of success of writing programs as they contribute to student learning. A subset of assessment, often used as a synonym, is *evaluation*, with its metaphor of comparative value. As the *Standards for Educational and Psychological Testing* establish, *assessment* is the more capacious term, "commonly referring to a process that integrates test information with information from other sources (information from other tests, inventories, and interviews; or the individual's social, educational, employment, health, or psychological history)" (American Educational Research Association [AERA], American Psychological Association [APA], and National Council on Measurement in Education [NCME] 2014, 2). With its origin in the Latin *assidere*, "to sit beside," we prefer the term *assessment* as the more appropriate term for a discussion of writing programs. With Susanmarie Harrington (2013), we agree that assessment yields meaningful narratives and facilitates sound decisions.

In the field of educational assessment, testing, and measurement, *outcomes* refers to "the end results of a curriculum for those it was intended to serve" (Weiss 1998, 8). Internationally, the existence of outcomes can be traced to the eight-legged essay, the orthodox genre used to test candidates for posts in the Chinese civil service during the Ming dynasty (1368–1644), as that genre was related to cultural outcomes (Elman 2000, 2009). The essay, used to examine candidates on classical learning, was believed to be the ideal cognitive exercise for judges to determine future societal leaders. In the United States, outcomes can be identified in the grammar schools of the New England Puritans of the seventeenth century (Morison 1936). As an enrollment growth of 500 percent occurred in postsecondary education between 1945 and 1975, Americans began to define outcomes as a series of measures to determine the relative efficacy among different educational systems (Cohen and Kisker 2010). With earlier beginnings, a similar history can be found in the United Kingdom (Wooldridge 1994).

For our purposes, the term *outcomes* as it is associated with writing program assessment is defined as the common cognitive, interpersonal, and intrapersonal domains exemplified in consensus statements such as the *Outcomes Statement* and the *Framework for Success* for first-year writing. In similar fashion, the Body of Knowledge Initiative (Coppola 2010; Coppola and Elliot 2013) developed by the Society for Technical Communication is an excellent example of outcomes for advanced college writing that facilitates career development. While we believe in the importance of outcomes based on broad consensus statements, we also agree with Chris W. Gallagher (2012) that framing outcomes in terms of consequences encourages articulation of aims important to local communities of administrators, teachers, and students (53). We will turn to the important resonance between the broad and the local throughout this book.

How to establish the importance of both broad-based consensus and local relevance (Conference on College Composition and Communication 2009)? Such alignment begins with recognizing the importance of both broad outcomes (broad and general results of an expansive curriculum) and locally developed competencies (distinct and varied within institutions and among specific programs). Once outcomes are distinguished from more narrowly defined competencies, it is possible to reach consensus—subject to refinement and revision—across institutions (Pagano et al. 2008). Such is precisely the process reported by Kelly-Riley and Elliot (2014) in their study of the *Outcomes Statement* as it was tailored for instruction and assessment at three postsecondary institutions. As we show in chapter 3, the process of articulation—defined by Gallagher as the expression and alignment of institutionally appropriate educational aims—can then help writing program administrators to set priorities, establish strategies, assign responsibilities, and anticipate the impact of their planning activities.

As stakeholders reflect on the ways outcomes shape assessment, attention is drawn to the ways the program is to be measured (Chen 2015). Integral to this process is evidence-centered design, a conceptual model yielding a coherent measurement system integrating design, delivery, and evidentiary reasoning (Mislevy, Almond, and Lukas 2004; Mislevy, Steinberg, and Almond 2002). As institutional stakeholders collaborate to design the assessment, they form plans to gather validity evidence based on the ways students develop their writing ability, students' response processes as they engage with defined outcomes, the internal structure of the institution's assessment plan, the relationship of the writing outcomes to other performance variables such as course grades, and the impact of the assessment on the community (AERA, APA, and NCME 2014). Planning for attention to such systematic collection, developed *in advance* of the assessment, is the subject of this book.

Traditionally, the measure of outcomes involves two concepts related to the provision of evidence: *validity* and *reliability*. Both of these terms remain important for all stakeholders of an assessment.

As a conceptual measure, validity is best defined as an integrated evaluative judgment derived from evidence that a measure in fact assesses what it purports to assess and that its scores are used sensitively and appropriately. Conceptualizing validity as an interpretation and use argument, Michael T. Kane (2013) defines validity as follows: "The validity of a proposed interpretation or use of test scores at any point in time can be defined in terms of the plausibility and appropriateness of the proposed interpretation/use at that time. A proposed interpretation or use can be considered valid to the extent that the IUA—the interpretation and use argument—is coherent and complete (in the sense that it fully represents the proposed interpretation or use) and its assumptions are either highly plausible *a priori* or are adequately supported by evidence" (2–3). Adopting the IUA as a frame of reference is important for two reasons. First, it presents validity as a communicative act of interpretation, not as a stamp of approval. Second, the IUA presents validity as a concept involving consequence, not solely as an intellectual exercise. Recalling that our acts are contingent and, as such, impact the lives of our students is an excellent way to think about validity.

An example is in order. Claims for the validity of impromptu tests of writing have long come under criticism by researchers because these timed tests fail to cover the construct of writing ability (Purves 1995). Conversely, claims for assessments drawn from more robust representations of writing such as ePortfolio assessments (Cambridge, Cambridge, and Yancey 2009) have been generally well received, especially when samples of student work include trait scoring (Hamp-Lyons 2012; White 2005). These orientations toward validity focus on interpretations of the writing construct. While a theory of consequence has not yet been developed for writing studies research, recent validity investigation has focused especially on impact as researchers ask if scores are used to classify students in inappropriate ways (Inoue and Poe 2012; Slomp, Corrigan, and Sugimoto 2014; Poe 2014). So, for instance, timed, impromptu tests send a harmful signal that someone's writing ability can be inferred from such a constrained measure (Huot 2002); with equally dire consequences, assessments that severely constrain the writing construct may result in disparate impact discrimination for various student groups (Poe et al. 2014). IUA is an important concept, and attention to it compels us to focus both on our interpretations and the consequences they will have.

This new view toward validity therefore leads us to a new view about construct representation: given what we now know about the complexity of the writing construct (a topic examined in chapter 3 and shown in Figure 3.1), it is clear that full construct representation is not possible in any given construct sample. As William Condon (2013) has held, the representation of the construct in a given instance occurs along a continuum, ranging from rich to artificial representation of writing. As such, we hold that complete construct representation is not possible in any single given assessment instance. Such a view leads to the importance of writing program assessment if we are to understand how writing ability evolves in a given educational setting.

As a consistency measure, reliability is best defined as an estimate of the ways scores resulting from measurement procedures would be expected to vary across time and circumstance (Haertel 2006). In addition, as every writing program administrator knows, intertopic reliability is equally important if we are to understand how students react to writing tasks requiring different responses to genre and mode. Those committed to statistical measures value reliability since it allows precise estimates of consistency to be drawn from the data. Reliability of ratings, for example, is critical to establishing score consistency on writing samples, while reliability among writing tasks is important when two or more samples of writing are to be evaluated (Brennan 2006). Rather than viewing validity and reliability as oppositional or prerequisite concepts (Moss 1994), contemporary validity theory emphasizes sources of validity evidence based on the ways the writing task represents the construct under examination (Borsboom 2005; Markus and Borsboom 2013) and on the ways the assessment draws on categories of evidence

(Kane 2013). Hence, reliability of measurement—score consistency over time and task—should be understood as an important element (but not the controlling factor) of validity, providing evidence contributing to the validity argument.

Put simply, validity and reliability are not to be held in tension; both are elements of the validity argument that will be used to justify our interpretation of scores on the assessments we design. As a process, validity is not an up-or-down vote; rather, it is a series of integrated arguments used to justify our use of scores.

A REMINDER: REAL STUDENTS AND REAL INSTRUCTORS

The assessment of writing as part of a writing program usually has three traditional purposes: to consider and respond to individual students in a classroom or tutorial setting for pedagogical purposes; to assess the relative success of a writing program in achieving its objectives; and to act as a gateway to national programs or universities for individual students taking nationwide tests. A rising junior portfolio assessment undertaken to assure that an individual student has the necessary rhetorical knowledge and writing skills to achieve career and personal success exemplifies the first purpose (Haswell 2001). The second purpose is nicely demonstrated by the Consultant Evaluator Service of the WPA (Brady 2004) and the program review service conducted by the Council for Programs in Technical and Scientific Communication (Maylath and Grabill 2009). The third purpose occurs in programs such as the Advanced Placement Program in English and Composition for high-school seniors (Jones 2001) or the Graduate Record Examinations® for those seeking admission to advanced university study (Broer et al. 2005). Increasingly, a fourth purpose has been added: to determine if students are ready for career success (Burstein and Elliot 2014). At the present time, a writing program may be called upon to serve each of these four aims concurrently.

Locally, assessment of classroom writing takes place routinely and is usually a private transaction between the teacher and the student. A long tradition of teacher knowledge and narrative speaks to the pedagogical methods of individual teachers in the classroom (Peckham 1999; Shepard 2006; Shepard, McMillan, and Tate 1998), but in recent years more generalizable research has sought to probe into these individualized assessments to identify effective ways of giving and responding to writing assignments in a defined curriculum (Beaufort 2007; Feldman 2008; Haertel 2013). A considerable literature relating to devising appropriate writing tasks for students and to useful ways of responding to these tasks, including peer feedback and revision assignments, offers teachers many ways of using assessment as an integral part of teaching writing (Graham and Perin 2007; White and Wright 2015). Regionally, assessment of writing programs has become increasingly important as these programs are being asked to justify their existence as part of regional accreditation (Middaugh 2010). While we take the position that the interaction between student and teacher does not constitute a programmatic approach to writing instruction, we nevertheless need to keep in mind that it is precisely that interaction that forms the basis for all local and regional efforts.

While the chapters that follow allow us to provide the details of the challenges of localism, three key tropes—defined by Donald C. Williams (1953) as "the occurrence of an essence" (7) of any system of beliefs— may be used to frame writing program assessment. These concepts may be understood as unifying ideas that will allow those who design, redesign and assess writing programs to gather important information about student performance and program support.

TROPE 1: WRITING PROGRAM ASSESSMENT AS GENRE

In 1984, Carolyn Miller introduced a new way to think about genre. Concentrating on the shift from form to framework, she proposed that genre be considered an "open rather than closed" discourse classification that is, as such, "organized around situated actions" (Miller 1984, 155). Genre, she continued, had unexplored implications. Distinct from the reductionist concept of form, genre "is a rhetorical means for mediating private intention and social exigence; it motivates by connecting the private with the public, the singular with the recurrent" (163). Her final statement set the course for future study. When we learn a genre, we learn far more than a pattern of forms or a method of achieving ends. "We learn, more importantly, what ends we may have: we learn that we may eulogize, apologize, recommend one person to another, instruct customers on behalf of a manufacturer, take on an official role, account for progress in achieving goals. We learn to understand better the situations in which we find ourselves and the potentials for failure and success in acting together" (165). Learning to design a collaborative help document such as a user guide in Adobe RoboHelp, a genre unimagined when Miller wrote, is thus far more than learning teamwork, audience, and technology. Instead, we learn the "cultural rationality" of the field of professional, technical, business, and scientific writing (CIP 23.1303)

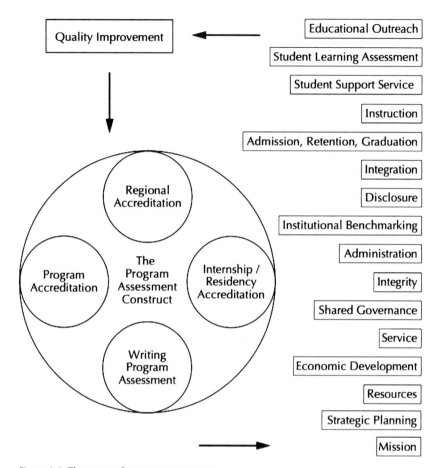

Figure 1.1. The genre of program assessment.

as that genre indexes the profession. And, although Miller never says it, the more we learn about genres in a profession, the more we can understand about that profession. Today, the work of tracing genre in organizations has been expertly taken up by Clay Spinuzzi (2003).

The assessment of writing programs is a genre, too. As one among others, we describe this genre in Figure 1.1.

Figure 1.1 depicts a compilation of the standards from the six regional accreditation agencies. Each of these US regional accrediting agencies publishes standards that postsecondary institutions must adhere to in their accreditation cycle. The Middle States Association of Colleges and Schools Commission on Higher Education, for instance, publishes its *Standards for Accreditation and Requirements of Affiliation* (Middle States

Commission on Higher Education 2014). Along with a host of supporting publications, regional accreditors identify standards—best thought of as sources of evidence—that must be presented if an institution is to be reaccredited. All institutions receiving Title IV financial aid must be accredited by one of these agencies.

Program accreditors are numerous and escape easy categorization. Familiar program accreditation agencies include the Accreditation Board for Engineering and Technology (ABET), the Association to Advance Collegiate Schools of Business (AACSB), the National Architectural Accrediting Board (NAAB), and the National League of Nursing Accreditation Commission (NLNAC). The final category of accreditation includes specialized residency and internship requirements such as those specified by the American Dental Association's Commission on Dental Accreditation. Here, for example, external evaluators examine evidence that a residency program documents its compliance with applicable regulations governing radiation hygiene and protection. The United States Department of Education (2013) maintains a database of all such programs; there can be found the broad educational aims of the regional agencies to the narrow aims of residency programs.

Centralizing writing program assessment within these assessment genres yields two major advantages for those who design, assess, and redesign writing programs: alignment and empowerment. Identifying resonances across the campus within the genre of writing program assessment allows teaching, research, and service commonalities to emerge across disciplinary boundaries. As those commonalities emerge, empowerment results as those responsible for teaching and assessing writing find themselves at the table with colleagues across the campus as they engage in similar program assessment activities. The resulting conversations and transparencies will help centralize the writing program as core to the institution's mission fulfillment.

However, we do not believe that reviewing a copy of *Standards for Accreditation and Requirements of Affiliation* (Middle States Commission on Higher Education 2014) will provide the unique framework needed for writing program assessment. Neither will applying *The Program Evaluation Standards: A Guide for Evaluators and Evaluation Users* (Yarbrough et al. 2011) to a specific writing program. It is here that the concept of genre is most powerful. Interpretation of the known sources of validity evidence shown in Figure 1.1 allows those who teach and assess writing to examine and demonstrate the central importance of rhetoric and composition/writing studies and its attendant subfields to the mission of the institution. Understood within the genre of program evaluation, these components used in higher education assessment—from mission to quality improvement—have a distinct historical origin in the later twentieth century (Keller 1983). The components take on distinct meanings that are extremely helpful to our profession:

- The mission of a writing program is aligned with the university mission, as well as with international and national forces shaping education.
- Strategic planning occurs with other fields so objectives can be established that reflect both writing program priorities and institutional initiatives.
- Resources can be allocated in a way that is comparable with other resource allocations across campus.
- Sources of economic development, from external funding to corporate consulting, may be identified and pursued with colleagues across campus in cases where common interests arise.
- Service roles of the writing program, especially in areas such as community development and service learning, may be pursued.
- Shared governance of the writing program may be planned so that the program's stakeholders—chief among these are students—may be involved in program planning and assessment.
- Various categories of integrity—fair process, professional conduct, and respect for diversity—can be identified to make sure that the writing program is leading the institution toward sound ethical and legal practice.
- In aligning writing program administration with other administrative campus functions, resource allocation can be strengthened, especially in cases where digital resources can enhance student success through rapid, timely assessment across courses taken concurrently.
- Institutional benchmarking, a key component of regional and program accreditation, can be used by the writing program to help the institution tailor its lists and build instructional, research, and service capacity across state and regional boundaries.
- Disclosure, a form of transparency closely related to integrity, can be highlighted in the writing program so sources of evidence, such as the performance of diverse student groups on various forms of assessment, can be highlighted and areas of curricular improvement can be identified.
- From admission to graduation, the writing program can extend its integrative influence across the undergraduate and graduate curricular life of the institution to prepare students for meaningful lives and productive careers.
- Emphasizing admission, retention, and graduation, the writing program can demonstrate its contributions to these key factors of academic success.

- The many elements of writing programs—from writing center conferences to writing-in-the-disciplines initiatives—can be understood as complementary to other campus initiatives for student-centered instruction.
- Student support offered by the writing program can inform, and be informed by, the wide range of student services offered across the campus.
- Student learning assessment, integral to the body of knowledge of those who teach and assess writing, can be shared with those across campus to ensure that a capacious, informed view of assessment prevails in the institution.
- Programs of educational outreach, especially those developed to address high-school students and future employers, can be developed by the writing program to broaden its impact.
- And quality improvement—that tired and misused phrase—can have additional meaning as the writing program is centralized with other programs across and beyond the institution to ensure that a truly visionary assessment model is advanced.

It is, nevertheless, insufficient to graft this framework onto a specific institution. Although Figure 1.1 has great merit, it must be tailored to local contexts—in our case, the writing construct as it is defined and modeled within writing programs at particular institutions.

TROPE 2: WRITING PROGRAM ASSESSMENT AS CONSTRUCT MODELING

While we have used the term *construct* earlier in this chapter, a fuller explication is in order. We are referring here to the idea of construct modeling as it was defined in 1955 by educational psychologist Lee J. Cronbach and philosopher of science Paul E. Meehl: "A construct is some postulated attribute of people, assumed to be reflected in test performance. In test validation the attribute about which we make statements in interpreting a test is a construct" (Cronbach and Meehl 1955; Embretson 1983). By theorizing the existence of constructs and methods of researching them, Cronbach and Meehl invented a future for the field of educational measurement that would allow the systematic study of psychological phenomena, of which writing is a notable instance. At a time when C. Wright Mills (1956/2000) would claim in *The Power Elite* that the military, industrial, political, and scientific complex had been let loose in the land, Cronbach and Meehl (1955) defined the future in other, more precise terms. They invented a future for the field of educational measurement that would allow the systematic investigation of psychological knowledge in the postwar nation. "Validation of psychological tests has not yet been adequately conceptualized," they claimed in the opening sentence of their *Psychological Bulletin* manifesto (381). And so they designed the idea of a construct and an accompanying method of validation.

Implicit in 1955 and more explicit today is the concept of modeling, which we define as the relationship between predictor (X, or independent) variable(s) and outcome (Y, or dependent) variable(s). As categories, variables can shift across time and circumstances (Bernard 2013; Odendahl 2011). In identifying variables as traits for writing assessment, Liz Hamp-Lyons (1986, 2012) ushered in an era of multiple-trait scoring of robust writing samples that, in turn, yielded detailed information relevant to the writing construct. The concept of relational modeling is of paramount importance for writing research (and thus for program assessment) for three reasons. First, as the predictor variables become defined, we can learn more about them and about the ability of our students to demonstrate that they have achieved them. Second, because they can vary within defined assignments, we can learn how one variable interacts with the other and therefore advance student learning through detailed knowledge about complex interactions. Third, variable modeling allows a wide range of information to be empirically gathered in systematic ways so large-scale curricular improvement may be made based on empirical evidence gathered at the classroom level.

As instances of construct modeling, the sociocognitive theory of writing and Phase 2 portfolio assessment are among the most important advances in our field over the past three decades. Both are germane to the topic of writing program assessment because both are instances of construct modeling. Historically, the work of Linda Flower and John R. Hayes in 1980 and 1981 led to an understanding of the process of writing as a complex web of writer, memory subprocesses, task, and environment (Hayes and Flower 1980; Flower and Hayes 1981). As Hayes recalled in 2012, despite its age, the model contains features that are still current in contemporary representations of writing—no doubt because of the validity of the think-aloud protocol analysis method that allowed the development of the model. Whatever its shortcomings (Trimbur 2011), the idea of modeling the construct of writing through empirical means became the centerpiece for our understanding of the act of writing as one of the most complex of human activities.

Absent, however, was a system to evaluate the writing products that could capture the complex model that Flower and Hayes had articulated. While holistic scoring had proved effective for assessing timed, impromptu essays, a single score could not capture variables such as metacognition or audience awareness. A new model was clearly needed. In two articles published in 2005, the first conceptual (White 2005) and the second empirical proof of concept (Ostheimer and White 2005), White agreed with the growing dissatisfaction with the widespread use of holistic scoring for many different kinds of purposes and showed that holistic scoring was inadequate for capturing the rich performances available in portfolios of student writing. Consequently, a reflective statement accompanying a portfolio would yield information on metacognition; similarly, a rubric based on goal statements of the curriculum from which the portfolio was taken would allow outcomes to be assessed by targeting a specific variable, such as audience analysis, that was part of the curriculum. In what he called "Phase 2 portfolio assessment," he proposed a method that advanced an embedded model of assessment, one that allowed the variables of writing ability to be assessed as they were integrated into instructional processes. By combining the flexibility and face validity of writing portfolios, a familiar part of many writing curricula, with emerging theories of reflection as an important construct in college writing (Yancey 1998), White proposed a new way to read writing portfolios, with a strong emphasis on students' reflection on their own writing in the context of course or program objectives. He also argued that Phase 2 increased both the reliability of scoring portfolios and the speed of scoring them, two problems that had held back the use of portfolios for program assessment.

Based on these research experiences and other related ones we will explore in chapter 2, we therefore propose that the heart of writing program assessment is a construct that can be defined and modeled in detail for students at various curricular levels. We advance just such a definition in chapter 3, Figure 3.1, and we show how some of its elements can be modeled in chapter 2, Figure 2.3. As to the novelty of such an approach to writing program assessment, it is important to remember that the concept of variable modeling we are advancing is quite recent. We believe it holds great promise for writing instructors and their students.

We now turn to the third main feature of this book, one in which the genre of program assessment and the concept of construct modeling are both contextualized.

TROPE 3: WRITING PROGRAM ASSESSMENT AS ECOLOGICAL STUDY

In 1990, White reminded writing assessment researchers that language use is integral to perceptions of reality. Referencing the work of Edward

Sapir (1963) and Benjamin Whorf (1956), White (1990) recollected the Sapir-Whorf hypothesis—our words strongly affect or even determine our world—and recommended that we should be more consciously aware of the ways language shapes perception if we are to remain free from—or at least aware of—its limits. As Whorf hypothesized, someone with a command of many languages may be freed from linguistic restraints on perception. But that was only a theory. Beginning in 1955, James Cooke Brown (2008) tried to test empirically the Sapir-Whorf hypothesis. He created a fictitious language, training subjects to speak it, and then tested their ability to think in ways more logical than before they learned the new language. The subjects, of course, did not think more logically. As we can readily see, the universe of generalization—critical thought—was so narrowly represented by the experiment that it had no possibility of success. (Of course, this is the reason multiple-choice tests of writing can never achieve meaningful construct representation: the slice of the pie is too thin.) While half of a century has certainly tempered devotion to the Sapir-Whorf hypothesis as the sole explanation of language use—in 1957, Noam Chomsky proposed that there are abstract principles of language that are not learned but genetically inherited, regardless of cultural origin—interest remains in investigating the ways language shapes perception. The publication of Daniel E. Everett's (2012) *Language: The Cultural Tool* assures us that the cognition + culture + communication method of understanding language is alive and well.

We live by our metaphors because they provide us with meaning making, invention, and knowledge-stabilizing functions (Bateson 1987; Lakoff 2004; Lakoff and Johnson 1980; Ruiz de Mendoza Ibanez and Perez Hernandez 2011). The metaphor for assessment we have adopted in this book is ecology. For date of origin, we take the publication of *Principles of Animal Ecology* by Warder Clyde Allee and his colleagues as a seminal work that examined the role of the environment in shaping distribution patterns. "Ecology," the authors wrote, "may be defined broadly as the science of the interrelation between evolving organisms and their environment, including both the physical and the biotic environments, and emphasizing interspecies as well as intraspecies relations" (Allee et al. 1949, 1). Just to make sure readers understood opportunities for metaphorical extension, the authors continued, "The definition of ecology as the science of communities may be valid in its total implications" (3).

In different areas of our field, the impulse for ecological metaphor is strong. If we take Marilyn M. Cooper's (1986) "The Ecology of Writing" as a starting point for use of the metaphor in writing studies, we can see the web extend to Fleckenstein et al. (2008) in "The Importance of Harmony: An Ecological Metaphor for Writing Research" and Kathleen J. Ryan's (2012) "Thinking Ecologically: Rhetorical Ecological Feminist Agency and Writing Program Administration." In assessment, the need for ecological modeling is eloquently expressed in "Addressing the Complexity of Writing Development: Toward an Ecological Model of Assessment" by Wardle and Roozen (2012). In professional, technical, business, and scientific writing, we see the value of the metaphor in "The Promise of Ecological Inquiry in Writing Research" (MacMillan 2012). In our related field of educational assessment, testing, and measurement, the 2010 American Educational Research Association presidential address of Carol D. Lee (2010)—"Soaring above the Clouds, Delving the Ocean's Depths: Understanding the Ecologies of Human Learning and the Challenge for Education Science"—proposes that there is a need for a new dynamic view of human learning and development, something very like a whale. The presence of such articles across traditional disciplinary boundaries suggests the need for a system of conceptualization that yields robust understanding of construct representation, affords a systems analysis framework to engage complex interactions, anticipates threats to the system, and allows planning within the local environment to achieve sustainable development and growth. We will turn to a fuller explication of an environmental framework assessing writing programs in chapter 5, where we will talk about the need for boundaries as part of program assessment pursued under an environmental metaphor. Ecological metaphors, as we will show, require hard-headed determination if they are to be pursued in order to avoid a tragedy of the commons—"the solemn and remorseless working of things," as Alfred North Whitehead (1925) phrased it, that works toward our shared destruction as we become unwitting participants in things as they are.

This third trope is not as perfunctory as it may seem at first. Understanding program assessment as an ecology reminds us that we are involved in complexities we both do and do not understand. Recognition of the limits of knowledge leads us to a fundamental belief: only an informed instructor, watching a student develop over time, can hope to make a valid claim about the totality of the writing ability of that student. Such a fundamental premise of program assessment will lead to the humility required if meaningful inferences are to be drawn from the information we collect.

The commons, as Garrett Hardin (1968) understood, is international. Enormous international forces contributing to the development of Web 2.0 technologies are shaping an international environment for writing. National, regional, state, and institutional writing stakeholders are rapidly realizing that demographics themselves—by 2024 the non-Hispanic white population will peak at 199.6 million and slowly decrease, while the Hispanic population will more than double—are shaping the United States into a truly pluralistic nation. Globalization, technology, and diversity are combining to create a new environment for writing programs and their assessment. In that uncertain environment, while the past will certainly allow us to establish themes and patterns of development, the answers lie ahead of us. Such is the complex cartography we map in this book. We employ it to recognize necessity, to identify gains, and to set an agenda for a hopeful future.

The concept of writing program assessment as a unique genre in which constructs are modeled within unique institutional ecologies provides a good way to understand the strength and limits of the case studies presented in the next chapter. While many of the elements of the case studies in chapter 2 can be refitted into the three tropes, designing writing programs with these concepts in mind illustrates the benefits of a systematic approach to writing program assessment.

QUESTIONS FOR WRITING PROGRAM FACULTY AND ADMINISTRATORS: TRENDS

Background

In this set of questions, we have taken the most important concepts from chapter 1 on trends in assessment and turned them into questions for writing program faculty and administrators. While this format follows that established by Witte and Faigley (1983), their questions regarding societal, institutional, program, and student constituencies are framed in terms of the external evaluations, which are conducted by those who visit but are not part of the institutional community. Our experience has taught us that a well-designed, publicly accountable program with a defined mission, selectively developed objectives, and key measures of program performance will be positively evaluated by any external agency associated with accreditation. Our questions are focused on the responsible faculty committees and administrators who will document their program for all those who are part of the instructional and assessment effort. This emphasis on local planning and assessment is consistent with our view that a meaningful program evaluation will be of greatest value to the program, despite the fact that the level of support of the program might hinge on the outsiders' reports.

The questions are intended to be used within the Design for Assessment (DFA) framework we propose in this book. As such, these questions are intended to accompany efforts to document writing program efforts and to plan for improvement in student learning and its assessment. For the particular set of questions that follow each chapter, we imagine that it would take an institution at least one year to articulate community-based answers. Indeed, since the DFA is intended to encourage the dynamic change that accompanies continuing curricular transformation, the answers for one year will be subject to change a few years hence.

Introduction

In "A Usable Past for Writing Assessment," Huot, O'Neill, and Moore (2010) propose the following: "To create a constructive culture for writing assessment demands more than a simple familiarity with assessment terms such as validity, reliability, rubrics, or outcomes. Rather, writing faculty and administrators need to know in greater nuance and depth not only contemporary definitions of assessment concepts, but also how these concepts have historically developed" (495). A way to answer the kind of inquiry these researchers propose was suggested by James Kinneavy (1971) forty years before: "Analyze the structure of the offerings in the department of English in your college catalogue. To what extend do historical periods, individuals, [and] genres structure the program?" (40). Just as the design of the English major has largely—but not wholly—departed from the historical and genre categories of past generations, we expect that writing programs will continue to change and adapt to new circumstances. But the programs' roots in classical rhetoric and their complex functions as central to college education are likely to remain at the core.

Questions

The following questions are intended to help those responsible for their institution's writing program identify important regional, national, and international assessment trends. Answering these questions will establish an important background for writing program assessment.

1. Using a ten-year mark as a milestone period, identify the framework that has been used in your institution's writing program for instruction and assessment. For example, if you now use *The WPA Outcomes*

Statement 3.0 (CWPA 2014) and the *Framework for Success in Postsecondary Writing* (CWPA, NCTE, and NWP 2011) as a basis for first-year program outcomes, what was used before that adoption? Establishing important milestone events lends an important sense of historical narrative and reflective awareness to the writing program.

2. What metaphors (Kahneman 2011; Lakoff and Johnson 1980; Leary 1990; Ruiz de Mendoza Ibanez and Perez Hernandez 2011) are used by the institution to describe the writing program, and what do these metaphors reveal about the way that the writing program is conceptualized in the institution? Conscious reflection on metaphors is important to establishing a sense of rhetorical awareness for the writing program.

3. How can you best describe the programmatic approach your institution uses for instruction and assessment of students in each of the following writing program components: preenrollment; required courses; the writing center; writing-intensive requirements in the upper division, including writing-across-the-curriculum and writing-in-the-disciplines initiatives; graduation requirements; postbaccalaureate requirements, including thesis and dissertation requirements; writing program administrator support; and the research agenda for the writing program? Establishing specific outcomes for all components of the writing program is important to the community served by the program—as well as to those external to your intuition who will eventually evaluate the program.

4. What kinds of validation evidence are used to demonstrate that the writing program is achieving its stated outcomes in each of the program components identified in question 3? Specifically, what arguments for interpretation and use of assessment information (Kane 2013) are used to justify the consequences of the assessment? One way to answer this question is to focus on the four purposes of postsecondary writing assessment: to consider and respond to individual students in a classroom or tutorial setting for pedagogical purposes; to assess the relative success of a writing program in achieving program objectives; to act as a gateway to national programs or universities for individual students taking nationwide tests; and to determine if students are ready for graduation and career success. Establishing a validation plan for instruction and assessment assures the institutional community that the work of students is being assessed in a meaningful way and the results of the assessment are being used to enhance student learning.

5. How does the writing program model the construct of writing longitudinally? For example, how is the writing construct modeled during the preenrollment period and communicated to students being placed into various levels of courses? Construct modeling (Hayes 2012)

assures the institutional community that writing is a complex process and thus combats reductive responses to writing instruction.

6. When assessment episodes (Ruth and Murphy 1988) are individual transactions between students and instructors, what mechanisms are used to document those transactions? For example, are grading contracts such as those described by Inoue (2014) used, and are the results from their use examined regarding their impact on ethnically diverse groups of writers? Documenting such individual transactions in a public way establishes instructor knowledge (Shepard 2006) as the center of instruction and assessment.

7. How does the writing program use constructive alignment (Biggs and Tang 2011) to link itself with other programmatic assessment efforts, such as regional and program accreditation, which are in turn linked to the mission of the institution? Specifically, how does the writing program use these available sources of evidence to determine institutional commitment and educational effectiveness? A good way to visualize the writing program in the context of other programs and their assessment is to fill in the specific regional, program, and internship/residency program assessment initiatives at your institution shown in Figure 1.1. After these are completed, then identify the sources of evidence shown in the figure—from mission through quality improvement—used in program assessment at your institution and the planned assessment of your writing program. Establishing such resonance between the writing program and other institutional agendas demonstrates that the writing program is part of a larger community conscious of the importance of institutional mission.

8. What genres will be used to communicate information from the questions to key stakeholders: advisory boards, administration, faculty, parents, professional organizations, students, and the general public? For example, while the historical background of the writing program might be expressed in a print document, writing program outcomes for different levels of instruction might best be posted on the web in digital format. Similarly, reflective statements on transactions with the writing center instructors, prepared by students, might best be communicated in podcasts linked to the writing center or the writing program website. From traditional reports to new digital forms, information about instruction and assessment should be designed to serve the information needs of various audiences.

2
LESSONS

In chapter 1, we identified components of a successful writing program, beginning with a defined construct model and ending with an overall strategic plan. Because the assessment of student learning is a key element in writing program assessment, in this chapter we turn to case studies conducted by the authors on student performance in three curricular areas: preenrollment placement and first-year placement; writing across the curriculum (WAC) and writing in the disciplines (WID); and graduate studies. We begin by reviewing the development of a program-wide writing assessment at Louisiana State University (LSU). We then turn to WAC and WID programs of writing assessment at the undergraduate junior level and a program of writing assessment at the graduate level. The upper-division and graduate case studies are based on work at New Jersey Institute of Technology (NJIT). Taken together, these studies provide a comprehensive view of writing program assessments at the first-year level, across the curriculum, and through graduate study. Our extensive involvement with these programs—along with others in our long careers, such as the credit-by-examination assessment for the California State University system developed and administered between 1973 and 1981 when 31,092 students were examined (Elliot and Perelman 2012, 8; White 2001)—informs the framework for program assessment we present in this book. Specifically, the key figures we present as visual guides to our vision of writing program assessment— Figure 1.1, Figure 2.3, Figure 3.1, Figure 3.2, Figure 4.1, and Figure 5.1—are derived from our experiences with cases such as those we present here. These cases confirm our belief in the significance of understanding writing program assessment as a unique genre, in the necessity of construct modeling, and in the importance of understanding the impact of our actions ecologically.

A good way to approach the case studies in this chapter is through the lens of their instrumental value—that is, not as ideals but as examples to be adapted and used in local situations. The research we present should

DOI: 10.7330/9780874219869.c002

thus be approached as collective case studies. As Robert E. Stake (2006) defines them, these are studies chosen because their analysis leads to a better understanding, including better theorizing, about a larger collection of cases (89). Just such an approach is taken by Huot, O'Neill, and Moore (2010) in their analysis of a "usable past" for writing assessment. In the conclusion to this chapter, we move outward to examine the instrumental value of the cases to offer, from a distance of time and perspective, lessons learned.

Among those lessons is the honest realization that our best at the time was not the best that can be accomplished today. Based on the concepts presented in this book, we hinted in the previous chapter at a potential gold standard for program assessment. We are well aware that not every institution has the resources, commitment, or will to use that gold standard. Historically, we did not have the framework for that standard when we began and published the studies we will summarize in this chapter. Large-scale, institutional adoption of innovative assessment based on Phase 2 portfolio concepts with their multiple variable scoring models, as we discuss in the next chapter, requires substantial agreement on program objectives among both faculty and administrators. Substantial preparation is also needed. Objectives of the program must be set out clearly so students can connect their work to them and save their writing in their coursework in preparation for assessment episodes occurring on a cyclical basis. Faculty colleagues must own those objectives so they can refer to them in their syllabi and assignments. And the administration must be patient enough to wait for the program assessment to produce data. There is not a quick fix. In this chapter, we therefore present a silver standard, one based on coherent theory supportive of student learning. As we will show, that silver standard has yielded and continues to yield valuable results for a wide variety of stakeholders. Such studies set the stage for the new gold standard.

WRITING PROGRAM ASSESSMENT IN FIRST-YEAR WRITING

Sensitivity to the centripetal and centrifugal tension in a large-scale first-year writing program allowed Irvin Peckham to institutionalize a program-wide first-year assessment at LSU. His efforts fostered a culture of assessment—rhetorical in nature and extending beyond the traditional discourse of accountability—that recursively enriched the culture of teaching at the local level, a consequence of assessment broadly valued by our field (Adler-Kassner and Estrem 2009; Adler-Kassner and O'Neill 2010; Broad 2003; Elbow 2012; Harrington 2013; Huot 2002; Yancey

1999). Challenging instructor resistance to large-scale assessment, the culture of assessment encouraged instructors at LSU to work collectively rather than in private. The assessment encouraged program coherence and persuasively demonstrated improvement in student writing ability, an outcome appealing to the complex ecology of internal stakeholders, such as instructors and administrators, and external stakeholders, such as regional and program-accreditation agencies (Fleckenstein et al. 2008). Working within the frames of "outsiders," the program directors at LSU used the very rhetorical strategies they taught in the classroom to craft ways of using assessment results and the language surrounding them to persuade others to see what they saw.

Because first-year undergraduate pre-enrollment and course assessment is a fundamental function of writing programs, the first case study is the longest. It reveals four important areas of writing assessment germane to program assessment: the appropriate use of technological solutions to traditional challenges; the importance of understanding validity in terms of writing tasks; the importance of understanding reliability in terms of intertask equivalency; and the significance of consequence in terms of specific assessment constituencies. Because the LSU case study is the first of four complex studies, you may want to review it briefly now and then review it again after completing the book. The concepts and analyses in these cases are complex, and their value will become more apparent after grappling with the new vocabulary and empirical procedures we define in chapters 3, 4, and 5.

The Challenge

In keeping with our claim that assessments, like texts, come bundled in genres, we interpret the LSU assessment as a response to an exigence in a local rhetorical situation (Bitzer 1968; Yancey 2012). The culture of assessment that leads to a program assessment often begins with the clear need for placement of entering students. As we noted in chapter 1, as federal attention continues to focus on the transition between high school and college in terms of retention and graduation, writing program assessment will provide needed answers regarding the decisions we make and their justification in terms of student curricular advancement.

After one year as a writing program administrator (WPA), Peckham was convinced of the need to replace the existing method of placing first-year students in the first or second of a two-course sequence in the required writing program. Upon admission, students were placed on the basis of SAT or ACT scores. Accuracy of these placements was then evaluated during the first week of classes with a timed essay, a traditional diagnostic technique. Just as they were suspicious of standardized tests, program administrators were wary of a single, timed writing sample as a valid predictor of a student's ability to write in the significantly different kinds of rhetorical situations instructors created in their classes. LSU researchers were aware of the research showing a range of statistically significant correlations, from 0.20 (Bamberg 1982, 405) to 0.75 (Stiggins 1982, 101), between multiple-choice tests used in the standardized tests and timed writing used in local evaluation. This range further suggested that the different tests were tapping different variables of the writing construct—and thus might not be providing a useful account of student writing ability in academic genres in the first place. In addition, the relationship of standardized tests such as the SAT to parent income suggested a use of scores for admission and placement widely viewed as no longer acceptable (Kidder and Rosner 2002; Tough 2014). Regardless of all good-faith efforts, this traditional first-year placement process was not meeting the needs of the university in the twenty-first century.

The relationship between the writing construct and the way it was manifested in the writing task was the heart of the matter. LSU instructors considered thoughtfulness, research, and revision to be integral parts of the writing construct: the classroom assignments allowed at least three weeks for the students to complete an essay; the students had a plethora of information; during that period they spent time analyzing previous student essays in the target genre, researching information, discussing their projects, prewriting, outlining, circulating their essays in writing groups to get suggestions for improvement, and rewriting. Only then did the students submit revised and polished work. Although the assessment committee did not frame the problem as one of construct representation—the precise expression of the construct as represented in the writing task—committee members believed that placement procedures should reproduce as nearly as possible the rhetorical situation students would meet in their classes. If classroom assignments allowed a great deal of time to complete a writing sample, why didn't LSU use a similar method to place the students in the appropriate classroom? Why sit by and let the test underrepresent the construct?

To redesign the writing-placement program, administrators obtained a one-time grant of $10,000 to support the first year of the Online Challenge. The assessment committee was reluctant to construct a placement procedure that would involve gathering, organizing, and scoring portfolios with unpredictable differences in content that might result in construct irrelevance. Peckham had initiated a similar project, based on the University of Miami and University of Michigan models, in 1994 through 1995, so he was fully aware of the difficulties such a placement procedure would involve and the differences in the rates of scoring portfolios (at a rate of five per hour) and single essays (at a rate of fifteen per hour). White (2005) had not yet published "The Scoring of Writing Portfolios: Phase 2," which would yield robust construct representation and reliable trait scoring (Collins et al. 2013). Even that model, however, may have proved difficult to follow for placement purposes because the Phase 2 model depends on a coherent curriculum with specific course objectives and is designed for course-embedded assessment, not for placement.

Because the $10,000 grant would not cover the cost of brochures, mailing, staff, and readers for five thousand essays (the approximate number of incoming students), the assessment committee decided to score only the essays of those students who were willing to do the required reading and writing in the summer in order to challenge the results of their ACT/SAT placement. Under the leadership of Les Perelman, founder of the iCampus MIT Online Assessment Tool (iMOAT) project at Massachusetts Institute of Technology, Peckham worked with Elizabeth Coughlin and Yared Tamine from DePaul University, Marlene Miller from the University of Cincinnati, and Steve Youra from Cal Tech to develop a sophisticated online assessment platform that would facilitate an online assessment so students from anywhere in the country could participate without having to be on campus for the duration of the assessment.

In "Online Placement in First-Year Writing," Peckham (2009) has described the iMOAT platform and the construct validity assumptions behind its design in more detail; in essence, the program allows test administrators to construct multiple online assessments for an unlimited number of students. The administrator can register thousands of students in a single batch and create a calendar to regulate the times when students can log on to the platform. Students can then retrieve articles to be read and at a later time log on again to retrieve a writing task based on that series of articles. The LSU Online Challenge gave students four days to write and submit their essays online. If classroom assignments allowed a great deal of time to complete a writing sample, the use of iMOAT at LSU would allow a similar method to place the students in the appropriate classroom. The placement test would no longer underrepresent the construct.

In order to reproduce the writing situation for the last essay in the genre sequence of the first semester course—a benchmark assuring that only qualified students would be exempted from the sequence

(Cizek and Bunch 2007)—the LSU assessment committee required student challengers to read a significant number of articles to become informed on a specific issue. The committee predicted accurately that approximately 90 percent of the incoming students would prefer to accept the ACT/SAT placement rather that spend several summer days writing an essay about a subject such as oil drilling in the Arctic National Wildlife Refuge in order to gain course exemption— a reminder that the convenience of efficient testing can override the desire for robust construct. It is not only the researchers who dread inconvenience. In order to encourage as many students as possible to participate, the committee opted to require only one essay, in spite of the research documenting several essays in several genres as indicators of a student's writing ability (Cooper 1984; Cooper and Odell 1977; Elbow and Belanoff 1986). The committee also thought students who decided to challenge their ACT/SAT placement would put significant effort into their attempt to gain exemption; consequently, readers would be looking at some of the best writing the students would be able to produce in the genre under examination.

Concurrent with the technological solution provided by iMOAT, attention was paid to inductive development of criteria that would capture student responses to the writing task and yield accurate and consistent scoring. The assessment committee members followed the careful procedure for establishing an organic protocol used by Godshalk, Swineford, and Coffman at ETS in 1961 (Elliot 2005, 160) and later designed for classroom application in the 1970s by the Bay Area Writing Project and by Charles Cooper in the 1980s for the California Assessment Project (Peckham 1987). The committee met for five days to write their own essays in response to the writing task, read each other's essays, and developed a preliminary list of scoring criteria they thought were important in the specific genre. Afterwards, they read student submissions, chose sample essays representing different degrees of achievement, refined their initial list of central features, and wrote descriptions of essays at different levels of achievement on the basis of the central features. This careful process of rubric development is an important aspect of the case. These procedures have become rare in recent decades, so it is important to remember them because more and more shortcuts are in play that diminish the reputation of group scoring of essays. Far too often, the criteria and scoring rubrics are hastily and poorly developed (Broad 2003). Indeed, it is common now for rubrics to be handed down by committees or administrators who have little knowledge of the students or the curriculum to be assessed—or even to borrow from other programs with different kinds of students and curricula, a practice that can put in question the validity of the scores themselves and, thus, the entire assessment.

Thus, LSU designed a targeted assessment that was clear about the specific skills and the specific genres being assessed for the purposes of placement into entry-level writing. If writing program administrators pay attention to the specific genres and skills central to their required writing programs, they should be able to design, with the considerable effort required for such an important process, a responsible placement process that will help them determine whether writers need first-semester or second-semester instruction. The procedure developed at LSU fit the local situation, a response, perhaps, to the overriding tenet of assessment: with due attention to research in the field, colleagues can construct a placement process that is a specific response to the local situation.

Serendipity and Technology

One project design led to another. Although participation in iMOAT was free for the first three years—a consequence of LSU's being one of five universities who were signatories to the Microsoft grant spearheaded by Perelman—Peckham knew that in three years, LSU would have to pay $15,000 a year to continue with iMOAT. Peckham also knew that the dean would not support the 250 to 275 students participating in the Online Challenge. So he imagined another use for iMOAT—assessing student achievement at the end of the first semester using a protocol identical to the one used for the Online Challenge. Here was a case of embedded assessment. He would consequently be assessing student writing ability for about 3,500 students (the number enrolled in the first-semester course); thus, the cost for iMOAT per student would be a little over four dollars per student. The congruity between placement and embedded assessment was appealing: place motivated, qualified students into challenging courses with an assessment incorporating a robust sample of the writing construct and then use that same technique to investigate writing improvement.

Peckham theorized there would be several advantages to abandoning the old end-of-semester assessment—an up-or-down judgment of proficiency—that would appeal to the dean, two of which would unarguably get the dean's attention: the new Semester Assessment could identify students who clearly did not need another semester of instruction, thus saving the cost of the per-student instruction in the second semester; and it could track improvement in student achievement by quantifying their abilities at the beginning and end of the semester. Faculty attention was directed toward two equally important areas: the new assessment program established a coherent set of criteria for evaluating student achievement in a well-defined genre central to the writing program; and the new program provided instructors with a relatively objective, independent evaluation of student achievement they could use when assigning final grades. As for the students, the carrot of potential exemption from the second-semester writing course encouraged them to work throughout the semester—not just on the assessment day—to improve their writing in order to demonstrate the kind of writing ability that would justify exemption. For all key constituencies of the assessment, the impact was both favorable and transformative. The signaling effect (Bowen, Chingos, and McPherson 2009, 131–33) was clear: LSU cared about the writing ability of its students; instructors were willing to go to great lengths to assure valid assessment through painstaking test-development work; and students were encouraged to see assessment as a naturally occurring part of their curriculum.

Results of the Online Challenge

By using iMOAT, LSU was able to create a placement test that simulated course context. Nevertheless, challenges remained.

As might be expected, there was evidence that a shift in topic affected the quality of student writing. The average score for the Online Challenge ranged from 4.99 to 7.16 on a scale of 2–12 in the years 2003 to 2009. The student population with the Online Challenge was quite consistent—the average ACT scores ranging in single sessions from 25.2 to 26.4—but there was no statistically significant correlation between these two measures (-0.8). Here was further confirmation of research suggesting that the range of correlations between multiple-choice tests and timed writing tests (Bamberg 1982; Stiggins 1982) tapped different variables of the writing construct. It should also be no surprise that, as a result of standardization stemming from limited construct representation, the ACT scores showed less variation than the writing tasks. Comprised of seventy-five multiple choice questions on usage/mechanics (n = 40) and rhetorical skills (n = 35), the ACT English section taps a different, more limited aspect of the writing construct than the Online Challenge does. Yet the lesson learned cuts both ways. The greater the breadth of the assessment as it is designed to capture the writing construct, the greater the score variance will be. If standardization and resultant national comparison to other institutions is desired, then the ACT English is the superior measure; if broad construct validity important to local setting is desired, then the Online Challenge is the preferred measure. Regardless of the type of assessment chosen, however, each must be validated in the institutional setting for its intended use. As Poe et al. (2014) have argued, "While locally developed measures are vital, they are not a proxy for validity" (604).

Drilling down more deeply, intertask reliability proved problematic. Students may have been more able to respond to the relatively apolitical task of a bottled water topic than to the clearly politicized task asking students to analyze different reports and claims about the weapons of mass destruction in Iraq, even though the articles administrators chose represented a range of positions on the issues. When we combined the political and relatively apolitical topics, we found that students performed at higher levels on the apolitical ($M = 6.51$, n = 295) than on the political ($M = 6.03$, n = 497) topics.

Results of the Semester Assessment

A sound demonstration of student improvement as measured by early and late course assessments means very little unless the program features objectives that appeal to both the writing studies community and to outside stakeholders. As a consequence of a survey of writing tasks in a variety of disciplines at LSU, course objectives had a firm base in genre theory. In addition, program objectives were derived from the *WPA Outcomes Statement* in their attention to rhetorical knowledge, critical thinking, reading and writing processes, and knowledge of conventions. Because any single assessment episode based on any single task has the potential to underrepresent the writing construct, the structure of the Semester Assessment did not allow for a full representation of all objectives of the first semester of the writing course. The Semester Assessment did, however, provide information on the basis of the following abilities: to understand a specific rhetorical situation; to undertake a critical reading of secondary research; to integrate information from other sources into the student's own writing; to write clearly; and to demonstrate control of conventions for standard edited English and cited references.

With limitations acknowledged, the program was able to document clear evidence of gain in the students' abilities to write in the family of informative genres. The number of students participating in both projects was small relative to the number of students who normally participated in the Semester Assessment (n = 3000) each year because only 6 percent to 8 percent of the incoming class (n = 250 students) opted to participate it the Online Challenge, and only 60 percent of them ended up in

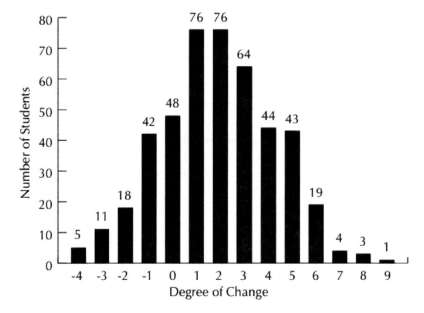

Figure 2.1. Gain in student achievement on 2–12 scale, 2003–2009 (n = 454).

the first-semester writing class, where, at the end of the semester, they were required to take the Semester Assessment. Yet because the Semester Assessment was embedded in the curriculum, comparisons were possible.

In Figure 2.1, we see the cumulative distribution of students who scored lower, the same, or higher on a 2–12 scale from the years 2003–2009 when their scores on the Online Challenge and Semester Assessment were compared.

Figure 2.1 demonstrates substantial achievement among the 454 students who participated in both the Online Challenge and Semester Assessment during those years. Only 5 out of 454 students had scores that were four points lower at the end of the semester than their scores on the Online Challenge. Only 48 students had scores that remained the same. Seventy-six gained by one point, 76 gained by two points, 64 gained by three points, and 44 gained by four points. At the high end, 4 gained by seven points, 3 gained by eight points, and 1 gained by nine. In the aggregate, these gains demonstrate that a significant majority of students improved. Table 2.1 further disaggregates the information.

As the table shows, student score gains far outweigh score declines. Indeed, by 2009 the program appears to be at its strongest in the reporting period, with 80 percent (n = 68) of the students demonstrating higher scores, with only an 8 percent (n = 7) score decrease.

Table 2.1 Breakdown of writing ability increase, 2003–2009 (n = 454).

Year	Average Increase	Percent of Students Who Increased	Percent of Students Who Decreased	Number of Students Who Increased	Number of Students Who Decreased
2009	2.33	80%	8%	68	7
2008	1.73	67%	20%	53	16
2007	2.26	81%	11%	66	9
2006	1.70	73%	16%	51	11
2005	1.16	59%	33%	36	20
2004	1.80	70%	18%	31	8
2003	1.68	69%	17%	25	6

Of course, demonstration of student gain is not the sole reason to conduct program assessment. An important element of any program-wide assessment is the feedback loop. The LSU program relied on several methods to continue to validate their assessment processes. The easiest method was to have instructors respond to a survey within a week of having completed the scoring. The survey was a combination of objective and free-form questions, the dominant purpose of the latter being a reflection on what instructors saw in student writing that marked progress and what they noted as common weaknesses, ones they might want to focus more clearly on in subsequent instruction. Also included in the survey were questions about the current focus of instruction and the method of assessing student writing. Responses to these surveys were then summarized and discussed in small workshops when the instructors reconvened for the following fall semester.

At the end of Peckham's tenure as WPA, the assessment program had become institutionalized. Most instructors looked forward to the week when they would get together as a group for three half days to talk about student writing, discuss criteria and sample student essays, and score patterns. The program began with three years of voluntary participation and ended with six years of mandatory participation. The instructors and graduate students had become skilled readers, many of them acting as table leaders. In the last two iterations, Peckham no longer functioned as lead reader for the training sessions, having consigned that role to two of the instructors who had been among the five instructors who developed the writing tasks, benchmark papers, and scoring guides. In the last iteration, the entire Semester Assessment was run by the instructors.

Consequence

Along with positive consequences for faculty and students, information generated from the Online Challenge and the Semester Assessments served as the basis for a report on the university writing program (UWP) to the Southern Association of Colleges and Schools (SACS) Accreditation Review. Indeed, the dean and chair both used that report as a model for other assessments. The administrators of the UWP were able to use the assessment scores to document improvement in both students and instructors by calculating the average scores in the years 2005–2008 to provide evidence that students were exceeding expectations, meeting expectations, or not meeting expectations (the categories suggested by the University Assessment Committee). Using scores to establish the categories of meeting or exceeding expectations, the research conducted by UWP found that 82 percent of the students either met or exceeded expectations and 18 percent did not meet expectations. The UWP used those scores as the baseline against which they measured achievement in subsequent years.

In the fall of 2009, the UWP was able to report an increase in student achievement. From 2003 to 2008, 82 percent of the students met or exceeded expectations. In the fall of 2009, that number rose to 87 percent. In their report, the UWP also compared the increase in student achievement with the fall of 2009 to demonstrate substantial average gain ($M = 2.33$, n = 84). UWP administrators were also able to report, on the basis of the Online Challenge and Semester Assessment scores, that in the fall of 2009, 91 percent of the students showed some evidence of improvement compared to 9 percent who did not improve. Using quantitative arguments, the UWP was able to demonstrate in their SACS report that students were learning how to improve their writing and instructors were improving their abilities to teach writing in the family of genres that were the focus of the program. Through information obtained in workshops, focus groups, and surveys, the UWP was able to document specific pedagogical shifts that were a consequence of the assessment, particularly in the instructors' use of genre-specific criteria to evaluate student writing.

The UWP also included specific data demonstrating the feedback loop—the use instructors were able to make of the assessment and their reflections on the assessment. In their surveys, the UWP compared instructor responses on two criteria: whether the scores students received in the assessment gave instructors good information they could use when determining a final grade, and whether the assessment was a reasonably accurate indicator of student ability to write in the genre framing the writing task in the assessment. Positive responses to both questions rose, from 61 percent in 2005 to 74 percent in 2009.

The UWP was able to use such information to demonstrate the progressive successful integration of assessment, curriculum, and pedagogy—a dialectic in which instructors obtained information from the assessment that, in turn, informed their pedagogy. Such a process fosters the discovery of information that holds the potential to improve the assessment, which recursively improves instruction. For all stakeholders, the assessment had a demonstrable impact.

WRITING PROGRAM ASSESSMENT BEYOND INITIAL REQUIRED WRITING COURSES

As a writing assessment program occurring early in the undergraduate curriculum, the LSU case reveals the benefits of technological solutions to traditional challenges. The case demonstrates the importance of developing construct-rich writing tasks and of understanding consequence in terms of specific assessment constituencies. Each of these lessons may apply equally to writing assessment beyond the entry level. By extension, examination of upper-division writing allows examination of the role of ePortfolios in program assessment. As we will demonstrate, an ePortfolio designed to be assessed yields rich sources of information that can be used to advance student learning. Our examples will focus on the conceptual alignment of program and assessment objectives, the usefulness of scores based on multiple variables of writing, the potential for both descriptive and inferential statistical analysis stemming from this kind of scoring, and the longitudinal use of such information.

As we argued in chapter 1, writing programs must extend their influence beyond the first year if they are to advance the educational and research mission of their host universities. To encourage such extension, we turn now to assessment as it occurs in writing across the curriculum, writing in the disciplines, and graduate writing programs. Examples are taken from NJIT and, on the graduate level, from instructor participation with the Society for Technical Communication. In essence, the NJIT cases are extensions of the LSU model but with a broader view of the writing construct (tapping more of the variables shown in Figure 3.1) facilitated through the use of ePortfolios and the varied writing genres they contain.

Writing Across the Curriculum

The movement today known as WAC has a rich and important history and a promising future (Bazerman et al. 2005). Of course, the study of rhetoric was an important part of American eighteenth- and nineteenth-century college education, an advanced study for future clergy with a tradition linked to classical roots in Aristotle and Quintilian. But the first use of the modern concept began, according to Les Perelman (2014), at Massachusetts Institute of Technology: "It began in the 1890s but then was replaced with a literature class in the late 1900s. It started again in the 1920s for just a few years. It started again in 1952 and has been continuous since then." More recent efforts to expand writing instruction beyond the first-year course have their origin with Barbara Walvoord in a 1969–1970 faculty seminar at Central College in Iowa. As an area of study, WAC refers to the pedagogical and curricular attention to writing occurring in postsecondary subject-matter classes other than those taught by those in the field of rhetoric and composition/writing studies. "The movement," as Bazerman et al. (2005) define it, provides "systematic encouragement, institutional support, and educational knowledge to increase the amount and quality of writing occurring in such courses as history, science, mathematics and sociology" (9). Often, these courses are designated as writing intensive and, at their best, include the kinds of writing tasks that expose students to varied genres and audiences as students write in both print and multimodal environments. Research has also been conducted on the assessment of writing-across-the-curriculum programs (Hughes 1996; Yancey and Huot 1997).

Recently, Condon and Carol Rutz (2012) have advanced an excellent taxonomy of writing across the curriculum. Based on metaphors from physics, their taxonomy employs construct modeling in writing program design, emphasizing both location (effort, impact, and identity) and momentum (program outcomes). If we can locate a WAC program's position in the context of the institution at a given moment, Bill Condon and Rutz propose, we enable planning for momentum and establish progress toward local program objectives through defined outcomes. In a classification that includes program ranking (foundational, established, integrated, and change-agent status), the conceptual system is based on objectives, funding, organization, integration, and indicators of success. Their taxonomy aligns well with the model we present in chapter 3 in depicting a tagmemic approach to the use of ePortfolios.

Direct measurement of student writing ability complements and enhances the taxonomy. In a writing-intensive course, an ePortfolio

Table 2.2 Core competencies from upper-division writing-across-the-curriculum course: Writing about Science, Technology, and Society.

STS Core Competency	Description
STS Analytics	Establish competency in drawing research conclusions, particularly in STS-related fields of policy, economics, and culture.
Collaboration	Demonstrate accuracy and efficiency in group setting, including working well in traditional and digital environments.
Communication (Traditional and New Media)	Articulate ideas lucidly through traditional forms of print and digital media.
Leadership	Assume key roles in collaborative work.
Information Literacy	Employ a variety of search techniques, both traditional and digital, to inform analysis

designed to capture a defined construct model based on the core competencies of the program provides an excellent vehicle for program assessment. An example—shown in Table 2.2 and Figure 2.2—shows how portfolios can focus such an assessment.

Table 2.2 and Figure 2.2 are taken from an upper-division, writing-intensive course offered for elective credit in a curriculum of general university requirements. In its dual purpose, the course —Writing about Science, Technology, and Society—serves as a good example of the ways that a writing program provides planned encouragement, institutional integration, and knowledge from the field of writing studies to increase the amount and quality of writing in a wide range of courses throughout the curriculum.

As a field of study, science, technology, and society (STS) is defined as "the study of the ways in which technical and social phenomena interact and influence each other" (McGinn 1990, 7–8). STS researchers examine the roles of science and technology in international and national relations, social institutions and groups, and ethics and values within and beyond the academy. Following Pierre Bourdieu (1991), Wiebe E. Bijker (2003) believes that those who study STS might serve as public intellectuals for the twenty-first century as they investigate topics such as the role of research and technology in developing nations, work with colleagues in science and engineering, and develop case studies that may potentially result in political intervention. Representative of the kind of curriculum ideal for WAC development, STS faculty members at NJIT have worked to design core competencies for students to ensure that the program will meet the objective of preparing students to take on the roles associated with a public intellectual.

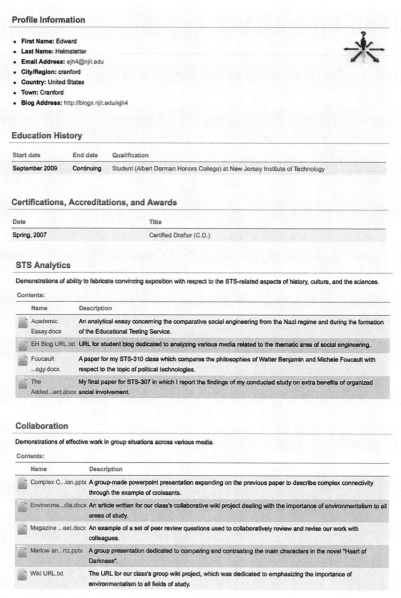

Profile Information

- **First Name:** Edward
- **Last Name:** Helmstetter
- **Email Address:** ejh4@njit.edu
- **City/Region:** cranford
- **Country:** United States
- **Town:** Cranford
- **Blog Address:** http://blogs.njit.edu/ejh4

Education History

Start date	End date	Qualification
September 2009	Continuing	Student (Albert Dorman Honors College) at New Jersey Institute of Technology

Certifications, Accreditations, and Awards

Date	Title
Spring, 2007	Certified Drafter (C.D.)

STS Analytics

Demonstrations of ability to fabricate convincing exposition with respect to the STS-related aspects of history, culture, and the sciences.

Contents:

Name	Description
Academic Essay.docx	An analytical essay concerning the comparative social engineering from the Nazi regime and during the formation of the Educational Testing Service.
EH Blog URL.txt	URL for student blog dedicated to analyzing various media related to the thematic area of social engineering.
Foucault ...ogy.docx	A paper for my STS-310 class which compares the philosophies of Walter Benjamin and Michele Foucault with respect to the topic of political technologies.
The Added...ent.docx	My final paper for STS-307 in which I report the findings of my conducted study on extra benefits of organized social involvement.

Collaboration

Demonstrations of effective work in group situations across various media.

Contents:

Name	Description
Complex C...ion.pptx	A group-made powerpoint presentation expanding on the previous paper to describe complex connectivity through the example of croissants.
Environme...dia.docx	An article written for our class's collaborative wiki project dealing with the importance of environmentalism to all areas of study.
Magazine ...eet.docx	An example of a set of peer review questions used to collaboratively review and revise our work with colleagues.
Marlow an...rtz.pptx	A group presentation dedicated to comparing and contrasting the main characters in the novel "Heart of Darkness".
Wiki URL.txt	The URL for our class's group wiki project, which was dedicated to emphasizing the importance of environmentalism to all fields of study.

Figure 2.2. ePortfolio of Edward Helmstetter, NJIT junior-year student. (Used by permission. Text unedited.)

Review of Figure 2.2 reveals a series of categories in the ePortfolio that are mapped to the STS core competencies in Table 2.2. That is, the writing construct used in the STS program informs the ePortfolio design. At this level the often-abstract elements of program assessment are

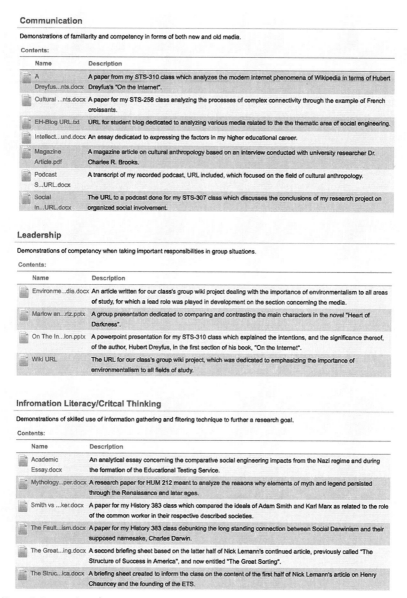

Communication

Demonstrations of familiarity and competency in forms of both new and old media.

Contents:

Name	Description
A Dreyfus...nts.docx	A paper from my STS-310 class which analyzes the modern internet phenomena of Wikipedia in terms of Hubert Dreyfus's "On the Internet".
Cultural ...nts.docx	A paper for my STS-258 class analyzing the processes of complex connectivity through the example of French croissants.
EH-Blog URL.txt	URL for student blog dedicated to analyzing various media related to the the thematic area of social engineering.
Intellect...und.docx	An essay dedicated to expressing the factors in my higher educational career.
Magazine Article.pdf	A magazine article on cultural anthropology based on an interview conducted with university researcher Dr. Charles R. Brooks.
Podcast S...URL.docx	A transcript of my recorded podcast, URL included, which focused on the field of cultural anthropology.
Social In...URL.docx	The URL to a podcast done for my STS-307 class which discusses the conclusions of my research project on organized social involvement.

Leadership

Demonstrations of competency when taking important responsibilities in group situations.

Contents:

Name	Description
Environme...dia.docx	An article written for our class's group wiki project dealing with the importance of environmentalism to all areas of study, for which a lead role was played in development on the section concerning the media.
Marlow an...rtz.pptx	A group presentation dedicated to comparing and contrasting the main characters in the novel "Heart of Darkness".
On The In...ion.pptx	A powerpoint presentation for my STS-310 class which explained the intentions, and the significance thereof, of the author, Hubert Dreyfus, in the first section of his book, "On the Internet".
Wiki URL	The URL for our class's group wiki project, which was dedicated to emphasizing the importance of environmentalism to all fields of study.

Infromation Literacy/Critcal Thinking

Demonstrations of skilled use of information gathering and filtering technique to further a research goal.

Contents:

Name	Description
Academic Essay.docx	An analytical essay concerning the comparative social engineering impacts from the Nazi regime and during the formation of the Educational Testing Service.
Mythology...per.docx	A research paper for HUM 212 meant to analyze the reasons why elements of myth and legend persisted through the Renaisance and later ages.
Smith vs ...ker.docx	A paper for my History 383 class which compared the ideals of Adam Smith and Karl Marx as related to the role of the common worker in their respective described societies.
The Fault...ism.docx	A paper for my History 383 class debunking the long standing connection between Social Darwinism and their supposed namesake, Charles Darwin.
The Great...ing.docx	A second briefing sheet based on the latter half of Nick Lemann's continued article, previously called "The Structure of Success in America", and now entitled "The Great Sorting".
The Struc...ica.docx	A briefing sheet created to inform the class on the content of the first half of Nick Lemann's article on Henry Chauncey and the founding of the ETS.

Figure 2.2—continued

implemented. As we will show in chapter 3, the integration of construct modeling and evidence-centered design has resulted in a digital design that allows Mr. Helmstetter, a major in STS, to showcase his best work on the web. In addition, brief reflective statements allow Mr. Helmstetter to situate his work and demonstrate his proficiencies with each core competency. Sections for his educational background (as a student in the Albert Dorman Honors College) and certificates (as a certified drafter) further allow him to demonstrate his capabilities to fellow students, instructors, and employers. While the limits of print do not allow full examination of the portfolio in Figure 2.2 (as is also the case with Figure 3.4, in which hyperlinks are equally unavailable), his uploaded files and reflective statements reveal his ability to work in various genres and address varied audiences in both print and digital environments.

EPortfolios designed in this way are ideal examples of constructive alignment in action (Biggs and Tang 2011). Broadly defined, constructive alignment is an integrated instructional and assessment framework used to map learning activities to outcomes. By extension, those using constructive alignment can link learning activities at the level of the institutional mission to the syllabus at the level of the course. While the processes and gains of constructive alignment are too extensive to treat here, mapping a series of objectives "up" to the institutional mission and "over" through the syllabus is an important element of writing program design. In an ePortfolio—the vehicle of constructive alignment—students can demonstrate their engagement with program-level objectives across time and circumstance. As a vehicle to capture student ability, the ePortfolio is thus designed for program as well as individual student assessment. As an expression of the relational model described in chapter 1, the ePortfolio—with its longitudinal collection of student work—is designed so it can be assessed. In measurement terms, the ePortfolio allows the predictor variables—in this case, analytics, leadership, collaboration, information literacy/critical thinking, and communication—to be evaluated as they contribute to the outcome of STS curricular competency.

Writing in the Disciplines

While the ePortfolio described above is in an experimental stage, another undergraduate course at NJIT—technical writing—has used these digital platforms since 2004 to document institutional effectiveness for a variety of audiences. Those audiences have included a decennial visit from the Middle States Commission on Higher Education and periodic assessments from the Accreditation Board of Engineering and Technology, the Association to Advance Collegiate Schools of Business, and the National Architectural Accrediting Board. If the course Writing about Science, Technology, and Society is a good example of a course in the genre of writing across the curriculum, then technical writing is an equally good example of writing in the disciplines. In the language of assessment, both courses represent the domain of writing—what we will refer to in chapter 4 as construct span.

Although writing in the disciplines (WID) is often associated with writing across the curriculum (WAC), they are distinct. While WAC focuses on students *learning to write*, WID focuses on students *writing to learn* in specific areas of study. As Bazerman et al. (2005) propose, WID involves "both a research movement to understand what writing actually occurs in the different disciplinary areas and a curricular reform movement to offer disciplinary related writing instruction" (9–10). Designed to be a course in which students examine what kind of writing actually is undertaken in their chosen disciplines, how professionals accomplish those tasks, and what aspects of the writing are most highly valued (Neff and Whithaus 2008, 7), technical writing at NJIT thus becomes a course that allows students to see themselves as disciplinary professionals. Indeed, when serving as a prerequisite course to capstone seminars in disciplinary areas, an upper-division course in technical writing becomes an ideal way for students to ensure that they have the competencies and skills to succeed in their professions. WID assumes that the essence of a college major field of study lies in the language, the definition and uses of evidence, the common tropes and metaphors, and the underlying reasoning processes that distinguish, say, a biologist from a historian. Distinct from the general writing approach in print and digital environments used in Writing about Science, Technology, and Society, the NJIT course in technical writing is designed to allow students to explore the special writing genres most often used in their disciplines. Here, the NJIT model for this component of the writing program follows the one used at the Massachusetts Institute of Technology (Poe, Lerner, and Craig 2010); that is, both models are based on the assumption that specialized ways of thinking and writing are inseparable and that such different practices demand knowledge of both writing practices and genres. Figure 2.3 shows the variable model that informs ePortfolio assessment in technical writing (Johnson and Elliot 2010). Table 2.3 shows the scoring sheet by which, after intensive review of sample ePortfolios to establish score ranges, the ePortfolios are evaluated by technical writing instructors.

As we will discuss in chapter 4, such complex student performances are often difficult to score. In early sessions, nonadjudicated scores on each of the eight predictor variables failed to reach statistical significance; and, following adjudication, ranges on the variables were often low (.29, $p < .01$). Over time, however, levels of interreader reliability rose—sending a clear message to the faculty to stick with the assessment in order to build reader community. The variables were always

Table 2.3. Scoring sheet for technical writing.

Technical Communication Scoring Sheet

Please evaluate the ePortfolio with attention to the variables identified below: 1 EPortfolio Design; 2 Clear Style; 3 Accurate Usage; 4 Task Knowledge; 5 Relevant Content; 6 Adapted Tone; 7 Graphic Cohesion; 8 Citation; and 9 Overall ePortfolio Score.

After you have scored these variables, provide a Holistic Score.

1 EPortfolio Design. The ePortfolio is attentive to user needs.

Very Strongly Agree	Strongly Agree	Agree	Disagree	Strongly Disagree	Very Strongly Disagree

2 Clear Style: The contents of the ePortfolio document style that is readable, concise, and cohesive.

Very Strongly Agree	Strongly Agree	Agree	Disagree	Strongly Disagree	Very Strongly Disagree

3 Accurate Usage: The contents of the ePortfolio document command of knowledge of conventions.

Very Strongly Agree	Strongly Agree	Agree	Disagree	Strongly Disagree	Very Strongly Disagree

4 Task Knowledge: The contents of the ePortfolio document clear understanding of assignments.

Very Strongly Agree	Strongly Agree	Agree	Disagree	Strongly Disagree	Very Strongly Disagree

5 Relevant Content: The contents of the ePortfolio document accurate and thorough articulation of ideas.

Very Strongly Agree	Strongly Agree	Agree	Disagree	Strongly Disagree	Very Strongly Disagree

6 Adapted Tone: The contents of the ePortfolio document that the student can adapt tone for audience.

Very Strongly Agree	Strongly Agree	Agree	Disagree	Strongly Disagree	Very Strongly Disagree

7 Graphic Cohesion: The contents of the ePortfolio document that the student can achieve cohesion by a variety of graphic means in print and digital environments.

Very Strongly Agree	Strongly Agree	Agree	Disagree	Strongly Disagree	Very Strongly Disagree

8 Citation: The contents of the ePortfolio demonstrate that the student can document sources so that the original can easily be found.

Very Strongly Agree	Strongly Agree	Agree	Disagree	Strongly Disagree	Very Strongly Disagree

9 EPortfolio Holistic Score

Very Strongly Agree	Strongly Agree	Agree	Disagree	Strongly Disagree	Very Strongly Disagree
The materials in the ePortfolio demonstrate excellent work in the class.	The materials in the ePortfolio demonstrate very good work in the class.	The materials in the ePortfolio demonstrate average work in the class.	The materials in the ePortfolio demonstrate below average work in the class.	The materials in the ePortfolio demonstrate work that is at a level near failure.	The materials in the ePortfolio demonstrate work that is at a level of failure.

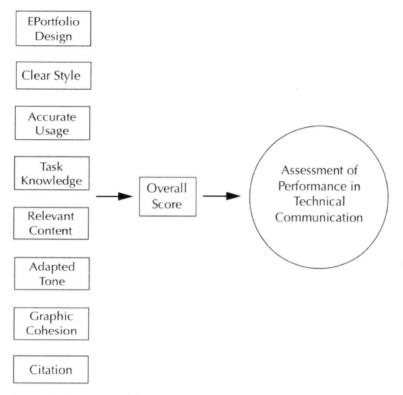

Figure 2.3. Construct modeling in technical writing.

well correlated, ranging from .55 ($p < .01$) to .79 ($p < .01$) over a five-year period (n = 636)—sending another message that whatever it was that the readers were assessing, one element was related to another. Furthermore, the internal consistency of the model—the relationship of the predictor variables to the outcome variable of the holistic score—was moderate, ranging from $R^2 = .68$ ($F(8,55) = 12.5$, $p < .01$ to $R^2 = .92$ ($F(8,24) = 21.48$, $p < .01$.). That is, from 68 percent to 92 percent of the relationship between the predictor variables and the holistic score was accounted for by the model. That message was even stronger—things held together. Because these analyses are powerful tools for program assessment, we will turn in more detail to them in chapter 4.

For now, it is important to realize that ePortfolios allow a wide variety of information to be used to justify their use in program assessment. With concepts of interreader reliability, correlation, and model strength accounted for in reports, program administrators can assure students, instructors, administrators, and accreditors that students are meeting expectations and improving over time.

Table 2.4 Improvement in awarded scores, 2004 (n = 61) to 2009 (n = 56).

Variables	Score: 2004 (Mean, Standard Deviation)	Score: 2009 (Mean, Standard Deviation)	Test of Significance	Level of Statistical Significance
Style	M = 7.77 SD = 1.28	M = 8.46 SD = 1.44	t = −2.76	p < .01
Usage	M = 7.54 SD = 1.4	M = 8.18 SD = 1.54	t = −2.34	p < .05
Task Knowledge	M = 8 SD = 1.22	M = 8.5 SD = 1.48	t = −1.99	p < .05
Graphic Cohesion	M = 7.84 SD = 1.52	M = 8.48 SD = 1.66	t = 2.19	p < .05
Overall ePortfolio Score	M = 7.82 SD = 1.34	M = 8.63 SD = 1.65	t = −2.86	p < .01

As was the case with the LSU program, reports of gains such as those shown in Table 2.4 are much welcomed in writing program assessment. The sampling plan formula shown in chapter 4 was used to randomly select ePortfolios that represented the total sample of the hundreds of enrolled students; as such, the numbers of students who are actually evaluated are smaller than the number of enrolled students in these technical writing courses. Because of the extensive time required to read robust representations of the writing construct such as ePortfolios, sampling-plan estimates are very important in program assessment.

Over a five-year period, scores on the variables identified in Table 2.4 were raised to statistically significant levels: with a score of 7 taken as the lowest competent score, there is evidence that students are meeting competencies and improving at statistically significant levels over time. Moreover, because the enrolled student population during this period performed at consistent levels on admission tests and was admitted at consistent levels on transfer articulation agreements, we can draw the following inference: because the technical writing curriculum encourages improvement, students in technical writing have achieved higher scores over time. Rather than isolate a single cause as the reason for that improvement, it is more accurate to infer that various environmental elements—from improved curricular delivery to increased student knowledge and engagement—accounted for the change. Of course, at some period a threshold will be met. It is, for example, unrealistic to think that mean scores of 10 or higher will ever be the order of the day or that scores at such levels will be statistically different from each other over time. As such, the language of writing program assessment must always be appropriately cautious. While the curriculum may continue to improve, beyond certain levels, scores will not improve. We must remind those primarily concerned with gain and its empirical measurement that we are dealing with real human beings in a learning environment and that they cannot be asked to demonstrate infinite improvement over time. (The pursuit of gain, of course, is part of a Western cultural belief that is not sustainable, as David Harvey [2010] has demonstrated.)

With this process of accountability and inference, instructors put into practice a defined construct of technical writing through the student samples (produced under naturalistic classroom conditions) and the rubric (designed to allow a range of scores). Thus, the domain of the model (Kane 2006, 19)—the desired interpretation of scores based on a performance activity as an estimate of the overall level of skill in technical writing—is gained through ePortfolios collected in the service of student learning and program assessment.

Writing Program Assessment at the Graduate Level

The volume of enrolled students in undergraduate technical writing necessitated the kind of power analysis-based sampling plan discussed in chapter 4. In programs where the number of students exceeds the available resources, a well-designed sampling plan assures that a designated confidence interval (CI) within which the parameter of interest will be included with a predetermined probability and that subsequent claims about student ability can be validated. However, in graduate programs, sometimes each student can be assessed, perhaps even more than once a year.

Such is the case in the MS in professional and technical communication at NJIT, one of the earliest programs in the nation to be offered entirely online. The challenges of instruction and assessment in such an environment were great, especially in 2004 when the first core competencies were developed. Since that time, in the fall semester, faculty have conducted formative assessments of student ePortfolios using a kind of report card derived from eight core competencies: writing and editing; document design; rhetoric; problem solving, personal traits, work skills; collaboration and team work; oral and interpersonal communication; specialized expertise; and technology. Tabulated results and summarized instructor comments are returned to the students by e-mail. In the spring semester, faculty conduct summative assessment using a Likert-scale scoring sheet similar to that shown in Table 2.3 based on the core competencies to review student ePortfolios. So established is the program that faculty were able to collaborate with colleagues at Texas Tech

University to design a model of technology transfer related to interinstitutional program assessment (Coppola and Elliot 2007).

Of the many lessons learned from writing assessment at the graduate level, one of the most significant is the relationship between ePortfolio scores and course grades. Very early in the use of ePortfolios, when the program had only seventeen graduate students, program administrators discovered that there was no statistically significant relationship between the core competencies and the overall portfolio score, on one hand, and the key variable of cumulative grade point average (GPA), on the other. While the ePortfolio variables correlated at statistically significant moderate to high levels, there was no relationship between the scores on these variables and course grades. A score study suggested a reason for this lack of relationship. Evaluated on a 6-point scale by two readers, scores ranged from a low of 7 to a high of 12. Average scores ranged from 7.93 to 9.41. While these scores are certainly acceptable, they do not reflect what we found was the extraordinarily high average GPA of 3.91. Program administrators realized instuctors were telling two different stories: the ePortfolio scores—a measure of student ability—varied, but the grade point average—another measure of student ability—did not. During subsequent semesters, the scores from the ePortfolios were used to study whether course grades were indeed reflective of student ability. By 2007 (n = 27), a statistically significant, moderate level of correlation was demonstrated between the overall portfolio score and the cumulative GPA (.423, $p < .001$). Once inflated, course grades were now aligned with ePortfolio scores. While we will return to the interpretation of such measures in chapter 4, it is important to understand that program assessment can be used—just as it was in the LSU study—to encourage informed discussion of different measures of the same construct (i.e., scores and grades) and how alignment and disjuncture may be interpreted.

Programmatic assessment of graduate writing indeed allows many advantages (Coppola and Elliot 2010). Since these programs often invite advanced pedagogical research, there is an opportunity to experiment with new forms of learning that, if proven successful, inform undergraduate writing instruction and assessment. Many of the advances made in the graduate program—the use of online learning environments to promote e-learning, variable-driven construct modeling, continuous curricular refinement, and public reporting—are now directly used from the first to the senior year of the undergraduate program.

By extension, present initiatives by the Society for Technical Communication (STC) to form a Technical Communication Body of Knowledge

(TCBOK) for the field (Coppola 2010; Coppola and Elliot 2013) related to individual certification continue to inform program design and assessment. The construct span of the field of technical communication, shown in Figure 2.4, is among the first to attempt a full articulation of the field.

Figure 2.4 depicts both the field of technical communication (as expressed in TCBOK) and a process of assessment for key competencies (as expressed in certification). Significant areas—the variables of metacognitive practices about technical communication, career management in the field, production of knowledge and research—are unpacked in detail. Taken together, these variables are understood to result in best practices. Similarly, areas of proficiency established by the Society for Technical Communication—user, task, and experience analysis; information design; process management; information development; and information production—are also mapped to the body of knowledge and articulated in detail. Taken together, these variables result in certification—a process in which experts review a candidate's submission packet. In both the TCBOK and the certification project, we see the relational model explained in chapter 1. That is, a series of predictor variables (or *X*, the independent variables) contribute to a defined outcome (or *Y*, the dependent variable). Here we see a variable model similar to that underlying the *Framework for Success in Postsecondary Writing* (CWPA, NCTE, and NWP 2011). Defined as a series of domains that have been identified by experts as predictors of success for the practice of technical communication, the TCBOK is an excellent way of establishing the variables of technical communication within a relational framework. As we identify the domains of the construct of technical communication, we can then further define the way those domains are interpreted in specific settings. Once established, the model—mapped from general to specific—is able to be examined empirically for its strength and refined as relationships among the variables are examined over time (Coppola and Elliot 2013).

INSTRUMENTAL VALUE OF THE CASE STUDIES

In reviewing our case studies, readers will have observed that many of the NJIT practices follow the *Standards for Educational and Psychological Testing* (AERA, APA, and NCME 2014), the *White Paper on Writing Assessment in Colleges and Universities* drafted by NCTE and CWPA (2008), and *The Program Evaluation Standards* presented by the Joint Committee on Standards for Educational Evaluation (Yarbrough et al. 2011).

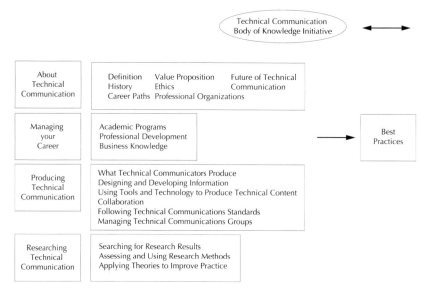

Figure 2.4. Construct span: Technical communication.

Nevertheless, while the practices we describe in this chapter may be mapped backward onto these documents, a comprehensively articulated framework employing recent advances in educational measurement has not until now been offered for the field of rhetoric and composition/writing studies.

In reflecting on these case studies, readers may recall the conclusion drawn in *Evaluating College Writing Programs* (Witte and Faigley 1983) following a review of postsecondary writing program assessments in Northern Iowa, the University of California, San Diego, Miami University, and the University of Texas. Evaluation strategies, Witte and Faigley found, that relied solely on pretest and posttest writing samples were inadequate. In *Developing Successful College Writing Programs*, White (1989) drew similar conclusions. Multiple measures, he found, should be used. "In program evaluation," he cautioned, "as in all other aspects of writing programs, we need to resist using or accepting simple or reductive definitions, procedures, tests, or inferences" (206). Whatever the charges against the case studies we have presented, reductionism should not be levied. Implicitly, each of the programs has followed the combined wisdom of Witte, Faigley, and White. In designing, redesigning, and assessing writing programs, we should focus on sources of evidence from these components—cultural and social context, institutional context, program structure and administration, curricular context, and

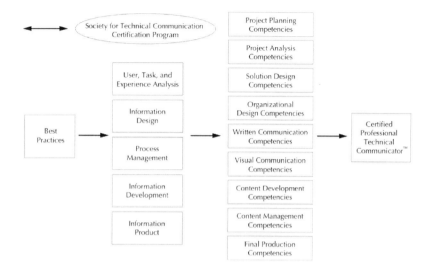

Figure 2.4.—continued

instructional program—as well as, of course, from evidence derived from student writing. In learning from our past, we should be aware of the need for careful conceptual definitions, humbled by the substantial resources needed to conduct an assessment, and alert to the potential of failure. It is fair to say that, at both LSU and NJIT, writing program administrators and instructors have acquired an overriding sense of humility.

What, we might now ask, is the instrumental value of these collected cases? Stake (2006) and Yin (2014) recommend that we use case studies such as ones described at LSU and NJIT to provide insight into an issue or refinement of theory. The cases, under this interpretative framework, can then be used to articulate the issues the authors confronted in their institutions. Because time and perspective have led to the belief that our cases are representative, we offer the following insights. Each should be regarded as an element of writing program design and redesign that can be used *before* assessment is begun:

- *Establishing a framework for consequence first, writing program assessment should place priority on the improvement of teaching and learning.* The LSU and NJIT programs prioritize the documentation of student learning to improve instruction through their emphasis on instructor train- ing, reflection, a recursive restructuring of pedagogy, and the assess- ment structure itself. Simply put, there is ample evidence that the interplay of instruction and assessment positively influence pedagogy and curriculum. Foregrounding a framework of consequence—that our assessment actions have moral as well as practical impacts that are context dependent, a topic discussed in the following chapter—yields substantial gain (Englehard and Wind 2013; Kagan 1989, 1998; Rawls 1971/1999).

- *Emphasizing a framework for theorization, writing assessment should be informed by current scholarship and research in assessment.* Both the LSU and the NJIT programs were based on then-current scholarship in genre (Bazerman 1999; Miller 1984) and writing assessment (Huot 2002). Ultimately, the programs might be understood to suggest the primacy of local situations and the principle of nontransferability of protocols. Current research, however, confirms the former and questions the latter. These value dualisms need not occur: localism and interinstitutional collaboration are not mutually exclusive. By aligning our past with our present, we can see that we are able to adjust the assessment systems developed by Witte, Faigley, and White. Recent developments in modeling writing programs, constructs, and their embedded ecologies allow us to do just that. As a long-standing and critical practice in our field, theorization is the ever-evolving essence of both instruction and assessment (Crusius 1989; Sánchez 2012).

- *Emphasizing standpoint, writing assessment should be based on continuous conversations with as many stakeholders as possible.* As Kristen Intemann (2010) has observed, standpoint theory is based on two main ideas: situated knowledge (location systematically influences our experiences) and epistemic advantage (standpoints of marginalized or oppressed groups allow distinctly valuable interpretations) (783). Following both theses, the LSU and NJIT assessment programs were predicated on a link between students, instructors, administrators, and colleagues in other disciplines. Over the years, the instructors increasingly developed confidence in what was being taught and the way in which it was being measured. The nature of the assessment program was widely shared with the department, upper-level administration, professors in other departments, and parents of first-year students. These programs became models for assessment at the university level.

- *Emphasizing research, writing program assessment should provide the foundation for evidence-based decision making.* Both assessments relied on several kinds of data-driven evidence, including longitudinal student performance, surveys of instructors, and focus groups. Information from these sources was fed back into constructive changes in the writing program.

- *Emphasizing documentation, writing program assessment should gather information in many forms.* Robert Coles (1998) defines documentary studies as "the attempt to ascertain what *is*, what can be noted, recorded, pictured; and that of presentation—how to elicit the interest of others, and how to provide a context, so that an incident, for instance, is connected to the conditions that informed and prompted its occurrence" (20). In writing program assessment, documentary studies is a rich and unexplored concept that embraces many forms of evidence, from the face validity of ePortfolios themselves to the scores given by experts to demonstrated core competencies.

- *Emphasizing accountability, writing program assessment should understand accountability as an occasion to document gains, identify challenges, and plan for the future.* While *cris de coeur* regarding the commercialization of higher education are common (Bok 2004), the LSU and NJIT programs took occasions of accountability to demonstrate wise use of resources. As milestone events, instances of accountability can be viewed as complex yet positive occasions to demonstrate the value of a writing program to local and national communities.

- *Emphasizing sustainability, writing program assessment should focus on ways that will allow the program to thrive.* As part of the ecological model presented by Wardle and Roozen (2012) to address the complexity of writing assessment in general, sustainability is a process of planning that focuses on past actions, present decisions, and future developments. As the LSU and NJIT programs both demonstrate, an emphasis on sustainability allows for key boundaries to be established—such as student-centeredness—so resources are allocated in terms of student need and development, not solely in terms of efficiency. We strongly support and seek to advance the ecological modeling advanced by Elizabeth Wardel and Kevin Roozen in its call for attention to documenting the literate development of students in a wide range of experiences with a defined aim: to offer stakeholders a robust account of writing experiences that inform students' growth as writers (107).

- *Emphasizing process, writing program assessment should view the documentary efforts of evidence gathering as a process to be undertaken, not a product to be produced.* Applying the process and postprocess models of our field affords a view toward assessment that stands in contrast to the view that assessment is a one-time response to a milestone event such as accreditation. Instead of attending to a written report for accreditors, those who design writing programs should view assessment as attention to the processes, policies, and procedures that become part of a continuing discussion to improve the writing program itself. Attention to the process of validation, rather than viewing validation as a stamp of approval, reinforces contemporary views of validity (Kane 2013) important to writing program assessment.

- *Emphasizing communication, writing program assessment should encourage and expect a variety of information to be presented in ways appropriate to a variety of stakeholders.* Both programs relied on instructors, with whom regular, planned meetings were held to develop instructional and assessment strategies so the projects could move forward. By participating in the project, instructors increasingly became experts in planned assessment practices that were communicated to stakeholders. In the design and implementation of communicative practices, the work of Linda Adler-Kassner (2008) stands as a model that, as we show in chapter 4, can be strengthened through genres of empirical reporting.

The programmatic approaches to assessment described in this chapter—aligned with national assessment models and indebted to previous writing program assessment research—generated a robust abundance of information that could be analyzed to determine best teaching practices. The programs created a platform for discussion among instructors who were active participants in reading and scoring writing samples and who discussed the judgments they used in their ranking system—processes leading to a redesign of classroom practices. The protocols of longitudinal assessment demonstrated to outside stakeholders the centrality of the writing program to the institution.

To develop a gold standard, we must now turn to a model that incorporates all of our learned lessons. To explain that model, we begin with a set of foundational elements for writing program assessment.

QUESTIONS FOR WRITING PROGRAM FACULTY AND ADMINISTRATORS: LESSONS

Background

In this set of questions, we have taken the most important concepts from chapter 2 on our case studies in assessment and turned them into questions for writing program faculty and administrators. When Witte and Faigley (1983) analyzed four sites of assessment using a pretest-posttest design, they found "few major insights concerning the teaching of writing or the operation of writing programs" (38). Assessment, they found, must be based on more than decontextualized pretest and posttest writing samples. We agree. In today's assessment-driven environment, we know that pretest-posttest designs are more silver than gold in their struggle to capture the sociocognitive variables of the writing construct. Vanishing, too, are ad hoc approaches as regional and program assessment demands have become systematic and cyclical (Yarbrough et al. 2011). The approaches we provide in chapter 2 are deeply contextual and serve as the basis for the questions that follow.

Introduction

In *Rhetoric at the Margins: Revising the History of Writing Instruction in American Colleges, 1873 to 1947,* David Gold (2008) examines archival information from Wiley College, Texas Women's University, and East Texas Normal College in order to encourage a nuanced view of the history of writing studies and the historiographical methods associated with our field. "I am interested in the institutions in this study," he wrote in his book's introduction, "because I am convinced they have something to teach us, something that the broad, general curricular histories have missed. Now, as in the progressive era, access to and diversity in education remain important questions." He then crafts questions that can accompany each of the questions we raise regarding analyses of specific institutional practices: "Can we recover the sense of community and community building that black, women's, and normal colleges fostered without reverting to institutional segregation and separatism? Can we join the study of the liberal arts with professional training? Can we foster civic values and participation in social discourse through rhetorical education? Can we instruct students in dominant discourse norms while still respecting the voices and experiences they bring to our classrooms?" (12).

Questions

The questions that follow are intended to help in the identification of best practices in instruction and assessment. Answering these questions is an important step in program assessment that allows local practice to be associated with broader trends.

1. If your institution uses traditional placement assumptions (Willingham 1974) for writing placement, how is the assessment used to accommodate individual difference in students (Carroll 1993)? For example, Peckham (2009, 2010b) chose to institute an Online Challenge allowing fuller representation of the writing construct rather than determining placement based on standardized test scores. Daniel J. Royer, Roger Gilles, and Gita Das Bender rejected the paternalism of writing placement and allowed students to have a role in their placement decisions (Royer and Gilles 1998; Das Bender 2012). Radically, Elliot et al. (2012) adopted the aphorism that "an admitted student is a qualified student" and worked to eliminate remedial classes while placing recovered resources into writing center expansion and student tutoring. In examining the process of placement, pay special attention to the following: the argument used to justify delay of degree through additional course work (Kane 2006, 23–25); the strategies of communication used to tell students about the placement test—specifically, the way the writing construct is to be assessed—before the testing episode; the strategies of communicating assessment results to students; the evidence used to justify the curriculum designed to prepare the students for college writing; and the impact of the assessment on diverse student populations, with assurance that the assessment is adhering to legal guidelines for avoidance of disparate impact (Poe et al. 2014).

2. What are the hallmarks of best instructional and assessment practices at your institution in writing studies, and what may be learned from them in terms of the pedagogical improvements that should be made in the writing program? For example, if an instructor is adapting National Writing Project collaborative practices (DiPardo, Storms, and Selland 2011) for postsecondary use to develop a common rubric for all sections of an upper-division professional writing class, how will those strategies be used to develop common rubrics for other writing-across-the-curriculum and writing-in-the-disciplines classes? How may the Conference on College Composition and Communication "Principles and Practices in Electronic Portfolios" (2007) be used to develop an ePortfolio assessment system that students can use across the writing curriculum—a system that will also be of use in their first jobs and applications to graduate school?

3. Using the concept of construct modeling shown in Figure 2.3, how is the construct of writing depicted so identified variables such as document design and style can be used to guide instruction and enable assessment? How can these variables be used to design meaningful scoring guides tailored to the course, such as those shown in Table 2.3?

4. Based on the Technical Communication Body of Knowledge shown in Figure 2.4, how can a body of knowledge be developed for the writing program and communicated to all its constituencies?

5. How will the writing program systematically expand its scope of influence beyond first-year writing? What writing-across-the-curriculum (Herrington and Moran 2005) and writing-in-the-disciplines (Neff and Whithaus 2008) strategies will be used to leverage the resources necessary for program expansion?

6. Based on conceptions of consequence (Gallagher 2012; Slomp, Corrigan, and Sugimoto 2014), how will the writing program demonstrate that its first priority is the improvement of teaching and learning? For example, how will core competencies be developed for designated levels of writing such as those shown in Table 2.2, and how will students be supported to respond to these in ways such as those shown in Figure 2.2?

7. What theories of composition and rhetoric (Crusius 1989; Sánchez 2012) and composition pedagogies (Tate et al. 2013) are promising for implementation within the writing program at your institution? What are the strengths, weaknesses, opportunities, and threats to implementation of theory-based practices of composition and rhetoric?

8. What theories of writing assessment (Huot 1996, 2002; Lynne 2004; Neal 2011; Rutz and Lauer-Glebov 2005) are promising for implementation within the writing program? What are the strengths, weaknesses,

opportunities, and threats to implementation of theory-based practices of writing assessment?

9. What theories of program evaluation (Chen 2015) from the field of educational measurement are promising for implementation within the writing program? What are the strengths, weaknesses, opportunities, and threats to implementation of theory-based evaluation practices from other fields?

10. Based on standpoint theory (Intemann 2010), who are the most important constituencies of the writing program, and how will their needs be addressed? For example, is a general faculty survey of student writing ability appropriate and useful? What about student surveys regarding their own perceptions of their writing ability and the importance of its development?

11. Recalling principles of evidence-centered design (Mislevy, Steinberg, and Almond 2002) and design for assessment, how will evidence that the writing program is meeting its stated objectives be assembled and communicated to different audiences to ensure that meaningful, timely information is presented to key constituencies?

12. Emphasizing the process of developing claims (Toulmin 1958/2003), how has your institution demonstrated its support of the writing program? For example, an excellent way to examine authentic administrative support is to compare faculty compensation for those who work in the writing program with the annual survey of compensation prepared by the American Association of University Professors (2014).

13. How will the writing program demonstrate its commitment to student learning? For example, will the writing program use strategies proposed by Linda Adler-Kassner (2008) to frame key constituency perceptions about instruction and assessment?

14. What genres will be used to communicate information from the questions above regarding institutional achievements and challenges to key stakeholders: advisory boards, administration, faculty and instructional staff, parents, professional organizations, students, and the general public? For example, if the writing program is planning to expand its scope of practice and function, a collaborative wiki might be developed so participants can share and record their proposed strategies in an asynchronous fashion. Using other digital technologies, a website might be designed to feature the instructors, with uploads of their syllabi, best assignments, and grading rubrics. Brief podcasts might accompany each instructor's section of the site in which clearly stated principles of writing instruction are available.

3

FOUNDATIONS

If we are to think clearly about writing program assessment, we need to untangle it from the issues involved with assessing the writing of individual students and assessing the outcomes of particular writing courses. This is no easy matter since the objective of writing programs is to improve the writing of individual students and the outcomes of writing courses. Each of these assessments poses its own challenges, which accumulate as we move from the student to the program—or, to try our new vocabulary, as we use the framework of constructive alignment to map the writing construct from the particular syllabus to the program mission (Biggs and Tang 2011). We have learned over the past three decades just how complex the measurement of student writing can be; the measurement of writing programs is equally complex.

The extent of this complexity is best understood by the example of assigning grades. Because they are poor surrogates for the complex and deeply human behavior expressed in writing, grades on student papers are less of a concern to writing instructors than are the comments they make to their students. There is so much represented in a single writing performance that any single symbolic judgment, especially on important papers, seems inadequate. Yet the transaction between the grading instructor and the student, from first grade through graduate school, is significantly colored by the grade assigned. Almost all American schools and colleges require grades from instructors as part of the certifying and sorting function given to education by society—a function instructors accept with grumbling and professionalism. We cannot take the space here to review the extensive literature on grading and response processes, but there is a distinct range of views from those instructors who see grading student writing as counterproductive to effective teaching (Elbow 2012; Zak 1998) to those who see systematic grading as a useful spur to student improvement (Straub and Lunsford 2006). In the middle are those urging fellow instructors to respond to student writing in various helpful ways,

DOI: 10.7330/9780874219869.c003

with or without conventional grades (Anson 1989; Lindemann 2001). Attempts to normalize or regularize instructor grading through scoring guides and controlled essay readings have been accepted for large-scale assessment programs, such as the Advanced Placement Program in English Language and Composition, but have not had much effect on the interaction between student writer and instructor, where instructors' individual standards determine evaluation patterns. The individualization of grading standards has also been influenced by differences in student populations—the standards, for instance, of upper middle-class postsecondary instructors who may not be accustomed to grading the writing of socioeconomically disadvantaged students may be different from the standards of instructors from working-class backgrounds who do work with those students. Perhaps this situation will change as the Common Core State Standards (National Governors Association 2014) become embedded in the nation's schools. Perhaps the standards will only serve to highlight inequality. The challenge for those who design and assess writing programs is to honor differences among teachers and students while fostering an environment for planned assessment.

For these reasons and many more, the grades instructors award students provide uneven indications for program assessments; that is, instructors are capturing their concept of the writing construct in a robust, naturalistic fashion that appropriately includes cognitive, interpersonal, and intrapersonal domains. If we reflect for a moment on the *Framework for Success in Postsecondary Writing* (CWPA, NCTE, and NWP 2011)—and, by extension, the Body of Knowledge Initiative discussed in chapter 2—the reasons become apparent. Where writing is concerned, instructors (and employers) judge students (and employees) along three domains: cognitive, interpersonal, and intrapersonal. When an instructor awards a grade (or an employer makes a comment), whether it is a formative or summative judgment, evaluation is often based on assessment of these three domains. Because the assessment is based on the instructor's broad horizon of understanding—itself a range from a specific response to a defined rubric to a generalized response to student behaviors—there is often misalignment of grades to formal assessments. The seminal research on this subject by Willingham, Pollack, and Lewis (2002) demonstrates that aligning criteria for measurement that include multiple domains results in substantially higher relationships between the assessment at hand and student grades. While many classroom instructors are resistant to aligned criteria—seeing them as akin to aligned curriculum and deprofessionalization—the kind of assessment advanced in this book aims to unify the pedagogy of localism with the need for demonstrable program results that can, in turn, be used to inform further pedagogical practice.

To map the alignment paths that allow us to make this move of constructive alignment from classroom to program and back again—while keeping classroom pedagogy at the forefront of such efforts—we now present foundational conceptual elements of program assessment. We have selected six concepts embodied in the following terms: construct span, construct representation, research multidisciplinarity, validation, vehicle, and cycle.

As a preview to the usefulness of these concepts, a brief example may be drawn from the complexity of navigating the space between individual grading and program assessment. Establishing the span of the writing construct allows us to target the benefits and costs of any given act of assessment in terms of construct coverage; representation of the writing construct allows us to judge the extent to which the writing task at hand captures the construct; multidisciplinarity allows us the advantage of new perspectives; validation allows us to examine categories of evidence as they are used in the process of making claims based on both grades and scores; the concept of vehicle allows us to select the most appropriate way to capture a particular element of the writing construct at any particular time; and the concept of cycle encourages us to integrate assessment and instruction as a regular pattern so the flow between them is natural. A moment's reflection on the case studies provided in chapter 2 demonstrates that these six concepts, philosophical and practical in nature, flow naturally from the present state of knowledge about educational assessment.

Before beginning, we wish to reiterate a point we made in the introduction. We wrote that we wanted to advance a powerful genre of research, writing program assessment, using methods and methodologies best begun and refined locally. As such we want to stress that writing program design and writing program assessment are complementary activities. Just as instruction and assessment are best when they occur naturally, so too is the case with the administration and assessment of writing programs. The six concepts we are about to present, therefore, apply equally to writing program design and writing program assessment. Because the program will always be involved in documenting its efforts to advance student engagement with the writing construct, a writing program designed and assessed within the framework we present will always be ready for an external evaluation.

CONSTRUCT SPAN: NOMOTHETIC CONSISTENCY

The first important concept in redesigning a writing program to facilitate recursive assessment is to map the writing construct as it appears in the curriculum at a specific institution. Because such mapping is both a philosophical and practical exercise, we here introduce two unfamiliar but useful terms: *nomothetic span* and *idiographic representation*. Here are their origins.

In 1894, the German philosopher Wilhelm Windelband (1980) made a distinction between two types of knowledge—nomothetic (associated with generalized taxonomy) and idiographic (associated with unique representation)—in an address given in Strasbourg. Taking as his case empirical science, he made the following distinction:

> In their quest for knowledge of reality, the empirical sciences either seek the general in the form of the law of nature or the particular in the form of the historically defined structure. On the one hand, they are concerned with the form which invariably remains constant. On the other hand, they are concerned with the unique, immanently defined content of the real event. The former disciplines are nomological sciences. The latter disciplines are sciences of process or sciences of the event. The nomological sciences are concerned with what is invariably the case. The sciences of process are concerned with what was once the case. If I may be permitted to introduce some new technical terms, scientific thought is nomothetic in the former case and idiographic in the latter case. Should we retain the customary expressions, then it can be said that the dichotomy at stake here concerns the distinction between the natural and the historical disciplines. (175)

Deepening his analysis, Windelband (1894/1980) then turned to a comparative distinction between natural science and history: "Natural science seeks laws; history seeks structural forms. In the natural sciences, thought moves from the confirmation of particulars to the comprehension of general relationships; in the historical sciences, it is devoted to the faithful delineation of the particulars" (178). Indeed, it is this delineation of the particulars—"to breathe new life into some structure of the past in such a way that all of its concrete and distinctive features acquire an ideal actuality or contemporaneity"—that is understood to be "the source of the relationship between historical accomplishment and aesthetic creativity, the kinship between the historical disciplines and *belles lettres*" (178). Students of the English novel will notice a parallel here to Henry Fielding's insistence in *The History of Tom Jones, A Foundling* that he was not writing a fiction, which deals with particular persons and events, but a history, dealing with eternal types and conditions. The definition of history may be the opposite of

Windelband's but the distinction between nomothetic and idiographic is the same.

Windelband's terminology is extremely useful for our purposes because it allows us to both map the writing construct and determine its uniqueness. We will turn to that uniqueness as we present the second core concept. For the present, let's examine the concept of construct (nomothetic) span as it appears in Figure 3.1.

Figure 3.1 provides a hypothetical taxonomy of the writing construct as it might be defined across an institution's postsecondary curriculum—from first-year writing and beyond. The construct spans both written and multimodal communication (Fraiberg 2010; Murray 2009). Our conceptualization of the construct is both consistent with and informed by the competency domains of Pellegrino and Hilton (2012). Because volumes have been written on the concepts presented in Figure 3.1, our references provide only broad definitions.

- The top row spans the three environments in which students communicate: digital (blogs and wikis), print (from persuasive essays to laboratory reports), and blurred (such as ePortfolios, which contain a variety of genres). That which is manifested on the top tier may be defined as secondary orality—a deliberate and self-conscious use of language "based permanently on the use of writing as print" (Condon 2014; Ong 1982, 136).

- The second row captures a language-arts framework for writing. Included are instances of integration of writing with reading and writing with visualization.

- The third row is central to mapping the writing construct. Rhetorical conceptualization—"the faculty of observing in any given case the available means of persuasion" as Aristotle defines it (Corbett 1984, 24)—centralizes our profession, its attention to language, and its sources of knowledge. However, we agree with David Bleich (2013) in our distrust of selecting argument as the first among equals in the rhetorical landscape. Far better, we believe, is to advance rhetorical conceptualization as both discursive and nondiscursive (Langer 1942; Murray 2009).

- The fourth and fifth rows identify the cognitive domain of writing. Here we draw upon, and extend, the *Framework for Success* and the Body of Knowledge Initiative.

- The sixth row identifies the interpersonal domain of writing. Again, we draw on and extend the *Framework for Success* (CWPA, NCTE, and NWP 2011), the Body of Knowledge Initiative, and the domains identified by Pellegrino and Hilton (2012).

- The seventh row identifies the intrapersonal domain of writing, traditionally called the Big Five personality factors (De Raad 2000; Messick 1979; O'Connor and Paunonen 2007) which, in turn, have been expanded by Pellegrino and Hilton (2012).

Communication in Digital Environments	Communication in Print Environments	Communication in Blurred Environments

Writing and Reading Integration	Writing and Visualization Integration	Writing and Speaking Integration

Rhetorical Conceptualization

Genre Knowledge	Task Knowledge	Audience Knowledge	Writing Processes Knowledge	Problem Solving Knowledge

Information Literacy Knowledge	Conventions Knowledge	Metacognition Knowledge

Collaboration	Social Networking	Leadership	Diversity	Ethics

Openness	Conscientiousness	Extraversion	Agreeableness	Stability

Neurological System	Attention System	Visual System

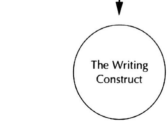

The Writing Construct

Figure 3.1. Nomothetic span of the writing construct.

- The eighth row, often neglected in construct mapping, attends to the neurological capacity (nerve function), attention capacity (the ability of the brain to attend to a task), and vision capacity (the ability of the brain to stimulate pathways into the visual cortex) necessary to perform those acts of reading, visualization, and speaking associated with the writing construct (Alvarez 2014; Borsting et al. 2012; Chen, Bleything, and Lim 2011; Rouse et al. 2009). Attention to these elements of the domain will allow examination of the relationship between vision problems and writing performance. Concepts of the writing construct must include an awareness of such capacities (Wood, Price, and Johnson 2012).

The writing construct itself is thus shaped and defined by these variables—categories that vary across time and circumstance but that can nevertheless be identified. Mapping the writing construct in this manner through campus consensus draws attention to the core environments, cognitive abilities, and affective competencies embodied in a rhetorical conceptualization of the writing construct. In addition, such mapping allows a multidisciplinary literature review to inform the process of construct modeling that follows in the curriculum.

Ultimately, and most powerfully, this kind of nomothetic mapping allows courses that encourage practice with cognitive, interpersonal, and intrapersonal domains to be identified across the curriculum. This kind of constant, environmentally based reinforcement interrupts the destructive perception of first-year courses in writing as inoculation events, a concept we satirized in chapter 1. Because the writing construct is fully mapped and reinforcement is longitudinally planned beyond the first year, the desire for transference is realistically accommodated (Schwartz, Bransford, and Sears 2005; Wardle 2013). We feel certain that, in the near future, it will be difficult for a writing program to be assessed in a valid fashion—perhaps even for it to exist—unless such a figure is available for all stakeholders as a representation, subject to revision and improvement, of the construct that consumes so much time, attention, and resources.

CONSTRUCT REPRESENTATION: IDIOGRAPHIC UNIQUENESS

The unique representation of the writing construct is found in the writing task. In Figure 3.2 we illustrate what Windelband called "the faithful delineation of the particulars."

The design of constructed-response tasks is where idiographic representation takes place. The success of the task assigned to students is the true test of theory, as every instructor struggling to develop appropriate

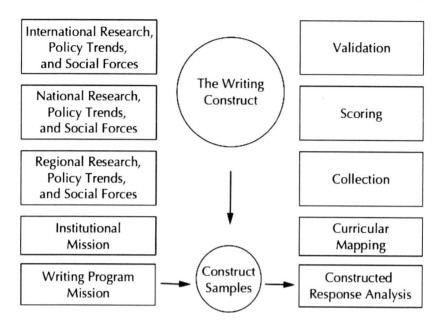

International Research, Policy Trends, and Social Forces

National Research, Policy Trends, and Social Forces

Regional Research, Policy Trends, and Social Forces

Institutional Mission

Writing Program Mission

The Writing Construct

Construct Samples

Validation

Scoring

Collection

Curricular Mapping

Constructed Response Analysis

Figure 3.2. Idiographic representation of the writing construct.

writing assignments well understands. Long understood to be the contact zone of writing assessment, writing tasks are an important part of writing program assessment in terms of documenting student learning. Research from the seminal *Designing Writing Tasks for the Assessment of Writing* by Ruth and Murphy (1988) to recent work by Robert J. Sternberg (2010) on college admissions demonstrates that writing tasks strongly impact the quality of writing responses. As all instructors know, eliciting the construct sample from the construct domain through a good writing task is an art and a science.

The term "constructed response," Randy Elliott Bennett (1993) has argued, is a superordinate classification for a broad range of tasks. His scheme for a categorization of the family of writing tasks is useful for its six types: selection/identification (the cloze elide task of deleting extraneous information from a paragraph); reordering/rearrangement (ordering and sequencing of information); substitution/correction (sentence combining); completion (sentence completion); construction (production of a total unit of thought), and presentation (a performance). The classification is especially useful in revealing how various item types underrepresent and more fully represent the writing construct.

In the kinds of robust construct representation required for writing assessment within a programmatic context—that is, for expression of the nomothetic span shown in Figure 3.1—we are exclusively concerned with those constructed-response tasks that result in demonstrations of writing performance. Constructed-response writing tasks, linked to a specific construct model, allow us to distance ourselves from the Pavlovian metaphor of stimulus-response and engage in deeply considered sociocognitive modeling of the writing task that, in turn, yield desireable measurement aims of fairness, validity, and reliability (Sparks et al. 2014). It is, in fact, best to speak of writing tasks, and not prompts, if robust samples of the writing construct are to be elicited from students.

An example demonstrates the relationship between Figure 3.1 and Figure 3.2. Peckham taught a junior-level course entitled Writing: Practice, Pedagogy, and History with a specific focus on motives for writing. This course is offered as part of the university's general university requirements, a series of courses taken by all students. Peckham took a Freirean approach, modified by the necessity of providing students with a knowledge base congruent with the purpose of a specialization in rhetoric, writing, and culture, one of the three undergraduate strands in the LSU English department curriculum. Influenced by John Dewey, James Moffett, and Paulo Freire, Peckham knew that he wanted to design the course so his students would engage in active learning and focus on peer review of their own writing. He determined to develop a curriculum responsive to the students' sense of their own needs. He therefore constructed the course around four objectives: to learn about the nature of composition studies; to learn something about what genres are and how they function to enable writers' abilities to respond to different kinds of rhetorical situations; to improve writing through work on cognitive, interpersonal, and intrapersonal; and to improve student friendship with writing. Reference to Figure 3.1 allows location of these course objectives, and reference to Figure 3.2 allows a way to map these curricular objectives in the construct samples taken in the course and thus identify sources of validity evidence that may be gathered from the expression of the course objectives in the course assignments.

In Peckham's case, he decided to design a book—a complex constructed-response task, with demands ranging from writer's tone to page layout—based on the experiences of the class. The last section of the semester became a project of constructing a book, with different groups working on the following themes: the experience of writing in the class; what students learned about writing; writing for self and class members (instead of to the instructor for a grade); writing in public and private journals; and the development and expression of voice. Each student was to write a chapter in the book adhering to the following guidelines: what they first thought about themselves as writers when they began the class; what they then thought about writing as an activity; what they learned about themselves as writers and about writing as a consequence of the writing that they did and by reviewing the work of others; an example or examples of writing that they completed in the course. Students were also to provide reflections on their writing along the following lines: ways to encourage writing—the kinds of writing experiences students would like to have in school and outside school; feelings about themselves as writers at the course's end; and a speculative statement on the roles writing might play in their future lives and careers.

In these constructed-response tasks, Peckham demonstrates a clear path from Figure 3.1 (the place of the task among others) to Figure 3.2 (the unique representation of the writing construct in the class). While he did not use ePortfolios, these complex student writing tasks could be scored by the careful process of rubric development discussed in chapter 2. Interpretation of those scores would then lend further validity to the project, allowing it to serve as a model for instruction in other upper-division writing courses within the LSU specialization in rhetoric, writing, and culture. Within such an integrated framework, curricular transformation would occur as more is learned about the writing construct as it gains specific definition in that context. Seen as programmatic, such a course project has significant consequences for students, instructors, and administrators. As Bennett (1993) correctly observes, use of just such complex constructed-response tasks is inherent to a unified validity framework of the kind we advance in this book.

RESEARCH MULTIDISCIPLINARITY: COMPLEMENTARITY

For Windelband (1894/1980), the nomothetic span of the sciences and the idiographic representation of the humanities remained "independent and juxtaposed." So great was this value dualism of this ontological reality, he told his audience, that it "defines the space of our cosmic scheme; it transcends all change and expresses the eternal essence of reality." Where did psychology—the ancestor of psychometrics and quantitative psychology, educational psychology, and educational assessment, testing, and measurement—stand in the scheme of things? Broadly, a discipline as important as psychology "cannot be classified unambiguously either as a natural science or as a science of the mind," he wrote. But regarding the specific method, there could be no doubt: "From the perspective of psychology as an investigation, however, its entire methodological procedure is exclusively the method of the natural sciences" (174). The division was complete, and we experience their resultant disjuncture today: educational measurement is nomothetic in nature; writing studies is idiographic.

In a chapter concerned with the nuts and bolts of assessment, what is the relevance of such dusty and distant disciplinary divisions? First, as Sir Geoffrey Lloyd (2009) has shown in *Disciplines in the Making: Cross-Cultural Perspectives on Elites, Learning, and Innovation*, Windelband's Austrian address exemplifies the role of elites in creating hegemonic status for disciplines along ontological and epistemological lines. Frederick C. Beiser (2011), who has brilliantly situated Windelband's speech, reminds his readers that the 1880s was a period in which the struggle for disciplinary autonomy was strong. It is therefore important to identify the origin of the long-standing disjuncture that interrupts research in our field.

Second, reflection on the address allows us to witness an era in which multidisciplinary inquiry was unimaginable—and to compare that era to our own. Here was a European culture that would, two years later, lead the young Albert Einstein to Zurich Polytechnic. So great was the sense of disciplinary isolation that Einstein's first dissertation proposal was rejected because he lived in such isolation that he did not realize Americans Albert Michelson and Edward Morley had already conducted the very experiments he had proposed. For Einstein and his culture, the world of collaboration that Bruno Latour and Steve Woolgar would describe at the Salk Institute a century later was as much science fiction as would have been sketches for the Large Hadron Collider (Latour and Woolgar 1979/1986).

Third, because of the impulse for disciplinary hegemony conducted in a cultural context of isolationism, we witness an instance of value dualism and value hierarchies that continues to have such a dramatic impact on our field one hundred and twenty years later. Defined by environmentalist Karen J. Warren (1990) as disjunctive pairs in which terms are seen as oppositional rather than complementary, value dualisms are often paired with value hierarchies, conceptualizations of diversity organized by metaphors associated with value. Observation of such oppressively conceptual frameworks—Ann E. Berthoff (1990) called them killer dichotomies—helps those in the writing community, especially writing program administrators, remain alert to these underlying prejudices against their work and therefore develop conceptual and practical strategies to neutralize them.

We now take our leave of Windelband because his speech has served its purpose. We have identified two important concepts and we recommend that they be seen in terms of each other. In sum, we advocate abandonment of value dualism and value hierarchy as we embrace both nomothetic span and idiographic representation.

Yet how would we address vast systems of knowledge as represented in the field of educational measurement and our own? Two perspectives are readily apparent: interdisciplinary and multidisciplinary. For advocacy of multidisciplinarity, we take as our star witness Stanley Fish (1989), who maintains that interdisciplinarity is impossible due to the nature of stance: an epistemological move toward a new line of investigational authority inevitably results in additional singularity. We agree. No one individual can honestly claim disciplinary knowledge of all that is needed to assess a writing program. When key concepts and practices of measurement—the topic of this chapter and the next—are fully understood, it eventually becomes clear that consultant expertise is needed. We identify in chapter 1 the range of individuals who will have to be part of the multidisciplinary knowledge-based team if an assessment is to have authentic meaning and impact. We advocate building collaborations with representatives of those fields of study.

VALIDATION: EVIDENCE AND CATEGORIES

In chapter 1, we presented the definition of a construct as a postulated attribute—that is, a stipulated assigned definition of what we are seeking to measure. The discussion of constructs and validity that follows applies to all educational measurement but is of particular importance in relation to program assessment, which can lead to profound consequences for writing programs.

Extending the definition of Cronbach and Meehl (1955) to the present, we find that much has occurred in six decades. The most comprehensive review of the history is provided by Robert L. Brennan (2006); the most comprehensive review of the theory is provided by Kane (2006). Regarding the history, a milestone moment occurred when Samuel Messick (1989) argued that validity was not a stamp of approval awarded on a particular day by an anointed group. Validity was best understood as "an integrated evaluative judgment of the degree to which empirical evidence and theoretical rationales support the *adequacy* and *appropriateness of inferences* and *actions* based on test scores or other modes of assessment. . . . Thus, the key issues of test validity are the interpretability, relevance, and utility of scores, the import or value implications of scores as a basis for action, and the functional worth of scores in terms of social consequences of their use" (13). In a stroke, as Kane (2006) has written in his seminal work on validation theory, "Messick gave the consequential basis for validity equal billing with the evidential basis" (21). In fact, one cannot but wonder if Messick's experiences with performance assessment—with writing assessment at the forefront of tasks that demand productive action, not bubble-and-booklet item completion—led him in 1995 to include consequence as a key form of validity evidence. "Because performance assessments promise potential benefits for teaching and learning," he wrote, "it is important to accrue evidence of such positive consequences as well as evidence that adverse consequences are minimal" (7). As Hillary Persky (2012) has reminded us, this was the period of *Trends in Writing: Fluency and Writing Conventions*, the 1996 National Assessment of Educational Progress report in which ETS staff members conducted assessment focusing on writing processes. With such an enormous amount of direct assessment of writing ability occurring at ETS during the mid-1990s, we wonder aloud if our field's insistence on direct, meaningful assessment supporting classroom practice and writing theory directly influenced Messick's attention to the importance of assessment consequence.

In the years following Messick's work, it became increasingly accepted that validity is not only a property of the assessment itself; validity evidence must also include the use (or misuse) of the results; we must attend as well to its anticipated (and unanticipated) consequences. In the quarter century to follow, the italics that Messick used made all the difference. Required for validation was construct coverage (*adequacy*), appropriateness (*logic*) and actions (*use*). In their very helpful expression of validity and writing assessment, O'Neill, Moore, and Huot (2009, Fig. 1, 30) illustrate how this kind of socially responsible thinking influenced the publication of the *Standards for Educational and Psychological Testing* (AERA, APA, and NCME 2014). Providing criteria for assessment design and guidance for evaluating score interpretation and use, the present sixth edition of the *Standards* offers a new Trinitarian model of investigation: fairness; validity; and reliability/precision.

However, it is important to remember that the details of consequence have not been fully worked out in either our field or in the field of educational measurement. Enormous effort has been put into understanding the conceptual and empirical complexities of scoring, generalization, and extrapolation. Despite the new emphasis on fairness in the *Standards*, no such effort has been made in the area of consequential validity; we therefore hold that the authors of the Standards have provided a necessary, although not sufficient, guide for writing assessment (Elliot 2015). Two of the reasons for this massive intellectual and moral failure are identified by Paul D. Nichols and Natasha Williams. First, the integration of the consequential and the evidential basis for validity remains controversial. A moment's reflection shows why: regardless of assumed powers of prescience, no one can know the impact of an assessment that has not been created. The reaction of some stakeholders (researchers and administrators) can be anticipated through a literature review, but the reaction of others (students and parents) cannot—especially since we rarely ask the latter. Second, the responsibility for gathering and presenting evidence of consequence remains undefined and unassigned. Is the use of results the responsibility of the maker or the user? Can the assessment designer really define the unanticipated use of scores? And, if it is the responsibility of the user, to whom, precisely, does that charge fall in the vast bureaucracy of educational administration? To establish a framework of responsibility for collecting evidence of consequential validity, Nichols and Williams (2009) focus on the fluid nature of ownership, breadth of constructs, distance from intended score use, and time from test publication. Their framework is admirable, and it remains the responsibility of those who design and redesign writing programs to grapple with the ever-emerging meaning of consequential validity within their institution, design categories of evidence that support the use of assessment systems, and identify groups and individuals responsible for gathering that evidence. If twenty-first-century writing researchers attend to consequential validity to the extent that twentieth-century researchers focused on interreader reliability, the most important group of stakeholders, our students, would surely benefit.

Concurrent with the publication of O'Neill, Moore, and Huot's (2009) *A Guide to College Writing Assessment*—and their attention to context as a key source of validity evidence—an important event in the history and theory of validity occurred: an argument-based approach to validation. Readers attuned to noun forms will note that we now shift from the noun form (*validity*) to a noun combined with a suffix (*validation*). The shift from stasis to action was accompanied by a new conceptualization, based on Cronbach (1988), which is well expressed by Kane (2006): "To validate a proposed interpretation or use of test scores is to evaluate the rationale for this interpretation or use. The evidence needed for validation necessarily depends on the claims being made. Therefore, validation requires a clear statement of the proposed interpretations and uses" (23). Robert J. Mislevy has best formalized the meaning of this view of validation through the use of Toulmin's (1958/2003) logic, the visual system of argument developed by Stephen Toulmin in 1958 and made familiar to writing instructors in textbooks such as Maxine Hairston's

(1981) *Successful Writing: A Rhetoric for Advanced Composition.* Using a system of situation-dependent arguments of evidence, warrants, claims, and qualifications, Kane (2006) proposes two types of validation arguments. The first, an interpretive argument, documents the network of inferences and assumptions leading from the performance to the conclusions and decisions on use. The second, the validity argument, serves as a check on the interpretative argument by evaluating its plausibility.

Such specificity now demanded in the process of validation must be accompanied by a categorical system of validation evidence. The *Standards for Educational and Psychological Testing* (AERA, APA, and NCME 2014) established five sources of validity evidence that might be used in evaluating a proposed interpretation of test scores for particular purposes: evidence based on test content, response processes, internal structure, external variables, and consequence. Under this evaluative method, researchers seek evidence of the overall relationship between test content and defined construct, fit between construct and performance, resonance between detailed test components and the construct, relationship between test scores and other variables tapping the construct such as course grades, and the unintended and intended impact of test use. In turn, Kane (2006) proposed four sources of evidence for an interpretive argument: scoring (studies of consistency and accuracy); generalization (studies of the specific assessment at hand in relation to the universe of generalization), extrapolation (studies of relationships among the construct at hand and related constructs), and implication (studies of consequence).

Abstract considerations of construct modeling and validation evidence are best understood in application. Consider, therefore, Figure 3.3, an adaptation of Kane's (2006, 2013) general measurement procedure for representation of the writing construct (shown in Figures 3.1 and 3.2).

In general, Figure 3.3 is intended as the key to validation of a writing program. And, if we may be so bold, its depiction of construct sampling and validity evidence is of central importance to the broad future of our field. As discussed in chapter 1, for a writing program to be accountable to its stakeholders, the program must be able to be assessed. We will return to this theme again in chapter 5 as we offer our Design for Assessment (DFA) model. For that model to take hold, each writing-assessment genre in place or planned will benefit from the model shown in Figure 3.3.

When combined with Figures 3.1 and Figure 3.2, Figure 3.3 reveals the complexity of complete construct representation in any one sample of writing—or, in any two or three samples, or even in an ePortfolio. Moving along a continuum of construct representation from a single

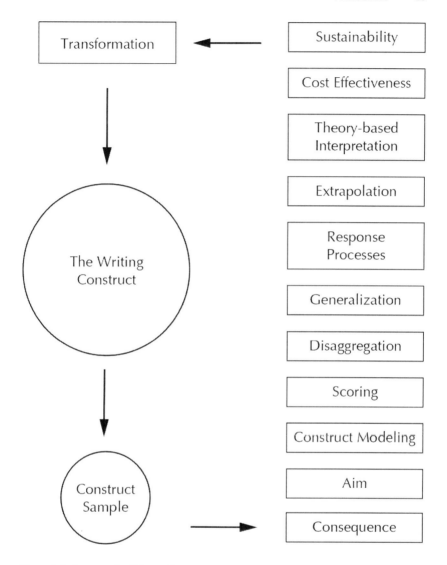

Figure 3.3. Sources of validity evidence.

timed, impromptu essay to a handful of writing samples to an ePortfolio increases construct representation. However, if the students at hand are majoring in chemical engineering and will spend their lives writing proposals for specialists and nonspecialists, then the value of a career portfolio, advanced in chapter 5, becomes apparent. Conceptualization of a writing program—instead of an instance of assessment—allows such construct coverage. That is, the construct sample will be modeled in various ways—and drawn many times under many circumstances—so that an institution's students may become proficient by experiencing the planned aims of the writing program.

Once we understand that a construct sample is an instance of the writing construct itself—the larger domain of writing—then it becomes clear that there are multiple sources of evidence that can be used to demonstrate that the writing program is doing its job. The distinct difference of the model we are advancing in this book rests with aim and consequence—the first two sources of evidence following the collected sample of the writing construct. Writing program assessment captures all genres of writing assessment; includes formative and summative assessment; and grapples with limited and robust construct representation at all levels of the curriculum, from admissions to placement, from end-of-course to upper-division certification for graduation. A writing program captures all these assessment aims. And, as we demonstrated in chapter 1, assessment of the writing program also includes documentation of institutional context, including resource allocation.

With aim and consequence advanced as the most important categories of evidence, the related categories fall into place:

- *Consequence.* Figure 3.3 calls for consequence to be determined early in the assessment, and we stress the importance of that determination for several reasons. While consequence may have been solidly linked to validity since Messick (1989) first made that connection, it is nevertheless still the case that consequence is often the last concern, or even of no concern, when an assessment is considered. In the model we propose for program assessment, consequence and its relation to fairness is determined directly after aim. For the end-of-course genre discussed in chapter 2, the consequence of assessing a researched paper at the end of first-year writing yields a valuable signaling effect: everyone knows researched writing is an important aim of the university's mission and hence research is integrated into the writing program. Moreover, an assessment of multimodal writing at the junior level will have a very positive washback effect indeed in conveying the message that the institution cares about the ability of students to communicate in digital environments.

- *Aim.* The aim of the particular assessment at hand determines its interpretation. Whether for placement or programmatic purposes, the wide range of assessment activities is deeply related to the construct sample. If that sample is narrow, then qualifications must be made regarding its relation to the writing construct; if that sample is robust, as we will argue is the case for ePortfolios based on the variable design associated with Phase 2 portfolios, then the collection of construct samples is much more likely to satisfy the desire for writing-construct representation.

- *Construct modeling*: As discussed in chapter 1, construct modeling is integral to writing program assessment. From the early work of Flower and Hayes (1981) to the recent *Framework for Success* (CWPA, NCTE, and NWP 2011), construct modeling allows the imaginative work of assessment to occur. And, as we will show later in this chapter, Phase 2 portfolio assessment—embodying the multiple-variable model that is rapidly shaping state-of-the-art contemporary assessment—itself embraces this model.

- *Scoring*: While reliability was of great, perhaps central, concern to researchers during the twentieth century, twenty-first-century researchers have learned that scoring is to be considered only part of validity evidence. As Brian E. Clauser (2000) has shown, evidence of reliable scoring is best viewed as evidence based on the judgment of panels of experts who develop the criteria, take care with implementation, and record information on reader consensus (interreader agreement) and consistency (interreader reliability). With attention to work by Stephen E. Stemler (2004), we will return to scoring in chapter 4. For now, let us consider scoring evidence as a result of the ways readers comprehend meaning, make reasonable and logical judgments, and understand the variables of construct modeling at hand during a particular assessment event or within a particular assessment genre (Bejar 2012).

- *Disaggregation*: Often unacknowledged as an important source of validity, disaggregation of scores is related to interreader agreement and reliability, as well as to consequence. In chapter 4, we provide tables in which scoring processes (Table 4.3) and impact (Table 4.1) suggest the importance of breaking down data. Indeed, as Inoue and Poe (2012) have argued, data disaggregation is of paramount importance as we continue to evaluate the fairness of our assessment procedures on a rapidly shifting American demographic. While White people still outnumber other groups (63.4 percent to 36.6 percent), the birthrate for African Americans, Native Americans, Hispanics, Asians, and people of mixed-race descent now totals more than 50 percent of all births in the United States (United States Census Bureau 2013). Along with socioeconomic factors, this remarkable demographic change in the United States is having a profound impact on educational contexts, and we will fail our students if we do not understand how our forms of assessment serve (or discourage) their potential for success. Score disaggregation is the first step toward the elimination of bias and disparate impact.

- *Generalization*: This category of evidence, as well as the next two, is taken from Kane (2006, 2013). For Kane, generalization is a category of construct inference. Does, we might ask, the construct sample taken in Figure 3.3 allow us to generalize about the larger writing construct? Such a category of evidence led Condon (2013) to offer a theory by which assessment genres might be classified into those with rich context (portfolios), scant context (the Collegiate Learning Assessment) and artificial context (the SAT writing section). A study of generalization would then examine the relationships among these three measures (or similar ones at a specific institution) to study the relationships among them—and then to draw conclusions regarding construct coverage.

- *Response Processes*: As the *Standards for Educational and Psychological Testing* (AERA, APA, and NCME 2014) recognizes, studies of response processes are often understood as pertaining to the examinee. Studies in which students are questioned about their responses to particular writing tasks remain at the center for construct modeling (Hayes 2012). In organizational settings, tracing the flow of documents and how individuals respond to them has revealed much about genre in organizations (Spinuzzi 2003) and would tell us much about how students respond to writing genres in a specific institution. However, studies of response processes need not be limited to the examinee. Validation may include how both instructors and their students evaluate the information provided by the assessment (13). When student and instructor responses are compared, much may be learned about the differences and similarities of assessment genres (Klobucar et al. 2013). Analysis of response processes is of critical importance to our field, especially in research on the reflective writing of students (Yancey 1998).

- *Extrapolation*: Extrapolation extends the construct sample into new domains. For example, studies may be conducted on the relationship of the ability of students to write well-documented assignments in a first-year writing class to the ability of those same students to use argumentative strategies including sources in a junior-level management class requiring researched work. In other cases, extrapolation evidence may involve relational studies such as the ones we discuss in chapters 2 and 4—the relationship, for instance, of ePortfolio scores to course grades and grade point averages. In general, as Kane (2013, 11) observes, extrapolation evidence will involve relationships between the performance on a construct sample and the performance on a related construct sample, perhaps in a larger domain.

- *Theory-based interpretation*: Theory-based interpretation depends on analyses demonstrating that the construct sample is adequately related to the broader writing construct so the assessment fits its aim. As Kane (2013) recalls, Cronbach (1989, 165) offered four criteria for deciding on whether or not a study should be conducted: uncertainty (Is the issue really in doubt?), information gained (How much certainly will be gained?), cost (addressed in the next category), and leverage (How important is the information to the audiences who will read the research?). Such questions are well suited to help define a theory-based study for a writing program. The study mentioned above—the relationship of the ability of students to write well-documented assignments in a first-year writing class to the ability of those same students to use argumentative strategies in a junior-level management class requiring researched work—might reveal a great deal about the need for researched writing across the curriculum and the ability to document writing genre relationships. If the samples are captured in an undergraduate ePortfolio that spans the undergraduate experience, the cost may be minimal and the gains may be great for a wide variety of stakeholders—from librarians who need to increase their databases and holdings to administrators seeking accreditation by the Association to Advance Collegiate Schools of Business.

- *Cost effectiveness*: In terms of time and dollars, Cronbach (1989) asked, how expensive is the investigation? As we will argue in chapter 5, this basic paradigm of reasoning should be replaced by cost-benefit-effectiveness analysis, a system developed by Levin and McEwan (2001) to evaluate costs and their alternatives with regard to their consequences. The intended use and language of cost-effectiveness analysis is ideally suited to the needs of writing program assessment if substantial faculty and curriculum development is a byproduct of the assessment, as often happens.

- *Sustainability*: Here the ecological metaphor provided in the introduction proves ideal as a category of validity. Achieving the objectives of the present without compromising the future is more than a slogan for writing program administrators. If there is disjuncture, for instance, between basic writing and the advanced aspects of the writing program itself—a situation Shawna Shapiro (2011) terms "the remedial rut"—then attention paid to bridging the gap could create an environment for students and their instructors in which the resources used to maintain a testing-intensive remedial curriculum focused on lexico-grammatical issues can be transformed into one in which a new basic writing curriculum fosters a broader construct sample that, in turn, supports a diverse student population. It is important, in fact, to entertain the proposition that an admitted student is a qualified student and make placements accordingly, based not on remediation but on intensity and appropriateness of instructional effort.

- *Transformation*: As we show in chapter 5, the assessment environment of the future will no longer support testing without a clear, well-articulated purpose based on a defined construct model. Absent will be tests that yield little information; present will be assessments used to improve student learning. If our predictions turn out to be true—and there is much evidence that they will—then all eleven categories of validity evidence must result in one end: an evolving and relevant curriculum designed to help students succeed personally and professionally. Retaining that which adds to student learning, while rejecting that which does not, will soon be the most important category in writing program assessment.

Once the writing construct is mapped and integrated robustly into the curriculum, the sources of validity evidence can be anticipated. The next conceptual move, therefore, is to continue to map the terrain in order to extend the impact of the writing program and assess the consequence of that extension.

A matrix identifying areas where the program objectives are expressed in individual courses is an important part of writing program design and assessment. A sample matrix for writing courses offered as part of a four-year college's general university requirements is provided in Table 3.1. The mapping is a modification of the writing program review process used by Nancy Coppola and Elliot (2010), based on the institutional mission of NJIT.

In this process of construct articulation, a method of linking the writing construct and the program that hosts its many manifestations is linked to institutional mission. Such a matrix centralizes the writing program within the institution. This centralization is the reverse of the derogatory view of writing sometimes held by student advisers: that writing is a requirement to be "gotten out of the way." In our view, writing is the central way for students to negotiate the institution and their own education.

In this process of construct articulation, a method of capturing the writing construct in its most robust form across the undergraduate and graduate experience is also needed. To do this, the writing program administrator must identify the core competencies (i.e., expression of the variables) of the writing program within specific writing courses. Table 3.2 is an example of just such a matrix with the following codes representing variables of the writing construct: 1. genre, 2. task, 3. audience, 4. writing processes, 5. problem solving, 6. information literacy, 7. conventions, 8. metacognition, 9. collaboration, 10. social networking, 11. leadership, 12. diversity, and 13. ethics.

As Table 3.2 demonstrates, there is no attempt to have each curricular offering be all things to all students. Only the required writing program curriculum and the ever-present writing center offer the kind of robust construct representation that yields in-depth experience with many variables of the construct and some grounding in their environmental context. Students are exposed to the cognitive, interpersonal, and intrapersonal domains in the first-year courses, after which core competencies carefully selected by program administrators are mapped and measured across the four years. In the sophomore year, where the essay is often a standard genre, task knowledge is featured so students can understand the demand of the constructed-response tasks of courses in literature and culture. Because they will write sourced papers, students are also given instruction in information literacy, from documentation to use of databases. In the junior year, knowledge of conventions is expected to be in hand, and the program administrators take a second opportunity to examine more of the core competencies, including attention to

Table 3.1 Writing program curriculum matrix: Part 1 (institutional objectives mapped to writing program core competencies).

Institutional Goals	Writing Program Goals	Core Competencies: Cognitive and Interpersonal	Core Competencies: Intrapersonal
Prepare students for productive careers and amplify their potential for lifelong personal and professional growth	Pursuit of writing as lifelong educational activity; awareness of writing as integral to individual and community advancement	Cognitive: genre, task, audience, writing process, problem solving, information literacy, conventions, metacognition Interpersonal: collaboration, social networking, leadership, diversity	Openness, conscientiousness, extraversion, agreeableness, and stability fostered in all courses and writing experiences
Conduct research with emphasis on applied, multidisciplinary efforts	Pursuit of research-based inquiry in writing; application of technology to writing circumstances to improve quality of individual life and community formation	Cognitive: genre, task, audience, problem solving, information literacy, metacognition Interpersonal: collaboration, social networking, leadership, diversity	↓↑
Strengthen sense of community	Pursuit of service in a variety of community settings; adoption of a leadership role in professional and citizenship activities; disposition toward engagement within and beyond the campus community	Cognitive: genre, task, audience, problem solving, metacognition Interpersonal: collaboration, social networking, leadership, diversity	↓↑
Promote ethical conduct	Pursuit of ethical conduct in all communication contexts	Cognitive: audience, information literacy, metacognition Interpersonal: ethical conduct	↓↑
Provide educational opportunities for a broadly diverse student body	Pursuit of diversity that celebrates cultural contexts; method of entrepreneurial inquiry when problem solving	Cognitive: genre, task, audience, problem solving, information literacy, metacognition Intrapersonal: collaboration, social networking, leadership, diversity	↓↑

audience and problem solving. These core competencies then underlie senior-year capstone projects. And, across the undergraduate experience, the writing center ensures that ways of addressing the full spectrum of writing program objectives are available to all students. The courses described in chapter 2 can surely be placed into this matrix,

Table 3.2 Writing program curriculum matrix: Part 2 (writing program core competencies mapped to individual courses).

Core Competencies: Cognitive and Interpersonal	1	2	3	4	5	6	7	8	9	10	11	12	13
Writing Courses													
First-year writing, including English language learning courses	✓	✓	✓	✓	✓	✓	✓	✓	✓	✓	✓	✓	✓
Sophomore year, including literature and culture courses		✓			✓	✓							
Junior year, including writing across the curriculum	✓	✓	✓	✓	✓	✓		✓		✓		✓	✓
Senior year, including writing in the disciplines in senior seminars	✓	✓	✓		✓	✓			✓		✓		✓
Writing center, available all years, including English language learning instruction	✓	✓	✓	✓	✓	✓	✓	✓	✓	✓	✓	✓	✓

and a cycle of formative as well as summative assessment can therefore be developed.

While we have concentrated on the writing construct, program assessment takes into consideration all of the factors that contribute to the success of a writing program. Table 3.3 identifies many sources of evidence that may be obtained from an institution's office of institutional research, its writing program administrators, its students through self-reports and writing performances, and from the instructional staff.

Many of these sources, such as the National Survey of Student Engagement and its appended module of thirteen questions on writing discussed in chapter 4, have defined construct models that may be used to provide evidence for interpersonal and intrapersonal domains (Paine et al. 2013). Indeed, the NSSE and the many standardized measures shown in Table 3.3 all may be understood as requiring validation through the categories of validity evidence identified in Figure 3.3.

In addition, each of the cells in Table 3.3 may be used to offer evidence for program assessment. Disaggregating performance data, for example, shows that writing program administrators are using standpoint analysis to ensure that the program serves all its students. Other sources, such as status and responsibilities of the WPA, can be used to evaluate program sustainability. Program administrators will find that their own versions of Table 3.3 are especially useful in combination with Figure 5.1 to identify categories of evidence that can serve as part of the writing program design.

VEHICLES: EPORTFOLIOS AND PHASE 2 ASSESSMENT

A print portfolio is a folder or binder containing examples of student work. An ePortfolio is a similar collection of student work, yet it is adapted to the writing construct as it is mediated in digital environments, and it embraces the potential of these environments to expand student proficiency in genre, persona, and audience. For generations, some faculties in the fine arts have been using portfolios for assessment and grading; the final examination in a class in drawing, painting, or architectural design, for example, often consists of a portfolio of the student's work, which is displayed, critiqued, and graded. Many writing instructors have used portfolios in the same way, and in recent years some writing programs have done the same as part of program assessment. Because portfolio use is directly connected to the curriculum and class activities, many schools and postsecondary institutions use portfolios for screening students for admission and advancement, assessing general-education program outcomes, and providing students with employment dossiers. As ePortfolios have come to replace print portfolios, the many advantages of digital formats have allowed this new version of the portfolio to capture even more of the writing construct than the older version, itself a much enhanced alternative to the single-sample, genre-constrained essay test.

One of the most thoroughly documented localized uses of ePortfolios is at Rose-Hulman Institute of Technology (Williams 2010). Broadly, Michael Neal (2011) has defined the two distinguishing features of electronic portfolios: these digital platforms may be used to enhance student connectivity to the curriculum and to other educational stakeholders, and they provide a source of student reflection on their learning processes and curricular experiences. In its specific application, the RosE Portfolio System (REPS) allows for efficient data collection across the institution. The results of these ePortfolio evaluations are then used by academic departments and programs to improve curricula and provide evidence of student achievement to external accrediting agencies. Using a carefully designed system based on institute-wide student learning outcomes, instructors score the student work posted to the REPS each year. The results are then reviewed by the Commission on the Assessment

Table 3.3 Examples of validity evidence for writing program assessment.

Institutional Research Sources	Writing Program Sources	Student Self-Reporting Sources	Student Performance-Based Sources	Instructional Staff Research Sources
High-school transcripts of English and related writing courses	Status and responsibilities of the WPA	Focus group results from student interviews on the writing program	Collections of undergraduate writing assignments with representative performance levels	Instructor participation in WAC and/or WID workshops
Admissions scores on standardized tests (e.g., ACT English, Reading, Writing; SAT Critical Reading and Writing; AP English Language and Composition, CLEP College Composition)	Institutional taxonomy of the writing construct	Student-volunteer curricular collaboration, including participation in writing program meetings, curricular design, and rubric-development and assessment	Collections of undergraduate cognitive domain performance ranges	Conference presentations
Placement scores on undergraduate standardized tests (e.g., COMPASS, ACCUPLACER), campus writing assessments (e.g., DSP)	Course syllabi, with common objectives mapped to the writing construct and established course goals	Reflective statements on course goals, with special attention to cognitive, intrapersonal, and interpersonal experiences	Collections of undergraduate intrapersonal domain performance ranges	Institutional and externally funded initiatives
Undergraduate course grades, institutional course evaluations, and National Survey of Student Engagement results	Individual and collaborative scoring rubrics; group score readers' recommendations on curricular transformation	Student recommendations on curricular transformation	Collections of undergraduate interpersonal domain performance ranges	Peer-reviewed articles and book chapters

continued on next page

Table 3.3—continued

Institutional Research Sources	Writing Program Sources	Student Self-Reporting Sources	Student Performance-Based Sources	Instructional Staff Research Sources
Undergraduate course cohort enrollment patterns, warning notices, final grades, grade point averages, and time to graduation; usage patterns on course-management systems; senior theses about writing	Instructor course reports	Student drafted, approved, and fulfilled learning contracts	Undergraduate student writing certifications and awards	Edited collections and professional books (single-authored, collaborations), including textbooks.
Number of undergraduate writing majors and minors, grade point averages, and graduate-school and/or job placement	Collections of writing assignments mapped to the writing construct and established course goals	Publications and reports from student organizations focused on writing (e.g., newspapers, magazines, digital communication, clubs, and learning communities)	Disaggregation of cognitive, intrapersonal, and interpersonal performance of undergraduate and graduate students by gender and race/ethnicity	Faculty and program awards
Scores from graduating students and admitted graduate students on standardized tests (e.g., GRE Verbal Reasoning and Analytic Writing; GMAT Analytic Writing Assessment)	Writing center use, protocols, and resource allocation	Participation of graduate students in writing center activities	Collections of graduate cognitive domain performance ranges	Citations of work done by program faculty

continued on next page

Table 3.3—continued

Institutional Research Sources	Writing Program Sources	Student Self-Reporting Sources	Student Performance-Based Sources	Instructional Staff Research Sources
Graduate writing course cohort enrollment patterns, final grades, grade point averages, and time to graduation; usage patterns on course-management systems; theses and dissertations about writing; doctoral, postdoctoral, or job placement	Minutes of meetings and action agendas	Participation of graduate students as teaching assistants	Collections of graduate intrapersonal domain performance ranges (e.g., ETS® Personal Potential Index)	Collaborative, inter-institutional research on the undergraduate and graduate level
Alumni, employer, and graduate school surveys	Examples of curricular improvement based on assessment results	Participation of graduate students as editors of peer-reviewed journals	Collections of graduate interpersonal domain performance ranges (e.g., ETS® Personal Potential Index)	Peer-review service; roles on editorial boards
Instructor level of education, salary, and ratio of full-time to part-time writing instructors	Interinstitutional collaborations	Collaborative presentations and publications of graduate students and writing program instructors	Disaggregation of cognitive, intrapersonal, and interpersonal performance of undergraduate and graduate students by instructor cohort	Service to professional organizations
Diversity of instructors by gender and race/ethnicity	Externally generated reports in print and digital formats	Sole-authored presentations and publications of graduate students	Disaggregation of cognitive, intrapersonal, and interpersonal performance of undergraduate and graduate students by gender and race/ethnicity	Participation by tenured, tenure-track, nontenured, and adjunct instructors in the undergraduate and graduate writing program, disaggregated by individual teaching load and course cohort

of Student Outcomes (CASO). Committee members then work with individual departments to affirm curricular progress, target areas of improvement, and redesign learning outcomes where necessary. On an international scale, Kathleen Blake Yancey (2012) has been instrumental in working with Darren Cambridge and Barbara Cambridge (Cambridge, Cambridge, and Yancey 2009) on the National Coalition for Electronic Portfolio Research. Current research conducted by the coalition has produced valuable findings on ePortfolio practice, integrative learning, identity formation, design of core competencies and learning outcomes, values articulation, and emerging technologies. To advance the knowledge base on ePortfolio use, the *International Journal of ePortfolio*—jointly published by Virginia Tech and the University of Georgia—advances the study of practices and pedagogies in research in educational settings. If the rapidity of digital expansion is any indicator of trends, print portfolios will soon recede as web-based ePortfolios continue to proliferate in educational and workplace settings. Indeed, it seems that the descriptive terms themselves are shifting: the various abbreviations now in use for electronic portfolios (*EPortfolios, Eportfolios, ePortfolios, e-portfolios,* and the like) will simply become *portfolios,* while those meaning *print portfolios* will need to specify the portfolios are *not* in digital form. While not quite ubiquitous at the present time, ePortfolios will soon become so (Wills and Rice 2013).

The great advantage of ePortfolios for assessment is that they can include numerous examples of student writing, produced over time and under a variety of conditions; they also allow students to include links to their work in blogs, podcasts, and collaborative wikis. Unlike the single constructed-response task, even one as well designed as that done by Peckham, the ePortfolios shown in Figure 2.2 and Figure 3.4 can show a student's actual writing performance across time and circumstance as the student encounters a wide range of tasks and genres, along with grading at (*not by*) a computer (Collins et al. 2013).

Uncontrolled conditions for collecting and scoring ePortfolios nevertheless pose challenges. Because close supervision of the production of portfolio contents is often difficult and sometimes inappropriate, several categories of evidence shown in Figure 3.3, needed as sources of validity, may be unreliable: without time constraints, the amount of time each student devotes to the task will differ. Sometimes, as a result of socioeconomic necessity in which students must work to pay rising college costs, artifacts uploaded to an ePortfolio may reflect time constraints instead of writing proficiency (a problem with all untimed response processes). In addition, students are likely to get help from various sources (consultations in the writing center to purchased papers from unscrupulous commercial firms), so it may be hard to know just what we are assessing (a problem of consequence). The development of writer authentication by input patterns may, however, solve the latter problem. With sophisticated methodology, Coursera was able to authenticate authorship in the recent Massive Open Online Course developed by Denise Comer of Duke University, which offered composition instruction to more than eighty thousand students across the globe. If we are assessing portfolios that show responses to a variety of assignments from different instructors, we may not understand the context of some classes or the assumptions behind the particular work (although we might ask students to provide this information as a matter of establishing aim); we may also be evaluating the assignments as well as the responses, as better assignments tend to elicit better writing (an issue of construct modeling under different circumstances). And, of course, regardless of the robust sample of writing under analysis, readers are still making observations on a given day at a given time.

The challenge for writing program administrators, then, is to maximize the advantages of this method of assessment while minimizing the disadvantages. Those who can perform this balancing act will find that ePortfolios are the most valuable means available of combining evaluation with teaching. As we have shown above, identification of the fundamental constructs embodied in courses through construct modeling and mapping affords a systematic way to use ePortfolios as the central way to capture writing performance within the writing program.

Scoring portfolios requires the development of two new documents as part of the assessment: first, a set of core competencies, or program objectives, set by faculty for the particular course, program, or purpose for which the portfolio is submitted, such as those shown in Table 3.2 above; and, second, a reflective statement to readers composed by the student that functions as an argument showing the degree to which core competencies have been met (or, perhaps, not met), using the portfolio contents as evidence, such as that required by Peckham in his course. To keep the discussion specific, consider Figure 3.4 below.

In this instance, writing program administrators used the *WPA Outcomes Statement* and the *Framework for Success* as the basis for core competencies: critical thinking, knowledge of conventions, reading and writing, and composing in electronic environments. Students were required to post reflective statements on how the work they uploaded to the platform related to the course objectives—which are, in fact, based on the variable model used in the course—as well as statements in which the

Profile Information

- First Name: Nilsa
- Last Name: Lacunza
- Email Address: nl29@njit.edu
- City/Region: Clifton
- Country: United States

Your Entire Resumé

Contact Information

| City/Region | Clifton |
| Country | United States |

History
Employment History

Start date	End date	Position
Summer 2009		Paid Internship at Liberty Science Center

Education History

Start date	End date	Qualification
Fall 2010	Spring 2014	Biomedical Engineer (Bachelor of Science) at New Jersey Institute of Technology

Liberty Science Center Internship

Critical Thinking

The ability to analyze diverse topics and derive an opinion that allows you to summarize the major points that you have read. Here are a few of my works where critical thinking was exploited.

Contents:

Change ca...eted.doc
Talks about the reason why we as individuals cannot come together for a cause through technology.
34KB | Monday, 06 December 2010

Gap year.doc
Entails my opinion of whether or not taking a year off after high school is a good idea.
32KB | Monday, 06 December 2010

Figure 3.4. EPortfolio of Nilsa Lacunza, NJIT first-year student. (Used by permission. Text unedited.)

aim, genre, task, and audience were identified. (The screen capture provides only the first layer of the ePortfolio, a limit of print.)

Although these do not appear at first to be particularly novel developments, when used together they transform assessment—and for the better in every sense. Since a Phase 2 portfolio assessment requires the

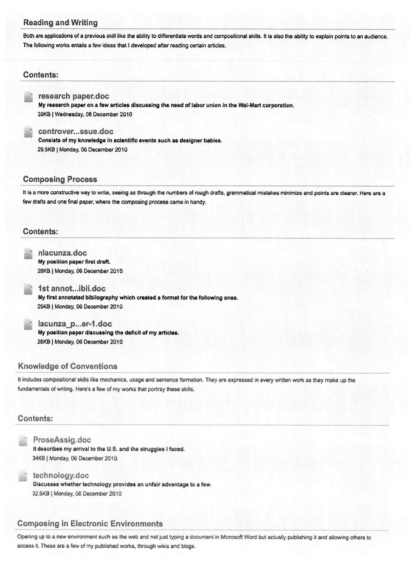

Reading and Writing

Both are applications of a previous skill like the ability to differentiate words and compositional skills. It is also the ability to explain points to an audience. The following works entails a few ideas that I developed after reading certain articles.

Contents:

research paper.doc
My research paper on a few articles discussing the need of labor union in the Wal-Mart corporation.
39KB | Wednesday, 08 December 2010

controver...ssue.doc
Consists of my knowledge in scientific events such as designer babies.
29.5KB | Monday, 06 December 2010

Composing Process

It is a more constructive way to write, seeing as through the numbers of rough drafts, grammatical mistakes minimize and points are clearer. Here are a few drafts and one final paper, where the composing process came in handy.

Contents:

nlacunza.doc
My position paper first draft.
28KB | Monday, 06 December 2010

1st annot...ibli.doc
My first annotated bibliography which created a format for the following ones.
25KB | Monday, 06 December 2010

lacunza_p...er-1.doc
My position paper discussing the deficit of my articles.
28KB | Monday, 06 December 2010

Knowledge of Conventions

It includes compositional skills like mechanics, usage and sentence formation. They are expressed in every written work as they make up the fundamentals of writing. Here's a few of my works that portray these skills.

Contents:

ProseAssig.doc
It describes my arrival to the U.S. and the struggles I faced.
34KB | Monday, 06 December 2010

technology.doc
Discusses whether technology provides an unfair advantage to a few.
32.5KB | Monday, 06 December 2010

Composing in Electronic Environments

Opening up to a new environment such as the web and not just typing a document in Microsoft Word but actually publishing it and allowing others to access it. These are a few of my published works, through wikis and blogs.

Figure 3.4—continued

student to construct the reflective letter in response to the course objectives, we need to consider that first.

The easiest and most direct use of ePortfolios is in a single writing class, as Ms. Lacunza's work demonstrates. The student loads the URL for the ePortfolio, and the work in the course to date is immediately available for conferences with the instructor or with tutors in the writing center. Because a reflective statement related to the course

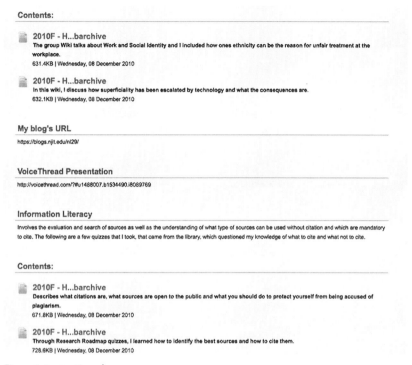

Contents:

2010F - H...barchive
The group Wiki talks about Work and Social Identity and I included how ones ethnicity can be the reason for unfair treatment at the workplace.
631.4KB | Wednesday, 08 December 2010

2010F - H...barchive
In this wiki, I discuss how superficiality has been escalated by technology and what the consequences are.
632.1KB | Wednesday, 08 December 2010

My blog's URL

https://blogs.njit.edu/nl29/

VoiceThread Presentation

http://voicethread.com/?#u1488007.b1534490.i8089769

Information Literacy

Involves the evaluation and search of sources as well as the understanding of what type of sources can be used without citation and which are mandatory to cite. The following are a few quizzes that I took, that came from the library, which questioned my knowledge of what to cite and what not to cite.

Contents:

2010F - H...barchive
Describes what citations are, what sources are open to the public and what you should do to protect yourself from being accused of plagiarism.
671.8KB | Wednesday, 08 December 2010

2010F - H...barchive
Through Research Roadmap quizzes, I learned how to identify the best sources and how to cite them.
728.6KB | Wednesday, 08 December 2010

Figure 3.4—continued

objectives is included, that statement serves as a foreword to the student's course accomplishments.

Before students can write such a reflective letter, they need to have a clear understanding of the objectives, or core competencies, of the course. A core-competency statement may be long or short, immensely detailed or fairly general, but the students need to understand its meaning in order to design their ePortfolios and compose their reflective statements. Since the statement, perhaps expressed in the genre of a letter, is essentially an argument, in the rhetorical sense, using the materials in the portfolio to show to what extent the student has in fact met the course objectives, a clear sense of what the competencies mean is crucial. When students have such an understanding, the reflective letter loses the narrative vagueness typical of such letters in the early days of portfolio assessment ("I learned a lot this term and worked really hard" or "You are the best instructor I've ever had") and gains structure and purpose ("You can see how I learned to revise by comparing the first paragraphs of the first draft of my second essay in Document 1 on page 9 to the third-draft opening on page 22 in Document 3").

The ePortfolio has important advantages for the student in a writing course. In the first place, it exemplifies the instructor's belief that writing is a process, not merely a product. Although the ePortfolio contains a series of products, as a whole it is evidence of the student's writing process. Some papers may be revised three or four times, and even the least capable writer notices the changes from early drafts to presentation copies. Furthermore, the ePortfolio demonstrates that the student is really writing for the self, or for other audiences in digital environments, not just for the instructor or for the grade. Almost all students take pride in the ePortfolio, want to preserve it at the end of the term, and are impressed at the quantity (if not the quality) of the work produced.

Individual instructors using this method for course assessments have many options for assessing the ePortfolio. For example, they might focus on one or two papers with multiple revisions to give a process grade on the student's ability to improve from draft to draft; such a grade is a responsible way to reward effort by writers who have not yet learned to produce excellent final products. Perhaps that process grade can combine with grades on the products to give a fairer term grade than one based wholly on final drafts. Again, instructors might allow students to focus the ePortfolio on a few papers they like the best, or instructors might define the ePortfolio as including several essential papers, with their notes and drafts. The point is to promote student ownership of the portfolio, despite the fact that the instructor must finally grade the work, and to demonstrate that the writing grade depends on more than a finely edited product. Or the writing staff may meet to grade ePortfolios from all sections of a writing course, sometimes with no instructors grading their own sections; the staff grade then has a strong influence on the student's course grade, though it usually is not determinative. The results of such a structured grading session then can feed directly into a program assessment.

Recognizing the value of ePortfolio assessment, we recommend it as the centerpiece of writing program assessment. This framework has several clear advantages for instructors as well as for the program. If the ePortfolio is to be scored by others, the instructor then becomes more a coach than a judge. The instructor in that case is helping the student prepare the best ePortfolio possible for the assessment. The core competencies—the variables on which the ePortfolio is designed—become aspects of the writing construct that the student wants to learn. The instructor's comments and grades become valuable clues to the way others will probably score the ePortfolio. Rather than giving a failing grade, for example, instructors can merely indicate that a portfolio with work of *this* quality, in their experience, will not receive a grade above the mean. Any system that turns the instructor into a valued coach is likely to assist in student learning and, incidentally, make everyone's lives much more pleasant.

Students sometimes find the unknown ePortfolio team even more threatening than the known course instructor and resist team grading, especially if, as we propose in chapter 4, a sampling plan is used so that each ePortfolio is not necessarily read. (Or, if students know that their own work may not be read or that there is no grade value, they may dismiss the activity altogether.) If the staff work together to define the ePortfolios so they express the objectives of the program and the scoring standards, and the assessment gains the support of the instructors, students will find the operation supportive rather than threatening. And once the staff members see the ePortfolio assessment team as "us" rather than "them," they can allay student concerns by their confidence in and support of the grading standards. Because key variables of the writing construct itself are being modeled for students, those responsible for the ePortfolio team must carefully and regularly consider ways to maintain the genuine collegiality of the program

We do not mean to suggest that Phase 2 scoring is problem free or the answer to all portfolio issues. Rather, we suggest that Table 3.4 be used to put Phase 2 scoring through its paces. It is derived from tagmemic theory, as first promulgated for composition studies by Young, Becker, and Pike (1970).

The importation of tagmemics into writing research led to some controversy, particularly from those tuned in to its particular and different use in physics. But its value for writing assessment and for conceptualizing effective writing assessments has never been fully explored. We find it particularly useful for explaining the developments in the field over the last fifty years. We can consider this development, following the historical view of Yancey (2012), as moving from multiple-choice testing (in tagmemics, a focus on particles), to essay testing (wave), to portfolios (field), to exigency (ePortfolios).

As is clear in this chapter, we advocate a criterion-based assessment system in which clear, precise core competencies—based on variables of the writing construct expressed in constructed-response tasks—are captured in an ePortfolio. In a norm-referenced system half of the students *must* be below average, but in a criterion-referenced system the proportion of students meeting a core-competency standard depends on the skills of the students and could be a low or a high proportion of the

Table 3.4 A heuristic framework for use of Phase 2 ePortfolios in writing programs.

	Contrast (Distinction)	Variation (Range)	Distribution (Contexts)
Particle (Static)	View the ePortfolio as an isolated, static entity. 1. What features of the ePortfolio differentiate it from all other writing assessment systems?	View the ePortfolio as one among a group of instances of writing assessment. 4. What is the range of construct measurement of the ePortfolio in relation to other systems of writing assessment?	View the ePortfolio as part of a larger context. 7. How is the ePortfolio classified among writing assessment systems?
Wave (Dynamic)	View the ePortfolio as a dynamic object or event. 2. What features of the ePortfolio differentiate it from the most similar assessment systems available?	View the ePortfolio as a dynamic process. 5. How is the ePortfolio evolving at the present time?	View the ePortfolio as part of dynamic context. 8. If the ePortfolio merges into the environment of its intended use, what are the costs and benefits?
Field (Network)	View the ePortfolio as an abstract, multidimensional system. 3. How are the features of the ePortfolio system related to known models of the writing construct in terms of fairness, validity, and reliability?	View the ePortfolio as multidimensional system. 6. How do the sources of validity evidence for the ePortfolio vary with each other?	View the ePortfolio as an abstract system within larger systems. 9. How might the ePortfolio under consideration become part of larger systems of use?

group. As a means of program evaluation, ePortfolios are currently the best methodology to capture the writing construct in its various forms now available, responding equally well to the new criteria for pedagogy and validity. For now, we recommend ePortfolios as part of the gold standard to advance the kind of writing program assessment described in this book. In Figure 3.5, we argue for their use.

Because we wish to support our claim that ePortfolios are a valuable addition to program assessment, we frame our arguments according to the Toulmin (1958/2003) model. As Figure 3.5 shows, the argument is situation dependent to a specific institutional site. The argument for Phase 2 portfolio assessment is an almost uncanny match with the framework of the Toulmin model. The match is quite accidental, which, in a way, makes the argument stronger. In common with much that is known in composition theory, Phase 2 portfolio scoring emerged not from theory but from practice. Faced with the problems of unreliable scoring (as a result of varied portfolio contents) and very high scoring costs, faculty favorable to the curricular benefits of portfolios sought out practical

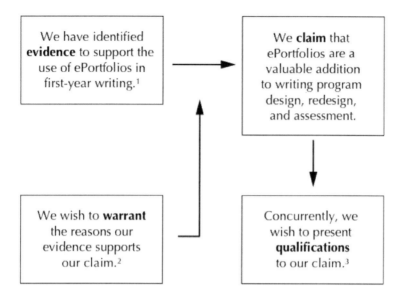

1. Congruent relationships exist among institutional mission, writing program objectives, and the ePortfolio's expression of the writing construct. Existing and emerging theoretical and empirical studies constitute a body of knowledge about ePortfolios.

2. EPortfolios serve a valuable role in the institution regarding defined models of learning and assessment and the use of technology to improve the lives of students.

3. Unless a multidisciplinary view of writing and its assessment is fostered, it will become increasingly difficult to understand the role of writing and its assessment in digital environments and thus to maintain the ePortfolio.

Unless the institution and its writing program are uniformly committed to quantitative and qualitative investigation of forms of writing contained in the ePortfolio as part of the writing program's ecology, the relationship between instruction and assessment will deteriorate and the ePortfolio's value will deteriorate.

Figure 3.5. A validity argument for ePortfolio use.

solutions. The attention to reflection as an essential part of the writing process at the college level, featured prominently in Kathleen Yancey's (1998) *Reflection in the Writing Classroom*, led to renewed attention to the reflective letter as the key element in an ePortfolio.

Thus the claim that Phase 2 portfolio assessment is more valid than previous performance assessment models rests on (1) its direct measurement of student writing over time, (2) its amenability to being scored according to multiple variables, (3) its ability to include measurement of revision strategies, (4) its ability to reflect and support the writing program and a construct of writing in tune with current research and pedagogy, (5) its requirement for student reflection about writing and the specific effects of the writing program, and (6) its ability to extend across the entire undergraduate and graduate curriculum and into the workplace as a demonstration of ability. Further, the reliability of scoring gained from the primary focus on the student's final reflection and the variable model integrated into the core competencies allows use of the data in support of the writing program in reports to outside parties accustomed to and expecting statistical evidence for success.

One common metaphor among those promoting portfolio assessment in its early days is a visual one: whereas a single assessment, whether multiple-choice test, essay, or some combination of the two, is a snapshot of student performance, a well-constructed portfolio is a moving picture. Now, with digital ePortfolio often containing images, links to various filmed scenes, and other innovations, that metaphor takes on new life and vigor. Indeed, ePortfolios have the potential, at least in theory, of helping us reimagine response process as either classroom grades or group scores. Digital environments, however, allow multimodal responses, and it may be these that hold the most promise. Because of their potential to richly capture writing constructs, ePortfolios allow us to anticipate and avoid statistical surrogation and other fallacies that present themselves in validity arguments (Kane 2006, 57–59). Responses to ePortfolios can be as robust as the digital environments that support them. A response can be a recorded response (audio or video), and program assessment could be constructed with this kind of rich response—rather than with how many students received scores on a scale. Fresh notions of reliability could even be incorporated in such a model. EPortfolios now can demonstrate their claim to be the most effective means of assessment of student work in writing programs, whenever there is time and support to use them appropriately. We are only beginning to understand their possibilities for instruction and assessment (Yancey, McElroy, and Powers 2013).

CYCLES: RECURSIVE ASSESSMENT

The final element of the basics of writing program assessment involves the cycle of assessment. We provide an illustration of that cycle in Figure 3.6.

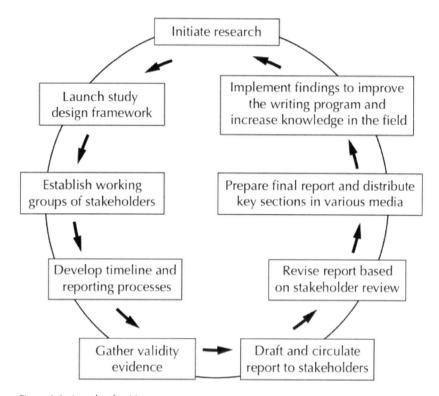

Figure 3.6. A cycle of writing program assessment.

While some of the assessment phases are familiar, others are novel. We stress, for example, the kind of alignment with forces external to the institution and the mission as central to the writing program's design and its assessment. In addition, we stress the importance of including a large variety of stakeholders, including students, to establish the writing program's mission and core competencies; indeed, if the writing program does not offer a degree, it is important to bring in colleagues from other fields so they may promote the use of varied genres within and beyond disciplinary boundaries. We also advocate that a planned assessment cycle operate on a spring-and-fall, odd-and-even-year basis so writing courses such as those shown in Table 3.2 can be assessed on a cyclical basis through the use of ePortfolios that can be used across the curricular experience. While the planned curriculum should always model constructs with students, there is no need whatsoever to have each core competency of the assessment under examination at all times.

In addition, we firmly believe that reports on the writing program in their draft forms should be shared for review and comment before they are released so the information they contain is both accurate and useful to a variety of audiences. And, in communicating those findings, we also believe that a formal, print report is only one way of communicating information. Indeed, if the nomothetic map is applied to communicating assessment results, then a wide variety of genre forms can be used—from blogs to podcasts—to communicate information.

Most importantly, as we will show in chapter 5, assessment information must be used to improve student learning in the curriculum. Because Phase 2 portfolio scoring is, in reality, a form of modeling the writing construct, assessment results reveal how students are performing on each of the core competencies. Such variable specific information is invaluable to stakeholders of writing programs. We turn now to the kinds of empirical measurement possible and how key techniques—and the important concepts they embody—can be used to transform writing programs.

QUESTIONS FOR WRITING PROGRAM FACULTY AND ADMINISTRATORS: FOUNDATIONS

Background

In this set of questions, we have taken the most important concepts from chapter 3 on our foundations of assessment and turned them into questions for writing program faculty and administrators. For Witte and Faigley (1983), there were five components of writing program evaluation: cultural and social context, institutional context, program structure and administration, curriculum, and instruction. Taken together in their interactions, these five components allow evaluators to examine the effects of the writing program (40). The six concepts we provide in chapter 3 are intended to augment both the evaluation and research contexts for writing programs and their assessment. Our concepts thus take a distinct research orientation that follows naturally from our emphasis on localism.

Introduction

It is of historical interest that White's (1985) *Teaching and Assessing Writing* appeared before his *Developing Successful College Writing Programs* (White 1989). Conceptually, we might have expected a second assessment book. Yet careful readers such as Richard Lloyd-Jones recognize that the two volumes are complementary. "White concentrates on providing information that will allow administrators to understand challenges to learning so fundamental that they define learning itself," he wrote in his foreword to the 1989 volume (White 1989, xiv). Because instruction and assessment must be unified, that unity must be communicated clearly (and loudly and formally) so others will listen in on the conversation. The questions that follow are intended to encourage just such communication.

Questions

The following questions are intended to prompt discussion on the fundamental principles and practices of writing program assessment. Based on regional, national, and international trends in instruction and assessment, the questions will facilitate an institution-based response to calls for accountability.

1. Based on Figure 3.1, how might visual design be used to capture the span of writing in all of its complexity as it is understood at your institution? In creating such a representation of the writing construct, you may wish to focus on the following: forms of communication and their expressions; rhetorical conceptualizations—cognitive, interpersonal, and intrapersonal domains; and neurological, attention, and visual systems. In addition, you should form the visual model with examples from across the curriculum and the disciplines, as well as new digital forms of writing used by students.

2. Recalling question 4 from chapter 2, how can this visualization serve as the centerpiece of a body of knowledge initiative for your writing program? Were such an initiative to be undertaken and communicated to students, how would such a statement inform instruction and assessment?

3. Based on Figure 3.3, how can the unique representation of the writing construct at your institution be visualized? One of the best methods to study the ways writing is conducted at your institution is to focus on the writing tasks students are asked to submit (Melzer 2014). Termed *construct samples* in the figure, writing samples can be analyzed according to various forces external to the institution that shapes them, as well as the internal forces of the institutional and writing program mission. The writing tasks can then be studied as they are embedded in the curriculum through mapping them to other tasks, examining the ways these tasks shape the writing construct for students, and describing the ways they may be used in ePortfolios as sources of validity evidence. As that validity evidence is gathered and used, the curriculum may be strengthened to advance student writing ability.

4. Following Kane (2006, 2013) and the Design for Assessment framework, how will the various sources of evidence stemming from study of the writing construct be used in the writing program? Based on Figure 3.3, what categories of evidence—from aim to transformation—will be used within your program to demonstrate its effectiveness in advancing student learning?

5. Once the span of the writing construct is identified and its distinct classroom use more fully understood, a matrix can be developed by which particular writing competencies can be established within the curriculum. Here is a further instance of constructive alignment (Biggs and Tang 2011). Because no single writing course can address all the complexities involved in writing, detailed planning will allow students to both broaden and deepen their communication experiences. Using a format based on Table 3.1 and Table 3.2, how will the span of the writing construct be identified within individual courses and writing center experiences so students gain exposure to the span of the writing construct? Because there is little evidence for transfer of specific skills (Pellegrino and Hilton 2012), how can the matrix be designed to encourage the deeper learning (Schwartz, Bransford, and Sears 2005) involved with transfer of general principles such as experience with genre and knowledge of audience (Yancey, Robertson, and Taczak 2014)?

6. As Table 3.3 demonstrates, collecting evidence about a writing program requires planned identification of sources. How will evidence be collected from your institutional research division, writing program administrator, students' self-reporting and performance-based collections, and instructors to document the performance of the writing program?

7. Following the design of the scoreable ePortfolio shown in Figure 2.2 and Figure 3.4, how might an ePortfolio be designed so students can achieve deeper learning through planned writing experiences and cyclical assessment? In this design, how will special attention be paid to student reflective statements so the ePortfolios are not reduced to mere digital filing cabinets? Using Table 3.4, how can the program objectives be most effectively communicated to students so their reflective statements show their understanding of those objectives and the degree to which they have achieved them?

8. Using Figure 3.6 as a model, how can an assessment cycle be designed so the results of the assessment are used to strengthen instruction while assuring assessment does not become too burdensome? In planning the assessment cycle, special care should be taken to anticipate the consequences of each assessment episode, identify the ways information will establish validity studies, plan communication of results, and use the findings to improve student writing ability.

9. Examine the *Common European Framework of Reference for Languages: Learning, Teaching, Assessment* (2001) and the responses to it (Little 2007; Weir 2005). As another framework for instruction and assessment, what components from this international framework can be used to strengthen program assessment at your institution? If you have English-language learners in your writing program, how can you adapt this framework to help these students succeed?

4
MEASUREMENT

In the introduction to this book, we called attention to the code used by the Classification of Instructional Programs for our field. In turn, we have used the term *rhetoric and composition/writing studies* (23.13) to refer to our professional orientation. Before providing an educational measurement perspective on the assessment of writing programs, it is important to examine a seemingly insignificant detail that accounts for many of our attitudes toward assessment: 23.13 (the four digits that represent intermediate groupings of programs) is categorized as part of English language and literature/letters (CIP code 23, the most general group of related programs). Although these bureaucratic matters appear remote from the writing and literature classes we teach and the programs we assess, these classifications matter.

Pragmatically, they matter because these codes are part of the system that postsecondary institutions use when submitting information for the Integrated Postsecondary Education Data System (IPEDS), the system of interrelated surveys conducted annually since 1965 by the US Department of Education's National Center for Education Statistics (NCES). So, when state policymakers and local university officials allocate resources, these are the buckets into which a coin is dropped or from which it is withheld: general writing (23.1301); creative writing (23.1302); professional, technical, business, and scientific writing (23.1303); rhetoric and composition (23.1304); and rhetoric and composition/writing studies, other (23.1399). Along with a system for allocating resources, within those seemingly descriptive codes live both a tumultuous disciplinary history and a distinct attitude toward knowledge.

The turf war between literature and composition has a long and inglorious history. The heat of the battle was best felt in the debate between Gary Tate and Erika Lindemann at a joint conference of the Association of Departments of English and CWPA, published in the pages of *College English* in 1993. For Tate (1993), "The Rhetoric Police had erred seriously" by elevating nonfiction prose and disciplinary discourse to "sacred

DOI: 10.7330/9780874219869.c004

heights." Literature, Tate argued, would help students "transcend whatever disciplines they associate themselves with while in college" (312). For Lindemann (1993), advocacy for the inclusion of literature in the composition curriculum was a nonstarter. "We cannot usefully discuss the role of imaginative literature (however defined)," she wrote, "without first asking what the purpose of a first-year writing course is." If the first-year course is to "provide opportunities to master the genres, styles, audiences, and purposes of college writing," then the textual consumption of literature-based instruction would do little good for students (312). The issue on many campuses is exacerbated further by personnel issues, an underlying bias among many literature professors against the practical nature of much writing instruction, resentment by the writing faculty of the differential in status and reward between them and the literature faculty, a lingering desire by some English faculty to use the required writing course to recruit English majors, and other matters that often appear to outsiders, and, increasingly, to insiders to be wasteful internecine warfare.

While this pattern was set early on in the history of English departments, when modern literature, American literature, creative writing, feminist literature, world literatures, and other noncanonical writing struggled for recognition, we hold that it is time to put this exclusiveness behind us. The liberal arts in the twenty-first century are under severe pressure from all sides and we need to work together to demonstrate the value of language arts (American Academy of Arts and Sciences 2013; Elbow 2002).

Because we reject value dualism and value hierarchy, our call for multidisciplinarity—in this case, between writing studies and educational measurement—becomes apparent as we turn to the measurement concepts in this chapter: descriptive statistics, sampling-plan design, null hypothesis significance testing, correlation analysis, tests of statistically significant difference, regression analysis, and effect-size determination. While some entrenched literature specialists may see this call as colluding with the enemy, we urge a broader view. Hamlet cannot retreat to his quarters in the castle; at last, he must confront his mother and Claudius in a harsh reality. When we look ahead, we see dark clouds for the humanities if we fail to embrace change. At present, this cloud is very like a whale—or, we might say to Polonius, a regression analysis that will fail to produce a statistically significant outcome.

Full explication of these topics would easily require consultation from the following fields: educational assessment, evaluation, and research (CIP 13.06); educational psychology (CIP 42.2809); and psychometrics and quantitative psychology (CIP 42.2708). This chapter does not attempt complete explication. Rather, we present what we have found to be key measurement concepts in terms of their application to writing program assessment from the point of view of those whose primary work is in writing studies.

Before starting out, we need to be clear about our reason for advocating empirical techniques for program assessment: preventing oversimplified measures of writing programs—measures that fail to support instruction—is simply not possible without the use of sophisticated quantitative and qualitative processes described in this chapter. The use of descriptive and inferential statistics is more effective in administrative meetings than the rhetoric often employed. Writing program administrators need the conceptual skills and empirical tools presented in this chapter if they are to serve the writing communities they represent. In the very near future, a doctoral program in writing studies that does not include training in empirical research, both quantitative and qualitative, will not be behaving responsibly toward its students. While it is our hope that the techniques we present in this book will be useful in all degree programs in rhetoric and composition/writing studies, as we noted in the introduction, we also strongly recommend that each of the doctoral programs in the Consortium of Doctoral Programs in Rhetoric and Composition offer at least one required seminar that provides students with the kinds of analytic knowledge we describe in this chapter.

We understand that many in our field have little or no training in statistics and may find the language that must be used in the following discussion daunting. So, as you read through the formulae and discussions to come, a little help from a colleague in a math-oriented field might be called for, perhaps only for the first time this rather simple but crucial step is undertaken. If further, in-depth study is needed, we suggest a standard research methods book such as that by H. Russell Bernard (2013) or Trochim and Donnelly (2008). Both of these books treat quantitative and qualitative empirical research equally. For those who will analyze data themselves, we recommend the most recent version of SPSS, the standard statistical software package for the social sciences offered by IBM. To accompany that platform we recommend books such as those by George and Mallery (2013) as step-by-step guides. For the equally complicated and demanding area of qualitative research, we recommend the NVivo platforms from QSR International and the excellent online guides.

If you decide at first reading of this book to skip the rest of this chapter for now, we will not just yet raise a ruckus, as long as you promise to return after a brief tour of these resources. It does take some time to feel comfortable with a new vocabulary, and you should certainly consult the glossary at the back of the book. The most important thing to remember when dealing with empirical analysis is that, as we will show, the statistics are not ends in themselves; rather, they are part of a rich system of reasoning that, when used thoughtfully, can lead to improved ways to teach and assess writing in a programmatic framework.

DESCRIPTIVE STATISTICS: IDENTIFYING THE LOCAL

Consider Table 4.1. This table from NJIT is a record for first-year writing over a fourteen-year period. The table records all admission-test scores in terms of national and state averages, placement based on locally developed measures, and grades for the four basic cohorts of students (honors, traditional, basic writers, and English-language learners).

This table illustrates the fact that a measure of success—defined as a grade of C or above—was needed to estimate the reliability of the placement system across time when the admissions scores remained consistent. As the table illustrates, although the admission-test scores were remarkably consistent, the course grades of C or above were not. Indeed, from 19 percent to 39 percent of the admitted class was placed into basic writing from 1998 to 2007—a range that suggests instability in the placement system. When the system was revised in 2008, the rates of success became more consistent, suggesting that the new placement system yielded the desired stability, defined as a grade of C or better. Such tables are critical to writing program administrators in providing information to all stakeholders regarding placement and grading of the incoming first-year students.

Once the writing program's student population is described, with attendant criterion measures—functional measures of performance such as admissions scores, course placement, and final course grades—assessment within the writing program can be initiated.

SAMPLING-PLAN DESIGN: MAKING INFERENCES

In cases involving very large samples, it is simply impossible to provide performance information on each student, especially when the performance is a complex act of writing such as those assembled in an ePortfolio. In these cases, information about the sampling plan used for the particular study at hand is essential. Because sampling-plan design is a very important part of program review, an extended example is in order.

Table 4.1 Longitudinal descriptive statistics: NJIT 1998 to 2012: Overview of admission and placement, 1998–2012.

	1998 (N = 678)	1999 (N = 710)	2000 (N = 729)	2001 (N = 740)	2002 (N = 685)	2003 (N = 770)	2004 (N = 713)	2005 (N = 809)	2006 (N = 907)	2007 (N = 858)	2008 (N = 939)	2009 (N = 1021)	2010 (N = 1006)	2011 (N = 1064)	2012 (N = 1017)
Admissions Test Scores															
National SAT Critical Reading: Mean Score	505	505	505	506	504	507	508	508	503	502	502	501	501	497	496
NJ SAT Critical Reading: Mean Score	497	498	498	499	498	501	501	503	496	495	495	496	495	495	495
Class SAT Critical Reading: Mean Score	546	534	533	533	545	540	544	529	520	535	523	537	526	536	549
Class SAT Critical Reading: 75th Percentile	600	590	589	590	590	590	600	590	570	580	580	590	587	588	600
Class SAT Critical Reading: 25th Percentile	490	480	480	490	490	480	490	470	470	480	460	490	460	480	490
First-Year Writing Placement															
Honors	102 (15%)	87 (12%)	78 (11%)	111 (15%)	82 (12%)	87 (11%)	81 (11%)	74 (9%)	102 (11%)	92 (11%)	88 (9%)	91 (9%)	62 (6%)	56 (5%)	63 (6%)
Traditional	357 (53%)	419 (59%)	417 (57%)	409 (55%)	385 (56%)	421 (55%)	394 (55%)	397 (49%)	408 (45%)	453 (53%)	704 (75%)	818 (80%)	766 (76%)	861 (81%)	826 (81%)
Basic Writing	161 (24%)	134 (19%)	178 (24%)	177 (24%)	179 (26%)	216 (28%)	200 (28%)	298 (37%)	355 (39%)	254 (30%)	103 (11%)	92 (9%)	157 (16%)	117 (11%)	101 (10%)
ESL Basic Writing	58 (9%)	70 (10%)	56 (8%)	43 (6%)	39 (6%)	46 (6%)	38 (5%)	40 (5%)	42 (5%)	59 (7%)	44 (5%)	20 (2%)	21 (2%)	30 (3%)	27 (3%)
Correct Placement: grade C or above															
Honors	92 (90%)	78 (90%)	59 (76%)	81 (73%)	74 (90%)	73 (84%)	78 (96%)	59 (80%)	86 (84%)	84 (91%)	81 (92%)	84 (92%)	60 (97%)	52 (93%)	60 (95%)
Traditional	298 (83%)	341 (81%)	342 (82%)	352 (86%)	346 (90%)	338 (80%)	329 (84%)	309 (78%)	316 (77%)	393 (87%)	602 (86%)	663 (81%)	631 (82%)	765 (89%)	698 (85%)

continued on next page

Table 4.1—continued

	1998 (N = 678)	1999 (N = 710)	2000 (N = 729)	2001 (N = 740)	2002 (N = 685)	2003 (N = 770)	2004 (N = 713)	2005 (N = 809)	2006 (N = 907)	2007 (N = 858)	2008 (N = 939)	2009 (N = 1021)	2010 (N = 1006)	2011 (N = 1064)	2012 (N = 1017)
Basic Writing	150 (93%)	118 (88%)	155 (87%)	146 (82%)	163 (91%)	194 (90%)	178 (89%)	270 (91%)	311 (88%)	225 (89%)	88 (85%)	71 (77%)	141 (90%)	110 (94%)	93 (92%)
ESL Basic Writing	55 (95%)	70 (100%)	54 (96%)	37 (86%)	34 (87%)	39 (85%)	33 (87%)	38 (95%)	39 (93%)	54 (92%)	40 (91%)	17 (85%)	19 (90%)	25 (83%)	25 (93%)
Course Failure: grades of D or F															
Honors	5 (5%)	6 (7%)	16 (21%)	27 (24%)	8 (10%)	14 (16%)	3 (4%)	13 (18%)	12 (12%)	6 (7%)	5 (6%)	6 (7%)	2 (3%)	2 (4%)	3 (5%)
Traditional	37 (10%)	65 (16%)	50 (14%)	44 (11%)	31 (8%)	60 (14%)	54 (14%)	71 (18%)	79 (19%)	45 (10%)	83 (12%)	124 (15%)	117 (15%)	71 (8%)	92 (11%)
Basic Writing	5 (3%)	10 (7%)	17 (10%)	30 (17%)	10 (6%)	20 (9%)	17 (9%)	23 (8%)	39 (11%)	26 (10%)	13 (13%)	17 (18%)	14 (9%)	3 (3%)	5 (5%)
ESL Basic Writing	2 (3%)	0 (0%)	2 (4%)	5 (12%)	2 (5%)	6 (13%)	5 (13%)	0 (0%)	2 (5%)	4 (7%)	3 (7%)	2 (10%)	1 (5%)	2 (7%)	0 (0%)
Course Withdrawals and Incompletes															
Honors	5 (5%)	3 (3%)	3 (4%)	3 (3%)	0 (0%)	0 (0%)	0 (0%)	2 (3%)	4 (4%)	2 (2%)	2 (2%)	1 (1%)	0 (0%)	2 (4%)	0 (0%)
Traditional	22 (6%)	13 (3%)	15 (4%)	13 (3%)	8 (2%)	23 (5%)	11 (3%)	17 (4%)	13 (3%)	15 (3%)	19 (3%)	31 (4%)	18 (2%)	25 (3%)	36 (4%)
Basic Writing	6 (4%)	6 (4%)	6 (3%)	1 (1%)	6 (3%)	2 (1%)	5 (3%)	5 (2%)	5 (1%)	3 (1%)	2 (2%)	4 (4%)	2 (1%)	4 (3%)	3 (3%)
ESL Basic Writing	1 (2%)	0 (0%)	0 (0%)	1 (2%)	3 (8%)	1 (2%)	0 (0%)	2 (5%)	1 (2%)	1 (2%)	1 (2%)	1 (5%)	1 (5%)	3 (10%)	2 (7%)

With statistician Kamal Joshi, Elliot and his NJIT colleagues have developed a general, very useful formula to achieve the lowest possible number of ePortfolios to score that are representative of all the students enrolled in a particular course. In the previous chapter, Table 3.2 identified courses offered in the junior year of a writing program. One of these—described in chapter 2—is a multisection technical writing course offered as part of the university's writing program. That course provides an excellent application of a sampling plan designed to yield a designated confidence interval.

Let us imagine that, in a given semester in which the junior-level course was scheduled for review, there were 216 students enrolled in nine sections of the technical writing course. Let us further imagine that ePortfolio readers that semester included two adjunct faculty, three instructors, and four senior faculty members—a mix that is often the case. Although neither the words *efficiency* nor *economy* appear in the *Standards for Educational and Psychological Testing* (AERA, APA, and NCME 2014) as key measurement concepts, it is clear that resource allocation is closely tied to construct underrepresentation, "the extent to which a test fails to capture important aspects of the construct domain that that test is intended to measure" (217). If an assessment of writing is captured by a multiple-choice test, that item type would be said to underrepresent the construct of writing; nevertheless, the test would meet the goal of efficiency. How do we then assess the construct of technical writing described in the model in chapter 2 and still meet the goal of efficiency with only seven readers on hand, with only a day allocated for the reading? This is where sampling-plan design comes into play—a system that allows us to assess efficiently the smallest number of students possible with the greatest possible confidence that our results are representative of the larger student population.

Here is a standard formula (Kerlinger and Lee 1999, 297–98) modified to address this case of sampling-plan design. The core formula appears below.

$$n = \frac{Z^2 \sigma^2}{d^2}$$

(1)

Where:

Z^2 = 1.96, the Z-value associated with a 95% confidence interval (CI, the upper and lower bounds for a statistic; for a 90% confidence level, the Z-value = 1.645; for an 80 percent confidence interval, the Z-value = 1.282)

σ^2 = the standard deviation (the spread around the mean) of the population

d^2 = the specified deviation defined as the deviation we can tolerate between the sample mean (the score at hand) and the true mean (a hypothetical concept defined as freedom from random error).

The correction for a finite sample is then applied:

$$n' = \frac{n}{1 + n / N}$$

$\qquad\qquad\qquad\qquad\qquad\qquad\qquad\qquad$ (2)

Where:

n' = estimated sample size
n = sample size estimated using formula 1 above
N = sample size of the population

Here is the step-by-step calculation.

Step 1. Calculate the specified deviation. It is best to begin with the specified deviation—the deviation the researcher can tolerate between the sample mean and the true mean. In the case at hand, the specified deviation can be determined as the standard error of the mean score of the overall ePortfolio score from the previous semester's reading (the overall score shown in Figure 2.3). Calculations based on the previous semester's readings ensure the information gained from the previous assessment is used to make the next set of decisions; the *Z*-value allows us to address the standard 95 percent CI for decision making—though lower CIs can be used when resources and time do not allow all the ePortfolios to be read. The standard error of the overall ePortfolio score used in this calculation is easily obtained from the descriptive statistics in SPSS, the statistical program most useful to writing program administrators because of its combined analytic power and user-friendly design.

Hence,

8.19 (mean score of the overall ePortfolio score from the previous semester's reading)
± .24 (the standard error of the overall ePortfolio score)

For the upper range of scores, we can be 95 percent confident that the scores will be 8.19 + .24 = 8.43; for the lower range, we can be 95 percent confident that the scores will be 8.19 - .24 = 7.95. In sum, the specified deviation allows us to be 95 percent certain that the range of scores from 8.19 to 7.95 will include an individual student's true mean score.

Step 2. Calculate the sample size. Now the specified deviation is established. Equation 1 above is then used.

Hence,

$$n = 1.96^2 \times 1.65^2 / .235^2$$
$$n = 3.84 \times 2.72 / .05$$
$$n = 10.44 / .05$$
$$n = 211$$

Therefore, to achieve a 95 percent CI, instructors would need to read 211 ePortfolios of the 216 total—not much of a reduction. However, equation 1 is designed for an infinite sample—a sample in which the total number of students in the sample is unknown. Formula 2 below allows us to make the correction for a finite sample—in the spring of 2009, the 216 students enrolled in all sections of the course.

Step 3. Make the correction for a finite sample. Equation 2 above is now used.

Hence,

$$n´ = 211 / 1 + (211 / 216)$$
$$n´ = 211 / 1 + .97$$
$$n' = 211 / 1.97$$
$$n = 107$$

Therefore, the target for the reading is a random sample of 107 ePortfolios of the 216 available. To choose the random sampling of students, writing program administrators such as those at NJIT obtain a list of all students taking the course. That list is then put in an alphabetized Excel file with columns for number (1–216), name, and website URL. Using the random number generator in Excel (or a sequence generated from a table of random numbers), we select 107 students sequentially according to the random numbers until the requisite number is met. The student names and their associated URLs are then loaded into an open source system so the ePortfolios themselves can be scored on (not by) a computer by the designated readers according to the variables shown in Figure 2.3 (Collins et al. 2013).

Such sampling-plan calculations rest at the heart of the next-generation program assessment described in chapter 5. If the idea is to study student achievement and refine the curriculum, there is no need that each student be examined in program assessment; rather, a well-defined sampling plan with random selection allows a confidence level to be established that will allow administrators and instructors to efficiently allocate resources under conditions of scarcity. At NJIT, for example, each semester seven instructors can handle the designated sampling plan for first-year writing in one day. After the sample is identified using the two formulas above, each instructor reads a total of approximately twenty-two ePortfolios (or eleven read twice), with time left for third readings due to discrepant scores. Rather than a burden—it would have taken twice as long to review the student ePortfolios from each section of the course—the end-of-term assessment episodes become community-building tasks for the writing program. Designing and report-ing sampling-plan calculations thus become central to every writing program administrator's activities so program assessment may proceed along evidentiary lines. The example shown here is basic and provides a good introduction to more complex forms of sample-size determina-tion (Maxwell 2000).

NULL HYPOTHESIS SIGNIFICANCE TESTING: THINKING HEURISTICALLY

Although much maligned, null hypothesis significance testing (NHST) is an excellent heuristic device for program assessment. The core of NHST is not, in fact, statistical analysis at all; rather, the system is designed to test the null hypothesis—that, in fact, no relationship exists.

A good example of NHST is provided by the interreader reliability analysis shown in Table 4.2. Before turning to the actual measures and what they reveal, NHST addresses the question of interreader reliability as follows:

H_0 = (null hypothesis) Considered individually, the variables in the port-folios have not been scored reliably.

H_1 = (alternative hypothesis) Considered individually, the variables in the portfolios have been scored reliably.

The nature of the heuristic is mutually exclusive: when one is true, the other must be false. So, we cannot have a case in which a variable both has and has not been read reliably. In the present case, a 2012 study of ePortfolios at NJIT, the condition required to reject the null hypoth-esis is singular: the .05 level of probability must be reached. If we attain our demarcation standard, we may reject the null hypothesis and accept the alternate hypothesis: considered individually, the variables in the portfolios have been read reliably. Of course, other accompanying stan-dards may be applied by the writing program administrator in the assess-ment and examined for their strength by the team assessing the writing

Table 4.2 Interreader reliability analysis, ePortfolios, 2012 (n = 54).

Competency	Nonad-judicated Pearson	Adjudi-cated Pearson	Nonad-judicated Weighted Kappa	Adjudi-cated Weighted Kappa
Fall 2012 ePortfolio Scoring (n = 54)				
1. Rhetorical Knowledge	.39**	.71**	.45**	.75**
2. Critical Thinking	.55**	.7**	.58**	.74**
3. Writing Processes	.41**	.72**	.43**	.76**
4. Knowledge of Conventions	.36**	.54**	.47**	.61**
5. Composing in Electronic Environments	.54**	.68**	.57**	.72**
6. Holistic Score	.21ns	.27*	.34**	.41**

*ns: not significant, * p < .05 ** p < .01*

program. These include, for example, the strength of the correlation itself. Timed, impromptu papers are regularly read at a .7 level of reliability as measured by the weighted kappa (a measure of reliability), one of the statistics recorded in Table 4.2 that is similar to the Pearson coefficient (a measure of correlation) as a measure of the linear relationship between two variables (Fleiss and Cohen 1973; Williamson, Xi, and Breyer 2012). However, more complex writing performances, such as portfolios, do not often achieve these levels. Note that none of the variables met this level before adjudication; indeed, the holistic score did not achieve the 95 percent confidence level before adjudication. However, following adjudication—in this case, scores at more than one point of difference by two independent raters that are given a third score to resolve the difference—all the ePortfolio scores except knowledge of conventions and the holistic score met or exceeded the .7 level of interreader reliability.

Were the .7 level to be established as part of the NHST for the non-adjudicated scores, then the entire reading would have to be considered invalid —the NHST could not have been rejected. However, in program assessment, we are not making decisions about individual students. We are, instead, gathering evidence about the program as a whole. As such, the NHST becomes a very good heuristic when used properly—as a way to help us think about complex relationships rather than a vehicle to prevent experimentation.

In the NJIT experience from 2010 to the present, experimental reading of 217 ePortfolios suggests the following ranges: nonadjudicated Pearson = *ns* (not significant) to .71, *p* < .001); adjudicated Pearson =

Table 4.3 Hypothetical strength of interreader reliability agreement for ePortfolios.

Range of Scores	Nonadjudicated Pearson	Adjudicated Pearson	Nonadjudicated Weighted Kappa	Adjudicated Weighted Kappa
ePortfolio Scoring				
High	.48 to .71	.57 to .86	.46 to .69	.57 to .85
Medium	.23 to .47	.27 to .56	.23 to .45	.28 to .56
Low	.1 to .22	.1 to .26	.1 to .22	.1 to .27

Note: Unless p < .05 on adjudicated scores, the scores should not be used for further analysis.

.56 to .86; nonadjudicated weighted kappa = .27 to .69; and adjudicated weighted kappa = .41 to .85. These ranges were read at the .01 level of statistical significance. Based on these levels, we offer Table 4.3 for writing program developers to model the level of interreader agreement with ePortfolios. The table assumes at least a .05 level of statistical significance—that is, a 95 percent chance that the relationships did not occur by chance. Importantly, the table includes both nonadjudicated scores and adjudicated scores so the complexity of scoring may be fully documented, revealing discrepancies often masked when only the reliability of adjudicated scores is reported. For those involved in writing program assessment, low reliabilities with nonadjudicated scores are occasions for further study to determine the sources of discrepancy between readers. Scoring complexities are not, in other words, reasons for alarm or censure.

Establishing such tables is very important lest we follow standards of reliability not designed to be used when robust construct representation is being examined. If one works with those unfamiliar with the measurement of complex constructs, it is important to remind such audiences that reliability estimates of samples drawn from timed, impromptu writing prompts will achieve a higher level of correlation between readers than will writing samples produced in response to more complex constructed-response tasks. In pursuit of robust construct representation, it is not appropriate to let standards obtained from elementalist measures interrupt programs of writing research.

CORRELATION ANALYSIS: EXAMINING RELATIONSHIPS

With reliability in hand, researchers can turn to other sources of validity evidence. Table 4.4 presents an interesting correlation analysis from a study that Andrew Klobucar and his research team conducted at

NJIT during the fall of 2012 with selected first-time, full-time students and instructors experimenting with writing in digital environments. The table illustrates relationships among and beyond measures of the writing construct: the SAT math section, the SAT critical reading section, the SAT writing section, ePortfolio scores, final grades, and cumulative grade point average. The ePortfolio variable model is based on the reading, writing, and critical thinking experiences in the *Framework for Success*.

Table 4.4 demonstrates the centrality—or, for skeptics, the relatedness—of ePortfolio scores to academic performance of first-time, fulltime students. As expected, the strongest correlations are found among the ePortfolio scores. Unexpected is that all sections of the SAT correlated, at statistically significant levels, with all of the ePortfolio scores. Evidence of commonality of related constructs learned while students were preparing for admission to the university, correlations such as .53 between the SAT math section and the ePortfolio variable of critical thinking, are demonstrations of independent though related constructs. Only composing in electronic environments and GPA, along with the holistic score and GPA, failed to meet the test of statistical significance.

Correlation tables provide a transparent, easily accessible way to document the many assessment activities of a writing program. While they do not demonstrate causation, methods of correlation analysis promote examinations of relationships. For instance, the correlation between SAT mathematics scores and the holistic score ($r = .39$, $p < .01$) suggests that there is a relationship between mathematics and writing performance, as measured by the two assessments. This finding makes good sense in that both are important for academic success and, practically, success in both mathematics and writing are necessary for students to advance through the curriculum. Such analyses are meaningful in that they allow demonstration of the kinds of competencies needed for academic success. Such analyses are naïve, of course, when they are misused to suggest that a score on a multiple-choice test of mathematics could magically predict a score on an ePortfolio assessment.

In sum: when locally developed measures such as ePortfolios are available, criterion variables such as admissions scores, course grades, and GPA provide invaluable information on the centrality of writing ability to the academic lives of students.

TESTS OF SIGNIFICANCE: ANALYZING DIFFERENCE

In many ways, the *t*-test—a basic test of significance between two mean scores used to reject the null hypothesis—is the workhorse of

Table 4.4 Summary of correlations, all measures, 2012 (n = 54).

	1	2	3	4	5	6	7	8	9	10	11	M (SD)
1. SAT Math	–	.48**	.55**	.49**	.53**	.42**	.38**	.49**	.39**	.13**	.28**	613 (71)
2. SAT Critical Reading		–	.71**	.42**	.36**	.28*	.38**	.52**	.4**	.16**	.22**	545 (84)
3. SAT Writing			–	.39**	.39**	.36**	.35**	.47**	.31*	.21**	.28**	540 (85)
4. Rhetorical Knowledge				–	.71**	.58**	.71**	.75**	.65**	.44**	.32**	8.39 (1.98)
5. Critical Thinking					–	.59**	.61**	.61**	.72**	.4**	.32*	8.28 (1.73)
6. Writing Processes						–	.71**	.42**	.46**	.41**	.35*	7.52 (1.76)
7. Knowledge of Conventions							–	.53**	.49**	.33*	.27*	8.22 (1.4)
8. Electronic Environments								–	.58**	.31*	.2ns	8.19 (2.15)
9. Holistic Score									–	.4**	.26ns	8.04 (1.63)
10. Course grade										–	.73**	3.01 (1.1)
11. GPA											–	2.88 (.86)

*ns: not significant, * p < .05, ** p < .01*

inferential measurement. Based on a ratio, the *t*-test allows us to see differences, at or beyond the 95 percent confidence level, between two groups. An example is in order. Recall that Figure 2.1 and Table 2.1 illustrated differences of increased mean scores over time in the LSU program. Table 4.5 presents a tabular view of the scores.

Were these scores different at a level of statistical significance? A one-way ANOVA—a technique used for comparing means—reveals statistically significant differences among the topics ($F(9, 1256) = 6.92$, $p < .01$) shown in Table 4.5. Disaggregation among the topics reveals much about intertopic reliability. In an analysis using Tukey's Honestly Significant Differences Test (HSD) ($p < .05$)—like the *t*-test, another comparison of means but one allowing multiple comparisons—task 1 yielded statistically significant differences with six of the topics (3, 4, 5,

6, 7, and 8). In terms of intertopic reliability, this task was the poorest. However, that task is the outlier: task 2 yielded statistically significant differences only with task 6; task 3 yielded a statistically significant difference only with task 1; task 4 yielded statistically significant differences only with tasks 1 and 8; task 5 yielded statistically significant differences only with tasks 1 and 8; task 6 yielded statistically significant differences with tasks 1, 2, and 8; task 7 yielded statistically significant differences only with task 1; task 8 yielded statistically significant differences with tasks 4, 5, 6; and task 9 yielded statistically significant differences with task 1. Task 10 yielded no statistically significant differences with any of the topics. Task 10 was clearly the best topic. Identifying the level of difference, and making analyses based on that level of difference, provides a wide range of methods by which to examine and refine assumptions regarding the ability of constructed-response tasks to yield adequate construct representation for the intended aim of the assessment. Heretofore, the committees charged with designing tasks for writing assessment would judge whether a particular assignment "worked," that is, effectively measured the construct being assessed; although establishing intertopic reliability remains a great challenge in writing assessment, with these new procedures those processes need no longer be entirely subjective.

In another study, Klobucar and his colleagues decided to conduct a range study. Writing program researchers wanted to know how an instructor very skilled in communicating in digital environments would work with the nomothetic map shown in Figure 3.1. One of the very best instructors was paired with honors students. In this range study—an investigation of just what was possible when high-achieving students were assigned to an unusually skilled instructor—the results were of great interest to writing program stakeholders. While the honors class was small (n = 17), ePortfolio scores were higher at statistically significant levels from the mean scores provided in Table 4.4 of students placed in traditional first-year classes: rhetorical knowledge = $M = 9.88$, SD = 1.65, $t(50) = -4.27$, $p < .01$; critical thinking = $M = 9.14$, SD = 1.46, $t(50) = -3.44$, $p < .01$; knowledge of conventions = $M = 9$, SD = 1.28, $t(50) = -3.1$, $p < .01$; composing in electronic environments = $M = 10.24$, SD = 1.2, $t(50) = -6.0$, $p < .01$; and holistic score = $M = 10.24$, SD = 1.2, $t(50) = -6.0$, $p < .01$). Among the highest scores the writing program administrators had seen, including ePortfolio scores from graduate students, such range studies allow student potential to be established empirically. Then, in related studies, examination can be made of ways to remove barriers to that potential.

Table 4.5 Statistically significant differences among Online Challenge topics.

Writing Task	n	M	SD	Range
1. Iraq and Weapons of Mass Destruction	76	4.92	2.41	2, 12
2. Rebuilding Iraq	132	5.92	2.48	2, 12
3. Somalia Immigrants	38	6.68	2.07	4, 11
4. Oil Exploration in ANWR	208	6.64	2.0	2, 12
5. Homelessness in the United States	154	6.66	2.29	2, 12
6. Efficacy of Bottled Water	134	7.02	2.37	2, 12
7. Dangers of Self-Revelation in MySpace	258	6.43	2.45	2, 12
8. Solving the US Immigrant Problem	144	5.76	2.26	2, 12
9. Advantages of Organic Food	47	6.34	2.11	2, 10
10. Using Cameras and Stoplight Violations	75	6.08	2.41	2, 12

Note: Statistically significant differences (p < .05) were recorded among each of the tasks except Task 10.

REGRESSION ANALYSIS: PREDICTING RELATIONSHIPS

Operating on the general linear model that underlies almost all empirical research, regression analysis is ideally suited to writing program assessment because the technique allows prediction of one variable based on the values of others. As Trochim and Donnelly (2008) note, terms such as *prediction* merely suggest that the theoretical relationship among variables should be able to be captured empirically. There should, for example, be relationships among the variables of the writing construct, just as there should be a relationship between these variables and course grades. A basic question that should be asked of all writing program assessors therefore involves the relationship between and among variables. For instance, there are moderate correlations among the ePortfolio variables shown in Table 4.4. The relationship between each of the independent variables (rhetorical knowledge, critical thinking, writing processes, knowledge of conventions, and composing in electronic environments) to the dependent variable (the holistic score) is expressed as follows: $R^2 = .56$, $F[5, 48] = 12.35$, $p < .01$). So, 56 percent of the variable is accounted for by the model. In other words, 56 percent of the variable of the holistic score represents the proportion of the variation of the independent variables to the dependent variable. The relationship of the entire ePortfolio set of scores to the course grade is less: $R^2 = .26$, $F[6, 47] = 2.69$, $p < .05$). One set of variables is related to—that is, predicts—the other, just as we theoretically imagine they do.

Often, readers interpret such regression analyses as low, but that need not be the case. In fact, as Table 4.4 shows, the correlation between holistic ePortfolio score and course grade is .4. If that is as good as it gets—and NJIT studies suggest it is—then a considerable readjustment must be made on the part of those who design and assess writing programs. Understanding what exists, rather than burdening writing programs with standards and measures designed for limited construct representation, is the far better role for those who teach and assess writing. It is indeed just such a perspective that has led us to prefer the term *relational modeling* (based on a robust ecological metaphor) to the term *causal inference* (based on an elementalist behavioral metaphor). Teaching and grading individual students is an art as well as a science, and program assessment should encourage the art as well as measure the results scientifically.

One reason understanding this caution is important is that misuse of statistics is a common problem in educational matters. We give as an example the use of data intended to demonstrate predictive validity in an attempt to undermine a writing placement program in a large university system. In this case, the program used preenrollment testing, including a writing sample, to place poorly prepared students into a basic writing program. The flawed study assumed that students so placed should also perform poorly when they advanced to the regular required writing program. But the data showed that these students performed in that course as well as students with high scores on the placement test. The study concluded that, since the placement test did not "predict" that outcome, it was itself a weak measure and hence should be abandoned. The actual flaw, of course, was the researchers' failure to consider that the entire point of the placement test was to provide enough basic instruction so that those very students would succeed—in other words, to defeat the test's "prediction" of failure. The flawed study was attractively decked out with charts and tables and was superficially convincing; it would have led to the abandonment of the successful placement program if not for the perception of its flaw by White, who was able to demonstrate to funding authorities that the study demonstrated the success of the program, the opposite of the conclusion asserted by the researchers.

While detailed explication of the criteria for establishing causal inferences is beyond the scope of this discussion, this example demonstrates the importance of establishing relationships according to four principles (Holland 1986; Schneider et al. 2007): causal relativity (causes must be evaluated relative to other causes); causal manipulation (each participant must experience similar instruction); temporal ordering (such exposure must occur within a specific pre-and postexposure time frame), and alternative explanations (through which the researcher must rule out alternative explanations). In the case of the placement test, the researchers had failed to consider causal relativity; that is, the students were supposed to improve and the prediction of failure was false. Also, the researchers failed to consider the alternative explanations of the prediction failures that were, in essence, evidence of success. In making causal inferences, the use of empirical information alone can never be valid unless it is accompanied by sound causal logic.

EFFECT SIZE: DETERMINING EXTENT

"How big is the result?" The answer to that question, determined by effect size, is best explained in terms of metaphor. In *The Research Methods Knowledge Base*, Trochim and Donnelly (2008) describe effect size as an analysis of signal-to-noise ratio. A signal is best imagined as the way an important variable of interest is captured. Noise, on the other hand, consists of all the random effects involved in trying to capture the variable—from temperature in the room during an assessment to the way a breakfast burrito is being digested by a reader. In selecting a construct sample from the writing construct shown in Figures 3.1 and 3.2, researchers want to identify a high signal-to-noise relationship so they may obtain a clear signal of their findings.

A good way to think about clear signals described by effect size is shown in an analysis of the National Survey of Student Engagement (NSSE). Conceived in 1998 and launched in 2000, NSSE provides information about two critical features of post-secondary educational life: the amount of time and effort students put into their studies and related educational activities; and the methods by which an institution deploys its resources and organizes to impact student learning. In 2007 experts in writing studies—led by Charles Paine, Robert M. Gonyea, Chris M. Anson, and Paul V. Anderson—developed 27 experimental questions about writing tasks and evaluation practices designed to deepen information from NSSE (Paine et al. 2013). After piloting the questions in 2008, a group of 75 participating colleges and universities formed the Consortium for the Study of Writing in College (CSWC), which included the set as part of a NSSE administration (Addison and McGee 2010). Between 2010 and 2011, over 70,000 first-year and senior students enrolled at 80 bachelor's degree-granting colleges and universities in the United States participated in the new writing survey. By 2012,

137 different institutions had participated in the CSWC, many of them across multiple years. Today, NSSE participating schools have the option to append a module of thirteen questions to the NSSE questionnaire to learn more about student experience with writing at their host institution. Those electing to participate in NSSE and use the writing module in 2014 were able to compare the answers of their students to student answers from 59 other United States institutions (Gonyea 2014).

Because such comparisons are available, their statistically significant difference can be determined by *t*-tests, as we discussed above. But what is the extent of that difference? A look at two variables from Figure 3.1, mapped to the 2012 NSSE CWSC survey at NJIT, reveals how effect-size measures help to determine the extent of comparative difference. Table 4.6 presents selected results of the 2012 NSSE CWSC survey at NJIT.

In the first three survey questions, NJIT students reported a score between 2 (few assignments) and 3 (some assignments), with a trend to the higher score. (The range extends from 5 [most assignments] to 1 [no assignments].) There is also a trend upwards from the first to the senior year; that is good news. The more students experience the NJIT curriculum, the more they gain experiences with genres requiring presentation and explication of empirical information and multimedia presentations. In addition, the asterisks indicate that there are statistically significant differences between NJIT and the CSWC benchmark schools. Now to the question, how big is the result? That is, how great is the signal-to-noise ratio, and can that ratio be expressed in a standardized way?

Jacob Cohen (1992) has established a power primer for effect size for various statistical tests. For effect size—the standardized measure used to judge statistical significance between NJIT students and CSWC students—Cohen recommends the following ranges: small = .20; medium = .50; and large = .80. Indeed, in their interpretation guide to effect size, NSSE presents exactly these levels for effect size, the practical significance of mean difference calculated by dividing the mean difference by the pooled standard deviation. Reference back to questions 1, 2, and 3 now demonstrates that there are statistically significant differences but that they are small to medium. A conclusion drawn from these questions might be presented as follows: with small to medium effect sizes, NJIT students report that some of their assignments require quantitative presentation of information and empirical analysis of that information. NJIT students also report that they create multimedia projects on some of their assignments. NJIT students report these genre experiences at statistically significant levels that are higher than CSWS students.

Table 4.6 Selected results of the 2012 NSSE CWSC survey at NJIT.

Nomothetic Map Question Identification	CSWC Questions	NJIT Mean First-Year (1,512, 20%) and Senior Class (1,415, 23%)	NJIT Mean compared with CSWC First-Year (18,518, 25%) And Senior Class (26,889, 32%)	Effect Size
Genre	1. In the current school year, in how many of your writing assignments did you describe your methods or findings related to data you collected in lab or field work, a survey project, etc.?	FY 2.90 SR 3.16	FY 2.72* SR 2.93**	.15 .19
Genre	2. In the current school year, in how many of your writing assignments did you explain in writing the meaning of numerical or statistical data?	FY 2.56 SR 2.83	FY 2.31** SR 2.58**	.22 .22
Genre	3. In the current school year, in how many of your writing assignments did you create the project with multimedia (web page, poster, slide presentation such as PowerPoint, etc.)?	FY 2.86 SR 3.29	FY 2.44** SR 2.91**	.39 .32
Task	4. During the current school year, for how many of your writing assignments has your instructor provided clear instructions describing what he or she wanted you to do?	FY 3.74 SR 3.63	FY 4.02** SR 3.93**	-.35 -.37
Task	5. During the current school year, for how many of your writing assignments has your instructor explained in advance what he or she wanted you to learn?	FY 3.51 SR 3.39	FY 3.81** SR 3.71**	-.32 -.33
Task	6. During the current school year, for how many of your writing assignments has your instructor provided a sample of a completed assignment written by the instructor or a student?	FY 2.57 SR 2.52	FY 3.02** SR 2.86**	-.38 -.30

*$p < .05$, ** $p < .01$

This is not the case, however, with questions mapped to task. In each case, NJIT students perform at lower levels on questions 4, 5, and 6. Additionally, there is a decrease in writing task instruction provided in advance from first to senior years. The negative effect size demonstrates, in the language of NSSE, that "the institution lags behind the comparison group, suggesting that the student behavior or institutional practice represented by the item may warrant attention" (National Survey of Student Engagement 2013). So, while NJIT is performing at moderate rates of acceptability on genre questions, the institution is lagging in task explanations on the part of the instructors.

If a target were established at a score of 4—that is, that most assignments would embody clear instructions delivered in advance of an assignment—then rounding up would reveal that only question 4 yielded such results at NJIT and nationally across the first and senior years. Such a target would allow program administrators to review syllabi for the courses in Table 3.2 to determine the extent to which the instructors are articulating genre and task specifications leading to construct representation. Using effect size as a method of comparing practical significance, instructors and administrators may use such information from the NSSE and the CSWS to identify which variables of the writing construct are being adequately addressed and which require more curricular work. As is the case with all empirical research, methods of determining and interpreting effect size continue to improve (Ellis 2010).

A final note on effect size is now in order regarding its relationship to regression analysis. If we estimate the effect size of the relationship between the holistic score and the course grade—a relationship often criticized, as noted above, by the correlation and regression analysis as low—we find an effect size of .87 ($d = 3.62$). Estimated by Cohen (1992) as a large effect size, such basic calculations will serve writing programs to substantiate the importance of robust measures of the writing construct.

QUALITATIVE EMPIRICAL STUDIES: EXAMINING UNIQUENESS

In his review of the most frequently cited authors in *College Composition and Communication*, Derek Mueller (2012, Fig. 2.2, 202–3) demonstrates that Linda Flower holds the top rank out of the 19,499 references examined between 1987 and 2011. As we noted in chapter 1, between 1987 and 1991, as Mueller notes, Flower reshaped our concept of the construct of writing through qualitative studies conducted with John Hayes. In essence, these studies helped us understand the writing construct, making quantitative studies possible, such as the ones shown in this chapter. At the present time, the Dynamic Criteria Mapping (DCM) technique invented by Bob Broad (2012) continues that empirical tradition of qualitative research.

While no one need be told that quantitative and qualitative research are two sides of the same empirical coin, it is important to remember that reporting standards are equally important to both. The more we know about how research is conducted, the more replication studies can be conducted and additional studies planned and conducted to increase our body of knowledge about the writing construct. In their prolegomenon for standards of qualitative and quantitative research, Howe and Eisenhart (1990) called for a quantitative-qualitative framework of standards based on five principles: fit between research questions and data collection and analysis techniques; effective application of specific data collection and analysis techniques; alertness to and coherence of background assumptions; and value constraints. In 2007, Melissa Freeman et al. (2007) proposed a set of guiding principles for qualitative research. Updating the proposal of Howe and Eisenhart (1990) to address the contemporary environment of accountability, Freeman and her colleagues identify commonalities of qualitative evidence and the standards qualitative researchers use to judge whether the claims they make are justified by that evidence: disclosure of data and evidence; justification of claims and interpretations; and articulation of theory and principles of generalization.

Tailoring such work to our field, we concentrate on documentation method, coding model, and content analysis method as shown in Figure 4.1. Establishing documentation methods such as structured interviews based on variable models used by Flower and Hayes (1981) or more recent computer applications (Hayes 2012) yields both clarity of findings and the potential of experimental replication and additional knowledge contributions. In similar fashion, exposition of the model of coding used, such as that developed by Glaser and Strauss (1967) or its application to DCM, allows readers to understand how the documentation method was used in the coding model. Finally, attention to the method of content analysis of written records, especially visualization of results from software platforms such as NVivo, yields a clear understanding of the interactions between documentation method, coding model, and technological applications that may further reveal, or constrain, construct representation of the study at hand.

Peckham's course—Writing: Practice, Pedagogy, and History—demonstrates a good example of the potential of combined empirical approaches. On one hand, quantitative review of student writing in each chapter of the book produced by the students could be undertaken with a variable set based on the course performance objectives: genre awareness and response to rhetorical context. A rubric based on the conventions of edited collections could easily be developed and scored using the kind of Likert scale shown in Table 2.3. Similarly, the affective objective—to improve friendship with writing—could be examined with DCM, as students submitted their reflective statements required as part of the edited collection. Coding according to these variables—termed "coding at the nodes" by Glaser and Strauss (1967)—could target the constructed response of the reflective statement: the kinds of writing experiences students would like to have in school and outside school; the degree to which students understood and achieved the course objectives; students' feelings about themselves as writers at the course's end; and students' speculative statements on the roles writing might play in their future lives and careers. Qualitative research findings address the seventh row of Figure 3.1, the intrapersonal domains associated with motivation (Yeager and Walton 2011).

The consequences of such research could be enormous. As more becomes known about the greatly underexamined intrapersonal domain variables of the writing construct, that information could then be used in the first-year program to foster what the *Framework for Success* labels "habits of mind." Fostered in the first-year curriculum—indeed, perhaps even becoming part of the Online Challenge so readers could know more about their admitted students through reflective statements—such qualitative research could have far-reaching consequences at LSU. And, in turn, if the quantitative research revealed an ability to achieve competence in the genre of edited collections, that new genre might be introduced into the first-year curriculum so students would increase their experiences in the nomothetic span of the writing construct, shown in Figure 3.1. Combined, such research could help students from admission through graduation from LSU.

Or, perhaps the simple statements of the students to Peckham could just be recorded and played for stakeholders wanting to know if the students were becoming independent learners. When Peckham asked the class if they needed any additional help to assemble the edited collection, they responded simply, "Don't worry, Dr. Peckham. We have it." Whatever happened in that class, students shifted from receivers of information to creators of knowledge. Could there be a better outcome?

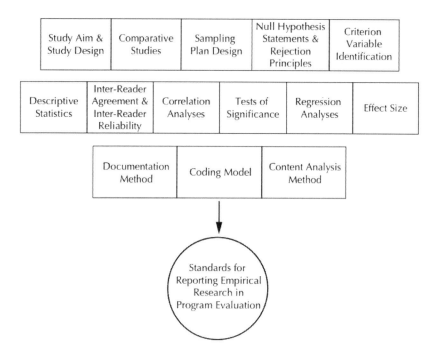

Figure 4.1. Reporting guidelines for rhetoric and composition/writing studies.

REPORTING GUIDELINES: ADVANCING RAD RESEARCH

Figure 4.1 is intended to make cohesive the seemingly disparate empirical quantitative and qualitative techniques briefly described in this chapter. It is beyond our power to set reporting standards for our field; indeed Freeman and her colleagues refused to use the term *standards* (Freeman et al. 2007), citing Foucault (1979) for good measure. While there remains an eternal fear of standards being used to discipline and punish, our experience nevertheless reveals that the areas covered in Figure 4.1 are good guidelines for those wishing to share results and promote collaboration across institutional boundaries. If program assessment research is reported with these guidelines in mind, that research is likely to follow the call of Richard Haswell (2005) and the gap identified by Benjamin Miller (2014) in rhetoric and composition doctoral dissertation research for the advancement of RAD research— that which is replicable, aggregable, and data supported. Each of the boxes represents a reporting aim—indeed, a disclosure—of the research design and findings.

- *Study Aim and Design*: Direct statement of the intent of the study allows classification of study types designed to gather evidence of the categories defined in Figure 3.3. Similarly, specifying study design, with special attention to the relationship between design selection and validation opportunities, allows additional study transparency.

- *Comparative Studies*: Comparative studies allow specification of the areas of the construct model under examination. Essential for meta-analysis research (Graham and Perin 2007; Graham and Sandmel 2011), comparative studies allow a body of knowledge to be built regarding the ways variables associated with the writing construct are used in the writing practices of different groups of students—a key method of strengthening curricular approaches.

- *Sampling Plan Design*: While studies of sampling theory are beyond the scope of this book, basic design principles such as the sampling-plan calculations presented in this chapter are within the grasp of all. Such disclosure allows readers to judge the comparative nature of the student population under examination—and, thus, the relevance of the results to the writing program at hand.

- *Null Hypothesis Statements and Rejection Principles*: The default of a .05 level of statistical significance is but an elementary principle of NHST statements and rejection principles. Identification of criteria for making causal inferences—causal relativity, causal manipulation, temporal ordering, and elimination of alternative explanations—helps readers identify the logic of causal inference (Schneider et al. 2007).

- *Criterion Variable Identification*: In experimental designs that are truly baseline and descriptive, the criteria for the research are the comparative studies themselves. Yet, a moment's reflection on Figure 3.1 reveals how much is now known about the writing construct. In program assessment, comparative measures of the performance at hand to related performance measures, from admissions tests to course grades to grade point averages, allow readers a sense of the relationship of the reported study to studies that may be successfully undertaken at their own institutions. While the limits of criterion variables are well known, as this chapter demonstrates, reporting the relationships between new and known measures proves invaluable to additional research.

The second and third rows of information have been covered in this chapter. Our categories of reporting standards, combined with the concept of construct modeling and the sources of validity evidence shown in Figure 3.3, are meant as guidelines for research reporting. Where areas are absent, additional guidelines should be added; where they are present, they should be elaborated. With a desire for comparative study of writing programs, we hope the proposed standards can be viewed not as barriers to freedom but, rather, as roads to writing program collaboration.

A FINAL NOTE ABOUT MEASUREMENT

In chapter 1, we noted the early adoption of the *WPA Outcomes Statement* by the publisher McGraw-Hill. Concurrent with that adoption were a series of research studies conducted to understand more fully the impact of the *Outcomes Statement* on local writing programs. White, Elliot, and Peckham each worked on that research, and one group of findings was published as a validation study of the outcomes themselves (Kelly-Riley and Elliot 2014). Using the validation framework shown in Figure 3.3, the authors focused on four forms of evidence gathered from early- and late-semester student performance (n = 153): scoring, generalization, extrapolation, and implication. With the exception of effect size, the study used each of the techniques presented in this chapter. The statistics were used to provide a basic framework for further research into the challenges of aligning broad consensus statements with locally developed educational initiatives. In many ways, review of that study is a very useful way to integrate the vocabulary and techniques presented thus far in our book and plan for their use.

As we noted in the beginning of this chapter, program review should be accompanied by a commitment to avoid value dualism and value hierarchy. The application of quantitative methods to research design is therefore to be taken neither as isolated from nor superior to knowledge of historical and theoretical research in writing studies. The kinds of empirical analysis demonstrated in this chapter should simply become part of the conceptual toolkit of all next-generation writing program administrators. For program designers and reviewers, such information assures both internal and external stakeholders that evidence of student learning is carefully gathered and applied in the service of the program. We will now conclude by turning to an environmental framework, termed Design for Assessment, into which the concepts and measurement principles covered thus far may be integrated.

QUESTIONS FOR WRITING PROGRAM FACULTY AND ADMINISTRATORS: MEASUREMENT

Background

In this set of questions, we have taken the most important concepts from chapter 4 on measurement and turned them into questions for writing program faculty and administrators. *Empiricism*, Davida Charney (1996) chided readers, is not a four-letter word. To demonstrate just how harmful dismissal of empirical research involving quantitative and qualitative methods could truly be, Richard Haswell (2005) offers two chilling predictions. The first is by Robert Connors (1997): "We are already pursuing research paths so disparate that many thoughtful people have feared the discipline will fly apart like a dollar watch" (18). The second is by Witte (1987): "A field that presumes the efficacy of a particular research methodology, a particular inquiry paradigm, will collapse inward upon itself" (207). Although we are well aware that it is not the only kind of knowledge important to our field, we agree with Charney and Haswell and argue for systematically produced knowledge. Our questions are intended to strengthen replicable, aggregable, and data-supported practice in writing program assessment.

Introduction

In their one-of-a-kind *Composition Research: Empirical Designs*, Janice M. Lauer and J. William Asher defined program evaluation as "the process of determining the worth or status of a writing program for several purposes: to provide a basis for making decisions about educational progress, to relate accomplishments to objectives, and to establish the effectiveness of instructional programs" (Lauer and Asher 1988, 228). They then turned to questions readers of program evaluations might ask. The list runs from purpose of the evaluation (formative or summative) to scope (as relative, important, timely, persuasive, and efficient). While the focus of this chapter—indeed, of this book—is to report research outward so any evaluator can answer questions relevant to program assessment, the questions Lauer and Asher pose provide an important focus on readers. Anticipating their needs is an excellent way to frame questions about measurement.

Questions

The following questions are intended to prompt discussions about quantitative and qualitative approaches to the empirical measurement of writing. Answering these questions will facilitate the development of measurement concepts that can be used to provide evidence that the writing program is serving its constituencies.

1. What program category do you most readily identify within the Classification of Instructional Program (CIP) codes developed by the National Center for Education Statistics? After identifying that category, define the research methods of that category, with reference to published studies. After such analysis, examine the relationship of that CIP

code and its program of research to the measurement methods provided in this chapter. Identification of research methods is a good way to understand the demands of writing program assessment.

2. We argue in this chapter that all doctoral students in composition and rhetoric should have formal courses in quantitative and qualitative methods of research design. If you have not had the benefit of such seminars, how will you develop the conceptualizations needed to use the empirical frameworks introduced in this chapter? Have you established a working relationship with the office of institutional research at your institution? Do you have plans to work through generalized books on empirical research such as that by Bernard (2013) or by Trochim and Donnelly (2008) with accompanying software such as SPSS? To apply such general research knowledge, do you have plans to follow the standard research taxonomy categories such as those described by Lauer and Asher (1988, Fig. 1, 16) in order to undertake replication studies that will allow empirical proficiency to be strengthened? If not, have you talked to possible consultants who will work with you to strengthen the research and reports you will be producing about your writing program?

3. What do you see as the advantages and limitations of embracing both nomothetic span and idiographic representation in the assessment of writing programs? A good way to understand such complementarity is by exploring the analytic methods in this chapter in terms of their ability to tell us something about the span of the writing construct across student populations and the way that construct is understood by individual students and faculty members.

4. Taking Table 4.1 as a model, how will you collaborate with institutional researchers to build an account of admission and placement information in terms of writing-course performance? What would such information mean to the following audiences: advisory boards, administration, faculty and instructional staff, parents, professional organizations, students, and the public? How could Table 4.1 be redesigned to meet the needs of each distinct audience?

5. How do you know that the sample of students at hand is of sufficient size to represent the broader population of students at your institution? While the formulas provided in this chapter may be unfamiliar, they will allow you to determine various levels of confidence so your findings from a particular study will have broader relevance to your community. Indeed, if the profile of your students is similar to that of the benchmark institutions used by your institution, your study may have relevance beyond the institution.

6. How can null hypothesis significance testing be used to help you identify the specifics of a research question? How can such thought

experiments help you identify the evidence you will need to reject the null hypothesis and confirm an alternative one?

7. Using Table 4.4 as an example, define a set of relationships among variables in any given study and examine the language used to describe the strength of those relationships. What does the use of that language reveal about the ways the literature has provided justification of those descriptors—or the way the researcher has simply decided to apply adjectives without justification?

8. Using Figure 2.3, identify the way the writing construct is modeled in one group of multiple-section courses at your institution. Then, based on that model of predictor and outcome variables, prepare a summary of ways you can capture the interaction of these variables based on Table 4.4. How would information from such a table allow you to better determine methods of instruction that would increase student exposure to the span of the writing construct?

9. Following the design of Kelly-Riley and Elliot (2014), imagine a pre-and posttest study in which students of similar ability and receiving similar instruction are examined on their abilities at the beginning and end of a course using comparable writing tasks. Using the variable model created for question 8, prepare a blank table based on Table 4.5 from that study. Were statistically significant gains to be established, what might that information tell you about the following: the students, their instructors, and the design of the assessment? How must claims based on such designs be justified and qualified? What do your answers tell you about the weaknesses and strengths of such designs?

10. At the end of the chapter we note that in many ways, review of the Kelly-Riley and Elliot (2014) study is a very useful way to integrate the vocabulary and techniques presented in our book. One way to practice with analytic tools is to experiment with the visual presentation of quantitative information, a field pioneered by Edward R. Tufte (2001). Taking Table 4.5 and the information on statistically significant difference presented in this chapter, refer to Table 5 in the Kelly-Riley and Elliot study. Which table is better suited for an audience of instructors and administrators? Which is better suited for an audience of researchers? Such comparative analysis is a good way to understand the elements of effective visual designs as they serve the needs of different audiences.

11. Using the variable model created in questions 8 and 9, change the outcome variable. For example, if you designed the model so that various traits were the predictor variables and the holistic score was the outcome variable, treat all of the traits and the holistic score as the predictor variables and use course grade as the outcome variable. What would a regression analysis tell you about the ability of the writing model to

predict course grades? Using Willingham, Pollack, and Lewis (2002), provide an analysis of the complexities of using course grades as an outcome based on the limits of any one sample of student writing.

12. Carefully review the four criteria needed to establish causal relationships (Holland 1986; Schneider et al. 2007). Then, read *Academically Adrift: Limited Learning on College Campuses* (Arum and Roksa 2011) and the review of that volume by Haswell (2012b). Using the four criteria, study the way Haswell implicitly uses these criteria to establish the invalidity of the College Learning Assessment Performance Task Score—the assessment upon which the book based its claim that student learning is both modest and limited. How can these four criteria, used in advance of a writing program assessment, improve the way program effectiveness will be interpreted?

13. Work with your institutional researcher to identify data from the National Survey of Student Engagement (NSSE) as it has been obtained from your school or its benchmarks. Then, using Cohen (1992) and Paul D. Ellis (2010) provide an interpretation of the meaning of the effect size of the survey results as they are compared within and beyond the institution. What does effect size reveal about the direction, magnitude, and interpretation of the results?

14. Design a study in which the quantitative approaches examined in questions 4 through 11 are combined with qualitative methods. For example, how might the qualitative approach of Dynamic Criteria Mapping (Broad et al. 2009) be used to elicit and examine student perceptions of the writing tasks used in question 9. How would such qualitative analysis help you better interpret the pre-and posttest study?

15. Using Figure 4.1 as an example, draft a set of reporting guidelines for quantitative and qualitative studies connected to your writing program. In terms of consequence (Gallagher 2012), what advantages would such a set of guidelines yield for constituencies of the program?

5
DESIGN

When White (2001) wrote "The Opening of the Modern Era of Writing Assessment: A Narrative," which was published in *College English,* he ended it with this prediction:

> As we enter the new century, we will be fighting old battles in new ways. The modern era of writing assessment has placed us at last on the right side of a series of social issues: for instance, we see writing assessment as a way to help students succeed rather than a way to screen out the undeserving, its more traditional use. We also see writing assessment as closely related to the teaching of writing in our courses and in writing-across-the-curriculum classes throughout the university. More and more, we have integrated writing assessment theory and practice into the general instructional programs of our universities and colleges, since they are so well based on performative and cognitive theories of learning. . . . Assessment, with its appeal to professionalism, certification, and standards (all ambiguous criteria, to be sure), has given us a way to reassert the values of our field and its ethical power. That power has been demonstrated in the public sphere, where the stakes are high. If we are indeed shaped in large part by our past, our management of assessment over the past twenty-five years can give us a certain amount of hope for the future. (White 2001, 319–20)

As we contemplate the future fourteen years later, we can see how much has changed. In 2001, many of us envisioned a continuing struggle between the "merely utilitarian view of writing" and the heroïc forces of English departments reasserting "the values of our field and its ethical power." Present in 2001 was an apocalyptic vision of Evil versus Good, the eternal value hierarchy, in a pitched battle for the soul of American education. When we compare that vision of assessment with that of this book, we have some indication of how far we have come in the last decade and a half. While darkness may remain, there is also a good deal of light, not present in other years, which offers shadowy visions of hope, sometimes very like a whale.

Let's take a moment to describe the present as it now appears to us. In their review of one hundred years of empirical studies in journals published by the National Council of Teachers of English, Roozen

DOI: 10.7330/9780874219869.c005

and Lunsford (2011) document a movement from an elementalism associated with positivism to the mixed-methods approach we associate with the theoretical orientations of postpositivism, critical realism, and constructivism. Referencing the work of Peter Smagorinsky (2006), Kevin Roozen and Karen J. Lunsford recall his characterization that the scholarship in rhetoric and composition/writing studies has moved away from "the search for universals" regardless of setting and toward more fully situated studies in order to take social context much more into account (12). "Over the last decade," they write, "a growing body of empirical research has revealed how the social context for writing is laminated with resources from multiple scenes" (202). Vitality is to be found in context.

The identification of writing program assessment with research is a new development among those in the field of rhetoric and composition/writing studies, significantly beyond the range of writing assessment faculty fourteen years ago. It is indeed proper to claim that writing assessment now has a defined history, a body of knowledge, and established research methods and methodologies. Each will be part of a promising future. In this final chapter, we turn to the presentation of our Design for Assessment (DFA) model—the conceptual glue that holds writing program assessment together—and a two-part case study to demonstrate its use. We know that without the existing history, knowledge, and research, the model would simply not be possible. And so we end, as we began, with an acknowledgment of our debts and our analysis of a challenging future sure to come.

HOW WE LIVE NOW: THE AGE OF CONTINGENCY

In terms of accountability, whatever claims we make about validity should be tempered with qualification. The elements of empirical studies described by Haswell (2005, 2012a) discussed in chapters 3 and 4, endure: such studies work from information resulting from a set procedure of observation, elicitation, or analysis; they describe a system of text analysis or a research method or a research tool, application, and report of results; they incorporate a comprehensive literature review of previous work on the topic at hand to confirm, qualify, or disconfirm previous study results with new information; and they offer contextual information that assists in understanding participants or texts in a study. This framework goes a long way, but, as we showed in chapter 4, an evidence-based view of validation is now such a complex process that contingencies are as present as claims. Whether we look at the educational measurement community or the writing community, the second decade of the twenty-first century has witnessed the end of reductive versions of validity as stamps of approval. As Richard Rorty (1989) taught, ours is an age of contingency—of language and of self and of community. If solidarity is to be found, it will come through both reflection and through action.

What, if anything, does history teach us that will help us to navigate this promising yet complex future? We may rightfully feel accomplished when we read Anne Ruggles Gere's 1980 call for a theory of evaluation that embraces both communication intention (variables such as rhetorical stance) and formal semantics (variables such as cohesion) and realize she has been answered, at least in part, by the conceptual model of the *WPA Outcomes Statement*—as well as the conceptual advances described in chapter 3 and the technical advances described in chapter 4. We know that assessment can be used productively to document the degree to which our instruction is doing what we claim it is doing; that assessment can improve teaching; that assessment can help us document the effects of our instruction to our stakeholders. We have learned to resist assessment strategies that are counterproductive to good teaching, to embrace those that are, and to offer evidence comparing both. As this book demonstrates, we are sufficiently confident in our evaluation theories and practices that we can provide a guide for writing teachers and writing program directors—who are perhaps not knee deep in empirical measurement literature—to use writing assessment productively to inform classroom practice and to provide evidence for stakeholders in a programmatic way. We do not suggest that we have reached the Golden Age of assessment or that reductive and destructive assessment practices have disappeared. But we now have the knowledge, experience, and examples that allow us to replace these relics of the past with best practices in the present.

In their recommendation for a usable past for writing assessment, Huot, O'Neill, and Moore (2010) remind us we must remain alert to the critically important role of instructor knowledge. As Steven North (1987) observed in his still-controversial analysis of composition studies from the early 1960s to the mid-1980s, the scholars and researchers had displaced the practitioners. Both the thrust and impact of the academic reform movement that drove the widely proclaimed and largely manufactured literacy crisis of the 1960s (Berliner and Biddle 1995) were to diminish instructional authority over knowledge. Psychometrician Gregory J. Cizek (2008) confirms North's analysis. In reviewing the monumental accounting of theories and methods in educational measurement—the 2006 fourth edition of *Educational Measurement* (weighing in at 779 pages and five pounds)—he laments the lack of attention to teacher knowledge. Clearly, research is needed on how teachers synthesize sources of classroom information to make decisions, use grading models for reporting achievement, and deal with potential sources of bias and their minimization in classroom assessment. We agree with the call for empirical studies, in the tradition identified by Haswell, on students in their classrooms. As Brian Huot (1996) has continued to advocate since postulating his theory of writing assessment, localism—of student, instructor, and setting—is critically important in assessment. With his colleagues Peggy O'Neill and Cindy Moore, he calls for a "productive culture of assessment around the teaching of writing and the administration of writing programs." If we create and embrace that culture, they claim, "the future of writing assessment will be much different from its past" (Huot, O'Neill, and Moore 2010, 512). Whether difference should be equated with improvement is uncertain, but the idea of a more creative and productive culture of writing assessment is worth imagining.

The problem to be solved is to discover ways of harmonizing this environmental view of writing assessment with the larger society's demands for empirical information that allows comparisons across institutions. From a stance inside our writing programs, we would perhaps imagine that this demand is impossible: the variations of funding, traditions, populations, curricula, objectives, and so on are so great that such large-scale assessments and comparisons are likely to be meaningless and misleading.

But this disjuncture is far from apparent to many of the administrators and funding sources for higher education on and beyond our campus borders. Everyone, those societal forces say, is accountable for reporting what they have done with the resources they have been given and comparing their outcomes with those of similar institutions. Writing programs unprepared to cope with this perspective will, we believe, be left behind in the competition for resources that every university and college is now experiencing. Those who have learned to take these matters in stride, turning such demands to the program's advantage, will prosper. It is our job to make sure the age of contingency is accompanied by the age of collaboration.

SOMETIME SOON: THE CASE OF BRICK CITY

Imagine the following case in the near future. At Brick City College, a primarily undergraduate public institution with approximately seven thousand students, a writing program administrator (WPA) has been called to a meeting with other program administrators in the College of Social and Humanistic Studies. Similar meetings are taking place in the College of Science and the College of Business. Although there are some graduate programs at Brick City, it is primarily an undergraduate institution. The Carnegie Classification for Brick City would therefore be as follows: "A&S+Prof/SGC: Arts & sciences plus professions, some graduate coexistence." In the meeting, all those present are responsible for either their department's degree programs or the core curriculum that every undergraduate must take. The agenda has been entitled "Accountability: Program Review."

The first image of the dean's slide set appears on screen, laptop, tablet, and smartphone. A list under the title "Essential Elements of Program Review" comes into focus:

1. *Program Mission*: The program must be aligned with the broad university mission and the mission of the college, with special attention to integration across programs.

2. *Program Management*: Specific program objectives must be established, defined by measureable objectives, and accountable through cyclical reporting.

3. *Research Support*: There must be an accounting of total R&D support by source of funds (federal, state and local, industry, institutional, or other).

4. *Scholarly Productivity*: There must be measurement of faculty productivity through designated categories identified in the university's new digital platform for annual teaching, research, and service activities.

5. *Instructional Efficiency and Equity*: There must be measurement of faculty load based on credit-hour production.

6. *Innovative Instructional Methodologies and Technologies*: There must be demonstration of innovation in curriculum delivery methods, including use of technology.

7. *Undergraduate Program Success*: There must be measures of student success. For comparative purposes, these measures will be analyzed by comparison with benchmark institutions (identified from the nation's framework for recognizing and describing institutional diversity—the Carnegie Classification of Institutions of Higher Education™) and comparative information from those institutions (gathered from the systems of interrelated surveys conducted annually by the US National Center for Educational Statistics—the Integrated Postsecondary Education Data System). Comparative measures will include the following: institutional characteristics, pricing and tuition, student financial aid, human resources, admissions, enrollment, graduation rates, and degrees

conferred. Special attention will be paid to retention, transfer, and graduation rates of the program under review. There must also be alignment with the university model of student-learning assessment. The university's local model of assessment must be integrated into the program whether it is externally accredited or not.

8. *Alumni Strength*: There must be measures of employment rate (by program and degree level), average salaries of employed alumni (weighted to average salary associated with CIP Code by the Bureau of Labor Statistics), acceptance rates to nationally ranked graduate programs, and rankings by industry employers.

9. *Community Engagement*: There must be demonstrated outreach and partnerships related to mutually beneficial exchanges between our campus and state, regional, national, and international constituencies.

The dean of the College of Social and Humanistic Studies gives the WPA and her colleagues a moment to scroll down the list. This, she says, is the way we will live now.

Because each of these variables can be measured, she continues, an index—the summative program evaluation, or outcome, based on the nine essential program review elements—can be derived. Integrating information given by the departments into these categories, she continues, will allow a fair and equitable system to be developed that will allow scarce resources to be allocated and meaningful comparisons with comparable institutions to be drawn.

Three concurrent thoughts run through the WPA's head. The first: the end of days has come. The description of Empire in J. M. Coetzee's (1980) *Waiting for the Barbarians* runs through her mind: "One thought alone preoccupies the submerged mind of Empire: how not to end, how not to die, how to prolong its era. By day it pursues its enemies. It is cunning and ruthless, and it sends its bloodhounds everywhere" (133). Her second thought is that she is nevertheless at the table and therefore has an opportunity to make a difference for the students in her program, and the instructors who teach them, by documenting curricular efforts and securing scarce resources. She recalls David Harvey's (2010) *The Enigma of Capitalism and the Crisis of Capitalism*: the irrationality of capitalism and its accompanying use of empiricism is the dark shadow just behind the dean's slide show. Here is nevertheless a chance to establish an epicenter for change by strengthening the presence and meaningfulness of her field within the daily life of the university. She also recalls Thomas Piketty's (2014) *Capital in the Twenty-First Century*: diffusion of knowledge and information will emerge as the most productive way to remedy inequality. Here is a chance for her to demonstrate that she knows precisely what a productive culture of assessment looks like.

Then she hears the dean say, "Remember, the aim here is not to collect data. No one cares how much data you have collected. We care most about what you did with the information you obtained in terms of improving student learning and thereby advancing the mission of the College of Social and Humanistic Studies and our university. Much is expected."

The WPA pulls up a screen on the tablet and writes to the director of institutional research: "I need your help to begin pulling down the data from . . ."

Then she thinks, "Ah, so this is what the localism looks like that we demanded for so long."

Thanks heavens, she acknowledges, that she has been working with the chair of the Department of English and her dean on the five-year strategic plan shown in Table 5.1.

Now in the second year of the plan, she has both experience and data on the progress she and her colleagues have made on the four strategic priorities of the plan as they were intended to advance the mission of the writing program: to support students' success in their transitions to Brick City, to document their academic success while at Brick City through ePortfolios, to enhance their roles as global citizens through exposure to contemporary world literature, and to encourage multidisciplinary collaboration through writing in the disciplines. These broad priorities have been focused on through a series of objectives related to each: elimination of noncredit basic-skills courses for first-year students; universal undergraduate use of ePortfolios in the core undergraduate curriculum; additional digital support for world literature; and an emphasis on writing in the disciplines for all capstone seminars in all majors.

For each of these priorities, those responsible for the priority, targets, communication strategies, and anticipated consequences have prepared a detailed set of objectives. One such matrix is shown in Table 5.2.

The table has allowed the WPA to achieve both direction and experience following a year of its use. For example, she has used the formula in chapter 4 to estimate the smallest number of ePortfolios that could be feasibly read under restrictions of time and funding, and she has been able to gain levels of interreader reliability similar to those shown in Table 4.3 at high to medium levels. The disappointment, however, was the number of replacements she needed to complete the sample because fully one-third of the sections of first-year writing were not using ePortfolios designed to be scored under Phase 2 assessment. Instead of

Table 5.1. Brick City College Department of English Five-Year Strategic Plan.

Our Mission: The Department of English is committed to the study of writing, literature, and the cultures in which both exist. Our aim is to ensure that Brick City students are able to communicate compellingly in order to play productive roles in their disciplines and in their communities.

Our Strategy Priorities: We will achieve our mission through strategic priorities aimed to help students succeed in their transitions to Brick City, to document their academic and student success through ePortfolios, to enhance their roles as global citizens through exposure to contemporary world literature, and to encourage multidisciplinary collaboration through writing in the disciplines.

Our Impact: In terms of consequence, we anticipate that over the five years of the strategic plan, we will provide all Brick City undergraduate students with hallmark experiences in writing, literature, and culture that will transform their undergraduate experience and strengthen their societal commitment.

Our Targets: We have identified four targets: to eliminate basic-skills classes for first-year students; to use ePortfolios for instruction and assessment across the curriculum; to offer a contemporary world literature elective in a digitally supported learning environment at the sophomore level; and to offer course-embedded writing-in-the-disciplines support for all senior students in their capstone seminars.

Our Assessment: Using a variety of qualitative and quantitative methods, we will document our curricular efforts, chart the work of our students, and use the information we gain to improve our instruction and deepen our knowledge about student learning.

Our Communication: To strengthen community involvement, we pledge to report our work to our constituencies—advisory boards, administration, faculty and instructional staff, parents, students, professional societies, and the public—in ways appropriate to each.

Priority 1: Transitions: First-Year Writing
    Eliminate basic writing through rapid course assessment and writing center support
    Implement advanced placement for proficient students
Priority 2: Student Achievement: ePortfolios across the curriculum
    Establish and use core competency proficiencies to document academic success
    Coordinate with departments and Office of Career Development to prepare students for workplace and graduate-school success
    Assess in first year, sophomore year, and senior year, with skill levels documented
Priority 3: Digital Learning: World Literature
    Feature contemporary authors including selections from fiction, poetry, stage, and film
    Offer digitally supported classes, including faculty podcasts for lectures
Priority 4: Writing in the Disciplines: Senior Year Capstone Seminars
    Ensure student writing proficiency in genres required in the major
    Ensure both print and digital writing exposure

using the variables she and her colleagues had designed—yielding student ePortfolios similar to those shown in Figure 2.2—many students had simply uploaded unreflective digital filing cabinets of files under categories of assignments. These digital filing cabinets were nearly impossible to score and thus had to be discarded from the sample, with Phase 2 ePortfolios to take their place. Hence, the sample was neither truly random nor ultimately representative. More work would remain during the next three years of the plan if she were to reach the 100 percent target she had set.

Table 5.2 Priority: Student achievement: ePortfolios across the curriculum.

Strategic Priority	Objectives	Responsible Groups	Targets	Communication	Impact
Priority 2: Student Achievement: ePortfolios across the Curriculum	Objective 1: Instruction: To ensure ePortfolios are designed to reflect core cognitive, interpersonal, and intrapersonal skills necessary for success	Faculty and instructional staff within and beyond the department; students Office of Institutional Research	First year: 100 percent of first-year writing classes use ePortfolios; sampling plan to assess ePortfolios at 95% CI	Department advisory board: spring meeting Administration: monthly dean briefings Faculty and instructional staff: collaborative wiki	To provide students with hallmark experiences in writing, literature, and culture that will transform their undergraduate experience and strengthen their societal commitment
	Objective 2: Assessment: To assure ePortfolios are evaluated on recurrent cycles in valid ways with Phase 2 assessment processes	Office of Career Development; alumni	Sophomore year: 50% of world literature classes use ePortfolios; sampling plan to assess ePortfolios at 95% CI	Parents: department web page Students: podcast series	
	Objective 3: Sustainability: To ensure that results from assessment are used to improve student learning		Senior year: 50% of targeted capstone seminars use ePortfolios; sampling plan to assess ePortfolios at 95% CI	Professional societies: regional conference; national conference; peer-reviewed publications Public: department web page	

On the other hand, sophomore level and senior students, seeing the value of ePortfolios to help them document their academic successes, were more than happy to use them. In addition, the writing-in-the-disciplines effort had truly taken off as colleagues worked across disciplinary boundaries to ensure that students were competent in the genres necessary to their major—laboratory research reports for chemistry students and proposals for business majors. Using resources recovered from the near elimination of basic writing, she was able to hire additional faculty for this embedded instruction in the senior seminars.

She was not that far from what her dean had requested, she realized, as she headed from the meeting back to her office. Her next step was to gather the information she had collected so it could be used within the dean's new index.

LOOKING BACK: KEY CONCEPTS

As we reach the end of this book—and before we examine our final framework for writing program assessment, Design for Assessment, and how it might be used by our fictitious WPA, let's review where we have been. Throughout the book, we have emphasized the key concepts below. Where specialized language is used, readers should refer back to the chapters in which the terms are introduced, use the glossary that follows this chapter, and consult the index for related terminology.

- The established field of rhetoric and composition/writing studies (CIP 23.13) provides the ontological basis for the design of writing programs and their assessment.
- Epistemologically, advancement of our field is best made by both disciplinary and multidisciplinary inquiry.
- Consideration of all who may be intentionally or unintentionally influenced by an assessment is the preferred axiological stance for writing program administrators in their instructional design and program assessment roles.
- Modeling of the writing construct—defining the variables of the writing construct and considering them relationally as a way to experiment with improved curriculum through constructed-response tasks and ePortfolio use—is a fruitful way of conceptualizing the essence of the writing program for it to serve its many stakeholders.
- The model itself, in turn, is best understood as embedded in the complex ecology of a program, the institution it serves, and its relationship with its internal (students, faculty, administration, and families) and external (state and regional elementary and secondary schools, employers of graduates, and benchmark programs) stakeholders.

- An historical orientation to writing program assessment allows comparison of the local ecology to regional, national, and international trends—a comparison that, in turn, lends instrumental value to the assessment regarding past and future directions.

- With attention to both the specifics of institutional context and the rigors of educational accountability, writing programs can be assessed in ways that allow them to be accountable to different audiences and for different purposes.

- Fundamental to the assessment of writing programs are sources of validity evidence gathered from the following categories: aim, construct modeling, consequence, scoring, response processes, disaggregation, extrapolation, generalization, theory-based interpretation, cost effectiveness, sustainability, and transformation.

- These sources of validity evidence are then integrated into a process of validation, exposition, and persuasion that, in turn, results in communication of the assessment in a variety of ways to a variety of shareholder audiences.

- In terms of writing performance assessment, the variable model associated with Phase 2 portfolio assessment—including print and digital forms both course centered and longitudinally designed—will yield substantial gains for all those associated with the assessment.

- In matters of measurement, abandoning preconceived notions of right and wrong, dialect values, or other a priori hierarchies that may not apply to the students, the institution, or the curriculum, allows an assessment to pay attention to both nomothetic span and idiographic representation of the writing construct in its many forms.

- In matters of measurement, analyses are most useful if they adhere to important reporting standards, including construct definition; descriptive statistics disaggregated to present information about diverse student populations; transparent sampling-plan designs based on power analysis; assessment aims stated in terms of null and alternative hypotheses; interreader agreement and interreader reliability analysis disaggregated to reveal scoring patterns; and correlation analysis, regression analysis, and effect-size determination of writing variables and associated criterion measures.

- Imagining a predicable future for the assessment of writing programs reveals a need for attention to the following contexts: institutional mission; program mission; program management; research expenditures; scholarly productivity; instructional efficiency and equity, with special attention to increasing the salary and benefits for writing faculty; innovative instructional methodologies and technologies; undergraduate and graduate program success; alumni response; community engagement; and faculty strength and student diversity.

- Attention to localism, sustainability, and professionalism are the best ways to counteract the reductionist tendencies accompanying the limitations and uncertainties that will be increasingly present in American society.

Encompassing the philosophical and the pragmatic, these themes serve as prelude to an overall framework for the assessment of writing programs we now propose. Perhaps, as we recommended in the introduction, you took a look at Figure 5.1 when you began reading. If so, the explication to follow will flow from the concepts and techniques we have offered thus far. While we regret withholding the framework until the last chapter, its significance would have been vague without a firm grasp of that which we have presented to this point.

LOOKING FORWARD: DESIGN FOR ASSESSMENT

In 2003, Mislevy, Steinberg, and Almond offered an innovative framework to connect the "web of inferences" between an instance of assessment and claims made about general student ability based on that singular instance. Their aim was to make explicit—in advance of an assessment—connections between validation arguments driving the conclusions, experimental designs, and operational processes such as administration, empirical analysis, and score reporting that are the machinery of the assessment. Basing his work on a 2003 research report, Mislevy and his colleagues termed the framework "evidence-centered design" (ECD). Proposed to make explicit the evidentiary reasoning such as that described in chapter 3 regarding the Toulmin model, ECD helps organize assessment design into cohesive, integrated thinking about assessment aims and their delivery capability. In the case of program assessments, these designs can be tailored and reused in different configurations to serve different programs of assessment. Their example of task-based language assessment provides a compelling model that, if used prior to beginning any assessment activity, results in highly specific articulation about the construct under investigation, the ways to gather evidence, the assessment's technical blueprint, and the delivery of the assessment itself. In the digital environments for instruction and assessment that are surely here to stay, as Mislevy and his colleagues note, the new territory before us will not be hospitable to the ad hoc, intuitive reasoning that all too often continues to inform assessment design.

Key to acceptance of the model is a point made many times in this book: validity, far from a unitary concept, is about precisely what Messick told us it was about in 1989—"the degree to which empirical evidence and theoretical rationales support the *adequacy* and *appropriateness* of *inferences* and *actions* based on test scores or other modes of assessment" (13). If new frameworks for the assessment of writing programs are to be developed, then—to put it coarsely—no one will care if samples of writing are assessed regularly if nothing is done with the results. All anyone will care about is whether the assessment has adequately captured the construct at hand, whether the inferences made from the assessment are based on appropriate evidence, and whether significant use is made of the results to improve student learning. If there is any one new trend that has recently emerged in the larger field of program assessment, it is that use of assessment results is the order of the day (Kane 2013; Middaugh 2010).

Informed by the ECD model, as well as the more recent advocacy by Kane (2013) for an interpretation/use argument (IUA) for validation discussed in chapter 1, we offer in this final chapter an assessment framework developed especially for the evaluation of writing programs. DFA integrates and tailors principles of ECD as they may be used or expanded to a writing assessment framework. Because DFA is a program-assessment model, it is informed by the recent revision of *The Program Evaluation Standards* (Yarbrough et al. 2011) from the Joint Committee on Standards for Educational Evaluation. With focus on utility, feasibility, propriety, accuracy, and accountability, the standards are designed to be of use to reviewers of program-evaluation proposals, practicing evaluators, evaluation sponsors, instructors, and students. As is the case with ECD, flipping these standards around to use them in assessments before they are designed—and tailoring them to the assessment of writing programs—affords a reflective practice we believe will characterize future writing assessment programs. Figure 5.1 presents the DFA framework.

As we have noted throughout the book, establishing the consequential validity of an assessment is of paramount interest to those who develop, revise, and assess writing programs. Seminal works by Messick (1989) and Kane (2013) on validity certainly do give equal billing to the evidential and consequential basis for validity (Kane 2013, 21). Yet these scholars simply do not identify consequence as the most important issue of assessment. Even in his highly creative and minimalist definition of validity—"A test is valid for measuring an attribute if variation in the attribute causes variation in the test scored (163)—Denny Borsboom (2005) makes no mention of impact. The word *consequence* does not appear in the index of his highly intelligent book. We do not fault our educational-measurement colleagues who are only recently making a concentrated effort to address an expanded view of validation focusing

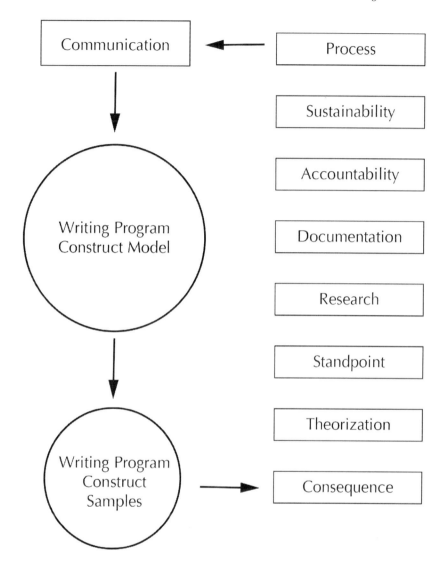

Figure 5.1. A Design for Assessment framework for the assessment of writing programs.

on consequence (Bachman 2013; Haertel 2013; Shepard 2013). Indeed, we are only turning to such issues in our own community (Poe et al. 2014). Because those in our profession spend their lives with students who work to find their voices and create their futures on the page or screen, we are especially attuned to the consequences—some intended, others unintended—of assessment. It takes a classroom instructor to offer the kind of radical definition of validity proposed by Asao B. Inoue (2009): "Racial validity, then, is an argument that explains the degree to which empirical evidence of racial formations around our assessments and the theoretical frameworks that account for racial formations support the adequacy and appropriateness of inferences and actions made from the assessments" (110). Surely here is a direction that will help redeem the intellectual and moral failure to develop our concepts of consequential validity. With modification required for our field, surely we can borrow from our health colleagues the aphorism that, above all, we should do no harm (McKee 2003).

As such, we define consequence as the impact, judgments, and changes that stem from the articulated mission, priorities, and practices of a writing program. With attention to the fairness of the assessment, consequence emphasizes that writing programs must use contemporary instructional and assessment practices mapped from the institutional mission statement to the syllabus with the sole aim of advancing student learning. An emphasis on consequence and fairness demands that writing programs be judged by their own articulated mission.

We define the second component, theorization, as the ability to define the writing construct and the samples of that construct used in the particular writing program under review. Here we adapt the categories offered by Timothy W. Crusius (1989) to explicate what a theory of writing must do in a specific institution: offer a typology, a nomothetic span capable of identifying how an institution defines the writing construct and how the many curricular-construct samples validly tap into that universe of discourse; isolate the ways, or "tactics of arrangement," in which each construct sample allows for construct representation (100); create a modal sequence that demonstrates how students learn, from admission through graduation, more and more about the writing construct; offer evidence of how the writing construct and samples of that construct are related to how students actually compose; offer evidence of how the writing construct and samples of that construct allow students to create voice and identity and serve the needs of audiences; and offer evidence of how the writing construct, as understood at a particular institution, relates to other construct models operating in other fields across the university. In advocating theory development as a core feature of writing program assessment, we certainly agree with Raul Sánchez (2012) in his suggestion that "a theory of writing might re-imagine empiricism as simultaneously a producer and recipient of theoretical knowledge" (238). Taking empiricism as ways of "looking at things in a systematic way and then making statements about them,"

Sánchez (239) is aligned with the impulse toward praxis that informed the theory of discourse offered by Crusius: "Our center, then, is ultimately praxis and therefore social or cultural in the sense that we gauge our success by the degree to which our students perform well in those kinds of discourse our culture deems necessary or valuable, including discourse that questions traditional values and the status quo" (112).

Attention to standpoint yields the sense of localism our profession has so long demanded. We define our third component, standpoint, as we did in chapter 2: pursuit of situated knowledge (location shapes our experiences) and leverage of epistemic advantage (marginalized groups have advantageous perspectives). With its orientation toward contextual justification, normative aims, and social epistemology, standpoint theory is a very good example of theories that provide strategies for articulating what we talk about when we talk about localism (Intemann 2010). The nomothetic map shown in chapter 3 (Figure 3.1) stands as the embodiment of a local vision of the writing construct—one based on formal research and consensus of experts. While the pressure of large-scale assessment will always be with us, expression and articulation of an institution's standpoint toward the writing construct yields an expression of the white heat of teaching at the local level—a force that, as Emily Dickinson meant it, could repudiate the forge.

The fourth component, research, is the foundation of DFA. Scholars from Huot (2002) to Neal (2011) have lamented that writing assessment is framed as a technology. Such framing, often focused on issues such as interreader reliability, has too often "obscured the essential purpose of assessment as research and inquiry, as a way of asking and answering questions about students' writing and the programs designed to teach students to write" (Huot 2002, 148). To counteract such reductionism, Neal has proposed attention to instruction and assessment in digital spaces through focus on connectivity (how and why students make connections among their texts, personal objectives, education, professions, and lives), textual revolution (recentering rhetorical principles in digital environments), and cognition (from short attention bursts to deep reflective thought). We do not think we are exaggerating when we say we are witnessing one of history's great transformations in perspective. As Ding and Savage (2013) have noted, what was often called "methodological nationalism" (Chernilo 2006) is yielding to intercultural, global research. Nation centered frames of reference are witnessing new cultural turns in which discourse—and the institutions and power relationships that instantiate it—is being reexamined. Receding is attention to industrial needs; advancing is a focus on "serious engagement with underexamined issues such as power politics, access and exclusion, ethics and equity, and social justice" (Ding and Savage 2013, 2). As illustrated in Figure 3.1, mapping the writing construct acknowledges the forces acting on it and provides a research agenda to better engage the validity model of Figure 3.3. A rich research agenda is the surest way, as civil rights pioneer and congressman John Lewis (2013) put it, "to get in the way."

The fifth component, documentation, is where models by Messick (1989), Borsboom (2005), Kane (2006, 2013), and Markus and Borsboom (2013) come into play. Attention to scoring, generalization, and extrapolation are of critical importance to writing program assessment. Yet, as Figure 3.3 illustrates, other aspects of validity evidence are equally important. What framework can unify all the sources of validity evidence we have identified in this book? What framework can unify empirical research that is quantitative, qualitative, and mixed method without giving hierarchical weight to one over the other? Complementary to the DFA framework we are advocating, documentary studies hold great promise. To complement the discussion of standards for empirical reporting we offer in chapter 4, we recommend *Doing Documentary Work* by Robert Coles (1998). Winner of the Pulitzer Prize for General Nonfiction for his *Children of Crisis* series, Coles is best known for recounting the struggles of Ruby Bridges and her family as she became the first Black child to attend William Frantz Elementary School in New Orleans in 1960. For Coles, the practice of documentary studies takes its disposition from the Latin *docere*—"to teach." To do documentary studies is to attempt a twofold struggle: "To ascertain what *is*, what can be noted, recorded, pictured; and that of presentation—how to elicit the interest of others, and how to provide a context so that an incident, for instance, is connected to the conditions that informed and prompted its occurrence" (20). With Coles, we want to summon the narrative of the verb *document* even as we accumulate proof. With Marilyn Sternglass (1997), we need to demonstrate exactly why support for our students is necessary as they strive, often bravely, to find their voices in the swirl of forces threatening to extinguish the authentic in favor of the bureaucratic.

The contextualizing power of narrative certainly drew a crowd that nearly exceeded the ballroom itself in 2005 as Nancy Sommers presented a short film, *Across the Drafts: Students and Teachers Talk about Feedback* at the annual meeting of the Conference on College Composition and Communication. A longitudinal study of four hundred students in the 2001 entering class of Harvard University, Sommers's study of instructor response—"the hero and anti-hero" convincing students that they could succeed or fail (114)—drew a capacity crowd not because of carefully designed tables of inferential statistics but because of students talking about their feedback experiences. And, it is certainly the impulse to document that has drawn so many researchers to Broad's Dynamic Criteria Mapping (Broad et al. 2009). A way to examine unmapped terrain of the writing construct as it is represented in the construct sample at hand, Dynamic Criteria Mapping surely fits the emphasis Coles gives to rhetorical formulations of what we really value and therefore should assess.

As a form of public responsibility, we define accountability as the use of contemporary project-management systems to analyze resources allocated to the writing program. Two forms of accountancy are ideally suited to the assessment of writing programs: cost-effectiveness analysis (Levin and McEwan 2001) and balanced-scorecard approaches (Kaplan, Norton, and Rugelsjoen 2010). Defined as "the evaluation of alternatives according to both their costs and their effects with regard to producing some outcome" (Levin and McEwan 2001, 10), cost-effectiveness analysis is well suited to educational assessments such as writing program evaluation. In place of the traditional system of cost-benefit analysis with its emphasis on value in monetary terms, cost-effectiveness analysis emphasizes alternatives for meeting effectiveness criteria. Especially suited to educational evaluations such as writing program assessment— cases where decision making must focus on educational interventions and their alternatives—cost-effectiveness analysis advances a method of ingredient identification. Any statement of the costs of a writing program assessment that ignores its value for the improvement of teaching and the advancement of student learning, for example, is unacceptable. Environmental in conceptualization, the ingredients method focuses on the identification of costs as well as units of effectiveness, benefit, or utility (47). Especially harmonious with the DFA model is the importance of integrating cost-effectiveness analysis as integral to the evaluation process, not as an afterthought—as is often the case with consequence—when the study is completed (247). If cost-effectiveness analysis stresses accountancy, balanced-scorecard approaches emphasize management. Acknowledging that "lofty vision and strategy statements don't translate easily into action at the local level" (152), Kaplan and Norton (2007) emphasize vision articulation, linking, planning, and learning in the operational-management process. Recently adapted to emphasize strategic partnerships of the kind emphasized in chapter 2 among institutions, a collaboration scorecard approach has been developed by Kaplan, Norton, and Rugelsjoen (2010) so collaborators can achieve benefits that no institution could achieve by itself. Combined with the strategies advocated by Adler-Kassner (2008) in *The Activist WPA: Changing Stories about Writing and Writers*, cost-effectiveness analysis and balanced-scorecard approaches hold the potential to mend disharmonies through the practice of informed pragmatism. While use of the Integrated Postsecondary Data Center may be an unfamiliar activity, comparing a benchmark institution's number of full-time instructors and average salaries from that database to one's own institution can be revealing. Linking objectives to effectiveness, part of cost-effectiveness analysis, could reveal critical disparities, especially in cases where graduate students and adjunct instructors are being exploited as cheap labor without minimal healthcare benefits.

Stemming from allocation of resources under conditions of scarcity, we define sustainability as an analysis that focuses on past action, present decisions, and future developments so key boundaries can be established to allow the writing program to extend its influence to the entire campus. As we have affirmed so often in this book, we rely on an environmental metaphor. In 1987, the Brundtland Commission defined sustainable development as growth that, in that now famous phrase, "meets the needs of the present without compromising the ability of future generations to meet their own needs." With the title *Our Common Future*, the report of the World Commission on Environment and Development (1987) wove cultural, technical, and economic issues together. Today, signs of ecosystem stress continue to emerge to the extent that recent researchers have taken a boundary approach. In 2009, Johan Rockström and his colleagues published a manifesto in *Nature* calling for the identification and quantification of planetary boundaries that must not, under any conditions, be transgressed. Absent from the four-page statement were the high-minded concepts of 1987; present were the realizations that climate change, rate of biodiversity loss, and interference with the nitrogen cycle "have already transgressed their boundaries" (Rockström et al. 2009, 473). As a result, the authors claimed, "Humanity may soon be approaching the boundaries for global freshwater use, change in land use, ocean acidification and interference with the global phosphorous cycle (473). The message is clear: without boundaries, complex systems will fail. Reflection back to the two figures in the introduction is in order. Unless a writing program is given the resources necessary to sustain its mission at a rate equal to other benchmarked programs, regional, program, and internship/residency accreditations may fail. The best way to ensure that all stakeholders meet their shared obligations of the program assessment cycle is to establish boundaries that may not be overstepped. Ranging from resource allocation on the part of the administration to empirical assessment on the part of the program administrators, boundary setting is an important, though often unexplored, way to ensure equity among postsecondary programs.

Informed by process and postprocess research on writing pedagogy, we define program processes as the varied actions that result in writing program success. Attention to processes, policies, and procedures assures that the assessment will be viewed as part of a continuing discussion by working communities interested in ways of improving the program. DFA emphasizes attention to process as a way to understand how the genre of writing program assessment operates within an institution. As anyone who has engaged the program review genre will attest, the early stages appear to be a litany recited for the pleasure of a mindless bureaucracy; the intended destination is a filing cabinet. However, during the process of collecting information and writing up reports, something shifts. The possibility of transformation occurs, and participants begin to feel that, in documenting the assessment, there are ways to make things better. Attending to process as a way to trace the genre of program assessment through organizations, as Spinuzzi (2003) has so ably done, allows the identification of activities, actions, and operations that empower stakeholders.

The final component of DFA, communication, appears so obvious that it should not need mentioning. Nevertheless, all too often assessment is viewed as a bureaucratic exercise leading to a printed, filed document never really intended to lead to program change. We have been describing a wholly different approach to writing program assessment throughout this book and, in particular, in this concluding chapter: an assessment designed with full attention from the start to open consultation, thoughtful consideration of the constructs embodied in the local context, awareness of the substantial literature on writing program assessment, accumulation of a wide range of evidence leading to student learning, full documentation of the validity of that evidence, attention to the consequences following from the program, and a richly documented report that leads to improvement as well as assessment of the writing program. To support the DFA model, we here recall Figure 1.1 to remind readers that writing program assessment is part of the family of postsecondary assessment and Figure 3.6 to suggest that the DFA study framework is not an event but a recurrent research process. As part of this family and its processes (Maki 2010), communication of information—ever rhetorical in orientation and thus sensitive to audience, purpose, and setting—must occur in both print and multimodal forms.

What might our WPA do with the concepts represented in Figure 5.1? Let's imagine she had read the very book you are now reading when she was a graduate student at one of the PhD programs in rhetoric and composition/writing studies. Combined with her graduate school experiences, she had come to believe, more or less, in the themes identified above because she found their music attuned to her experiences. As she designed her strategic plan, she had also used DFA principles from the very start.

When she opened her office door and sat at her desk after the meeting described in the scenario earlier in this chapter, she was thus able to open her computer and file cabinet to find rich sources of evidence she had been accumulating all along. Hers was not, therefore, a mad scramble at compliance; rather, it was an act that, while not quite celebratory, was nevertheless comforting. Here was a documentary act.

Following Gallagher (2012), she knew well that consequence must preceded outcomes, so she had worked hard with her chair and dean to bring the writing and literature faculty together under a common program mission for the department. Using constructive alignment (Biggs and Tang 2011), she was able to map institutional mission to program mission, program mission to syllabus, and syllabus to assignment. Sometimes the direction was clear, and sometimes it was not, but a process was underway.

As the concurrent process of local theory building had begun—Kane (2006) has called this occurrence "mini-theory"—it was becoming clear that information was coming in from the faculty regarding both genre and sequence. While the academic essay would remain the mainstay genre, student evaluations noted how much they liked working in multimodal environments, especially when collaborative wikis were involved. The faculty who taught sophomore-level literature classes noted that when the audience shifted—when, for example, the students developed wikis for other students who would take the class in the future—enthusiasm for the literature rose considerably. Substantial local evidence was accumulating that indicated that if multimodal writing assignments were interspersed with traditional academic essays, both tenacity and grades rose considerably.

In light of standpoint, such collaborations among the once-warring factions of literature and writing studies were lending themselves to greater identification of elements of the writing construct that led to student success. Attention was now being drawn to the interpersonal and intrapersonal domains of the construct, and the tutors in the writing center were beginning to ask very directed questions based on Brick City's construct model about the ways students approached assignments.

Such elements of process would be difficult to capture in ePortfolios directly, so surveys were being designed to get a better sense of the noncognitive domains of writing. These could then be compared to the reflective statements students prepared in the ePortfolios. After one year, good information was being collected on the relationship of Phase 2 scores to criterion variables such as course grades and grade point average. Because ePortfolios were used for program assessment—and never to hold a student back or question an instructor's grade—they were gaining momentum as a part of the environment of Brick City's writing program and as part of the classes that would truly help students display their skills for all to see. The pride was often palpable—and not just from the students.

And because the scores and the related analyses performed with the support of the Office of Institutional Research were always available, this aspect of DFA was increasingly becoming of more interest to administrators. As first-year remediation rates declined and grades remained the same, administrators seemed more and more willing to redirect those resources to the digital literature and writing-in-the-disciplines initiative. Just as the ePortfolios had great face validity for the students, so too did the statistical evidence have validity for the administrators. Documentary evidence came in many forms.

Because accountability was high in this new environment, funds had been secured from a number of sources, both from within and beyond Brick City. A group of local employers had seen the ePortfolios at the annual advisory-board meetings and had allocated seed funds for their expansion into the capstone seminars. And because presentations and publications were part of the DFA initiative from the beginning, early reports were being accepted at conferences. So, along with a demonstration of program mission and program management, the WPA could forward information to the dean to demonstrate external funding and scholarly productivity.

Instructional efficiency, she knew, would continue to be a problem. For some in the administration, the digital emphasis in world literature seemed like an opportunity to expand class size. If the lectures were always available, they argued, why not expand the classes to include additional remote-learning classes with larger class sizes? For the present, the WPA had been able to redirect such questions to the category of innovational instructional methodologies and technologies that would be of benefit to retention and graduation. With the literature faculty, she planned a new podcast series for the next year about writing in digital environments in order to create a series of digital artifacts that would help students complete the often-complex assignments that demanded small class sizes.

Was all of this sustainable? In terms of undergraduate success, it certainly was promising if the university wanted to continue its competitive retention and graduation rates. Brick City was far above national graduation and retention rates and thus had continued to receive excellent federal support. The predictions in 2014 had come true, and those institutions who had not been active in ensuring that admitted students gained the support they needed to succeed had either entirely lost funding such as Pell Grants or had their funding substantially reduced. But not at Brick City. Because the writing program had played a major part in raising the retention rates and was frequently cited as providing hallmark experiences for graduating students, it was apparent that resources were being used wisely to support student learning.

Because the processes of DFA had been inclusive from the beginning, both alumni and the business community had been involved. These colleagues had been invaluable in supporting both the digital-communication and genre-expansion efforts. Citing the importance of writing in both academic and nonacademic settings, these advisors had provided credible evidence of the need to continue the writing-in-the-disciplines efforts, especially the ePortfolios that would lend a competitive edge to graduates.

A few hours after the meeting, the WPA had uploaded to the dean's website the information she would need to begin work on the matrix. There were ePortfolio scores and their relationship to other student-performance measures; there were surveys and reports; and there were lists of faculty presentations and publications. Of the nine essential elements—in reality, categories of evidence—the dean had called for in the morning, our WPA was able to provide substantial, meaningful information for each. The hour was late but the job was done. In documenting the work of her colleagues, perhaps there was something to celebrate after all.

The implication of the longstanding call by the field of rhetoric and composition/writing studies for the type of localism illustrated in our case study is thus clear: the methods and methodologies of all writing studies research is given context and meaning in specific institutional sites. The current research practices described in Nickoson and Sheridan (2012) are most meaningfully undertaken when an important, significant construct model is examined collaboratively within and beyond institutional settings. Planned approaches to writing program assessment, developed locally and coordinated among institutions, hold the possibility to transform theory and research in our field (Rose and Weiser 1999, 2002).

THE SENSE OF AN ENDING: DOWN TO YOU

Imagine running into the three authors of this book, alone or together, between sessions at a conference, or, perhaps, at dinner. Maybe over late-night coffee and drinks.

At the end of our book, as at the beginning, we find the most immediate audience for our book. In these pages, we have chatted with friends in our field within earshot of those at other tables who have listened in. We have used language that did not exist when we were in school. That language has helped us map the territory of writing program assessment.

So much, you will say, remains to be done. Doesn't a history need to be written of writing program assessment? How representative are our experiences? Are the standards presented here constrained or ambitious? And what of this audacious DFA model? Isn't it just a theory? Will it work? How shall we begin?

In 1974, when the authors were younger, perhaps the very age you are now, Joni Mitchell (1974) released *Court and Spark*. It was a terrific album. "Help Me" came out as a single and hit the charts, reaching number two on Billboard during the summer. We listened on the beach as we read Robert M. Pirsig's *Zen and the Art of Motorcycle Maintenance*. While not exactly sure of our destination, we were all going somewhere. "Everything comes and goes," Mitchell sang, "marked by lovers and styles of clothes." It all seemed very right, sad and hopeful at once. Solidarity was in the air. Because we were brutes and angels, crawlers and flyers, we were at one with the song's final line: "It's down to you. It all comes down to you."

And so, dear reader, it does.

QUESTIONS FOR WRITING PROGRAM FACULTY AND ADMINISTRATORS: DESIGN

Background

In this set of questions, we have taken the most important concepts from chapter 5 and turned them into questions for writing program faculty and administrators. The Design for Assessment (DFA) framework we offer in this final chapter has multiple origins: the tradition of American Psychological Association documents beginning in 1954 recommending established testing standards; the unified validation theories of Messick

(1989) and Kane (2006, 2013); the challenges to those unified systems by Borsboom (2005) and Markus and Borsboom (2013); the evidence-centered design concept of Mislevy, Almond, and Lukas (2004) and Mislevy, Steinberg, and Almond (2002); the argument-centered logic of Toulmin (1958/2003) and its adaptation to measurement by Mislevy (2007); calls for localism by Huot (1996, 2002); calls for attention to race formation by Inoue and Poe (2012); calls for ethical considerations by Lynne (2004); and the ever-present theory of social justice by John Rawls (1971/1999). Because it is impossible to say which came first in the design of Figure 5.1, it is best to understand DFA under the universal framework of consequence: if we attend to the impact of what we do as the initial step in writing program assessment, then what follows will be—at the very least—sensitive to context.

Introduction

Mislevy, Steinberg, and Almond (2002) propose that an evidence-centered design (ECD) perspective toward educational measurement guides the way we conceptualize students, the way they are assessed, the rubrics we use, and the tasks we design. Such a design allows us to test our intuitions to see if they affect students the way we want them and believe them to do. In offering the DFA perspective for writing program assessment, we extend the model to assure that the development and assessment of the program is conducted locally—so when visitors come to call, that which is documented has been documented for a single purpose: to advance student learning.

Questions

The following questions are intended to allow local tailoring of the DFA model. Answering these questions will help your institution to build a well-designed, publicly accountable writing program with a defined mission, selectively developed objectives, and key measures of program performance—a program that will be positively evaluated by any external agency associated with accreditation while it demonstrates its importance and effectiveness to various campus constituencies.

1. In "Democracy, Struggle, and the *Praxis* of Assessment," Scott and Brannon (2013) claim that "assessment as a global programmatic mandate masks the local, specific, and situated practices of student writers and their teachers" (296). How can the genre of program assessment

advance the "open, democratic, intellectual life" Scott and Brannon advocate as essential to our profession? How does a poorly designed writing program assessment fail to support such an intellectual life?

2. What are the advantages and limits to the environmental view of writing program assessment? As a thought experiment, how could your own knowledge and experiences and those of your colleagues in the writing program enable program assessment to be used to advance instructor knowledge as an essential component of the writing program?

3. In the imaginary case study of the College of Social and Humanistic Studies, we present a likely scenario in which program review becomes a central activity of a postsecondary institution. Based on the nine essential elements of program review used to create the index of institutional effectiveness, design your own index of writing program effectiveness. How will you select the categories for the index? How will the index help you to communicate the aims of your writing program and secure the resources necessary to ensure its effectiveness?

4. Take a look back at the book and the questions you have answered thus far. Then, use Table 5.3 to answer the questions in the second column. Refer to the glossary for any unfamiliar terms as you create this table of tropes of writing program assessment tailored to your own institution.

5. Based on Figure 5.1, tailor the DFA framework to your local institution's writing program. As you define the core concepts in terms of your own institution, pay special attention to the consequences of DFA use on various writing program stakeholders. What advantages are gained by anticipating consequence as the first step in the program assessment process?

6. Based on Figure 5.1, define the cycle of assessment for the writing program. Based on the strategic plan drafted above, what might the assessment cycle be for the various writing program elements?

7. How will the varied efforts of the writing program be documented so any stakeholder can readily learn about the program and, if necessary, perform an independent assessment?

8. In the questions following chapter 1, we imagined it would take at least one year to articulate community-based answers to the questions raised by the DFA model. Based on the answers you have now provided at the end of each chapter, what is a realistic time frame for your institution to undertake assessment of its writing program?

Table 5.3. Writing program assessment: From belief system to practice.

Trope	Local Definition
Rhetoric and Composition/ Writing Studies (CIP 23.13)	What is the ontological, epistemological, and axiological basis—the working theory—for the writing program at your institution?
Modeling the Writing Construct	How is the writing construct modeled in the many locations—placement procedures, credit-bearing courses, writing center tutoring, and online student support—where writing is taught and assessed?
Ecology	How can you best describe the ecology of writing as it exists within your institution? How is that local ecology related to the field of rhetoric and composition/writing studies?
History	What does the history of the writing program at your institution reveal?
Accountability	How does the writing program presently document its accountability to its various constituencies?
Validity Evidence	What are the most promising categories of validity evidence at your institution?
Validation Process	How are these sources of evidence then used to strengthen the process of validation, exposition, and persuasion that are preconditions of effective communication?
Phase 2 Portfolio Assessment	How can Phase 2 portfolio assessment serve as a way to undertake longitudinal studies of student performance across courses and time?
Nomothetic Span and Idiographic Representation	Focusing only on the construct of writing, how does rejection of value dualism allow unfettered examination of instruction and assessment?
Reporting Standards	What reporting standards can be adopted at your institution to assure that high-quality research that is replicable, aggregable, and data supported is conducted and used to improve student writing ability.
Strategic Planning	How can a strategic plan be created for the writing program around the following writing program elements: institutional mission; program mission; program management; research expenditures; scholarly productivity; instructional efficiency and equity; innovative instructional methodologies and technologies; undergraduate- and graduate-program success; alumni response; community engagement; and faculty strength and student diversity? For each of these categories, identify the following: objectives, responsible groups, targets, communication processes, and impact.
Contingency	How does your writing program plan for contingent circumstances that may influence the improvement of student learning?

GLOSSARY

This glossary provides definitions of terms associated with writing program assessment as presented in this book. We have not attempted to be comprehensive in this large and complex field of study by duplicating existing assessment glossaries in the field of rhetoric and composition/writing studies (Johnson and Elliot 2010; Lauer and Asher 1988; O'Neill, Moore, and Huot 2009) and the field of educational assessment, testing, and measurement (Odendahl 2011; Yarbrough et al. 2011). Useful glossaries are also available in books on social-research methods (Trochim and Donnelly 2008) and basic statistics (Levin, Fox, and Forde 2014; Lockhart 1998); readers interested in extending their knowledge beyond our focus should consult such sources for key terms associated with qualitative and quantitative measurement. We do provide citations establishing origins and uses of these terms as they apply to writing program assessment throughout the book.

We are aware that different terms sometimes reveal similar underlying concepts and similar terms sometimes relate to different concepts. For a scholarly examination of this problem, consult the charmingly named *jangle fallacy* in psychological measurement (Pellegrino and Hilton 2012). As all scholars know, definition is difficult to control. Indeed, terminology is especially difficult to manage when adopting the multidisciplinary approach advanced in this book. We have therefore cross-referenced terms in italics so that the emerging body of knowledge regarding writing program assessment may be seen as a coherent taxonomy.

accountability. As a demonstration of accepted responsibility and wise resource allocation achieved by frameworks such as Design for Assessment, accountability allows instructors and administrators to present their curricular aims to key stakeholders, identify challenges of meeting these aims, and establish plans for the program's future (see Figure 5.1). The term is sometimes used in political discourse (outside the purview of this book) in reductive ways, holding single causes or individuals accountable for complex situations.

accreditation. As planned demonstrations of *accountability*, accreditation is awarded by membership organizations that voluntarily engage in a process of program review. During this process, evaluation teams determine the extent to which institutions and their educational programs are in compliance with designated standards ensuring academic quality (see Figure 1.1).

aim. As the stated objectives of an assessment episode, the aim of an assessment determines its interpretation and consequence (see Figure 3.3). Establishing *fairness, reliability,* and *validity* is essential to assessment.

assessment. With its origin in the Latin *assidere*, "to sit beside," assessment is an integrative process that uses a wide variety of *documentation* for the purpose of *accountability* (see Figure 1.1).

axiology. The axiology of an assessment deals with its underlying value and is influenced by the ontology (beliefs) and epistemology (knowledge) of the assessment *stakeholders*.

bias. Understood as the unintended or intended aspects of an assessment that may disadvantage or advantage certain groups in terms of gender, race/ethnicity, LGBTQ identification, or socioeconomic status, the identification and elimination of bias is important to establishing *validity evidence* used, in turn, to support the *validity argument.*

body of knowledge. As the domain of a profession, a body of knowledge is the expression of its concepts and activities. BOK initiatives are evident in *consensus models* such as the *WPA Outcomes Statement*, the *Framework for Success in Post-Secondary Writing*, and the Society for Technical Communication Body of Knowledge Initiative (see Figure 2.4).

causal inference. For a pattern of cause and effect to be established as a form of *relational modeling*, four conditions must be present: covariation, lack of spurious relationships, logical sequence, and theorization. Because of the difficulty of establishing causal inference in complex educational environments, *relational modeling* is also used to draw inferences regarding the *writing construct.*

cognitive domain. Along with *intrapersonal* and *interpersonal domains*, the cognitive domain is defined as those critical-thinking strategies used to accomplish a specific and usually complex mental task (see Figure 3.1).

communication. In writing program assessment, communication is defined as the process of providing information to a wide variety of stakeholders through diverse genres—from narrative strategies to empirical techniques—in both print and multimodal forms. (For communication processes associated with *strategic planning*, see Figure 5.1 and Table 5.1.)

confidence interval. As a range of scores expected to capture the mean score of a given population, a CI provides evidence that the parameter of interest will be included within a predetermined probability.

consensus models. Offered by experts, consensus models draw on empirical studies to define domains so that *nomothetic spans* may be developed that, in turn, produce instances of *idiographic representation.*

consequence. Informed by its relationship to *fairness*, consequence takes four forms: unintended negative, unintended positive, intended negative, and intended positive (see Figures 3.3 and 5.2).

construct. As an attribute (such as the ability of students to write effectively), a construct is the explanation—drawn from the *domain* of all possible *variables* associated with the attribute—of the behavior observed in the *construct sample.*

construct irrelevance. As a threat to validity, construct irrelevance occurs when an assessment *episode* includes *variables* in the *construct sample* that are not part of the *construct* under examination.

construct modeling. Prerequisite to *relational modeling*, construct modeling is defined as the study of relationships among variables (see Figures 2.3 and 3.3).

construct representation. As a precise expression of the *construct* as represented in the *construct sample*, construct representation is designed to give the most appropriate expression of the construct as determined by the assessment aim.

construct sample. Defined as a particular instance of a given *construct*, the construct sample is a specific and therefore limited instance of *construct representation* used in an assessment *episode*.

construct underrepresentation. As a threat to validity, construct underrepresentation occurs when a given assessment fails to measure the *construct* in a meaningful way.

construct validity. As a part of *validation*, construct validity provides evidence that the *construct model* used in a specific assessment episode has been defined appropriately for the assessment aim.

constructed response. A constructed response is the particular type of task used to elicit a student response in a given *construct sample*. In program assessment, the constructed-response task is the embodiment of *nomothetic span* mapped and expressed in *idiographic representation*. As such, a constructed-response task asks students to respond to a given task to demonstrate specific abilities in relation to the *writing construct*.

constructive alignment. Constructive alignment is an integrated instructional and assessment framework used to *map* learning activities to outcomes. Constructive alignment links learning activities at the level of institutional mission to the syllabus at the level of the course. Such mapping allows those involved in assessment of the writing program to *document* the ways the program uses available resources to advance student learning (see Tables 3.1 and 3.2).

core competencies. A detailed expression of the *nomothetic span* of a particular program, core competencies are those *variables* (or *traits*) identified as most important for student development and career success.

cost effectiveness. A form of cost-benefit analysis focusing on *ingredients* and their associated costs and *consequences*, cost-effectiveness analysis is especially useful in an economic framework for writing program assessment (see Figure 3.3).

criterion measure. As a comprehensive, real-life measure of a *construct* such as course grades or occupational employment, the criterion measure is independent of the assessment itself (see Table 4.4).

design. The art of anticipating function, design is an important aspect of the many activities of those who teach and assess writing. An emphasis on *Design for Assessment* interrupts the incorrect association of administration with mere bureaucratic management.

Design for Assessment. As an *accountability* framework and form of *relational modeling*, Design for Assessment (DFA) is a dynamic conceptual model that allows a postsecondary institution to identify the *variables* that impact the writing program and to *ecologically model* the variables to increase student success. The framework advances a component design emphasizing *consequence, theorization, standpoint, research, documentation, accountability, sustainability, processes,* and *communication* (see Figure 5.1 and Table 5.1).

disaggregation. A process of analyzing *scores* in terms of unique populations, disaggregation of assessment results provides *stakeholders* with precise information about all groups within the *sampling plan* (see Figure 3.3).

disparate impact. Disparate impact is defined as the unintended racial differences in outcomes resulting from policies or practices intended to be neutral and that on the surface appear to lack *bias*.

documentation. With its origin in the Latin *docere*—"to teach"—documentation is defined as the process of gathering evidence in order to provide information within a given context. Design for Assessment is intended to provide a capacious opportunity to document the efforts of all involved with the writing program to advance student learning (see Figure 5.1 and Table 3.3).

domain(s). As a universe of all known and potential instances of a given *construct*, a domain is defined as the observed and latent *variables* under examination (see Figure 3.1).

ecological model. An institutionally embedded form of *construct modeling and relational modeling*, ecological modeling calls for attention to *documenting* the experiences that inform students' growth as writers.

episode. As a specific instance of *construct representation* taken in a *construct sample*, an assessment episode is a planned occasion to gather validity evidence used, in turn, to support the *aim* of the assessment.

ePortfolios. Maintained by students across the curriculum and into workplace and graduate school, ePortfolios are *documentary* efforts that showcase *core competencies*. To be part of program assessment, ePortfolios must be designed to be *scored* by *Phase 2* methods (see Figures 2.2, 3.4, and 3.5 and Table 3.4).

extrapolation. Extrapolation is defined as the study of relationships among the construct under investigation and related constructs (see Figures 3.1 and 3.3).

face validity. As a general, impressionistic reaction to the ability of an assessment to cover a construct, face validity is a qualitative, often nonmeasurable component of the *validity argument*.

fairness. Defined in *assessment* as justifiable score use for population subgroups and individuals within them, fairness is pursued through the elimination of *disparate impact*. Along with *reliability* and *validity*, establishing fairness is an essential *aim* of *assessment*.

generalization. Generalization is the study of scores as they represent the *construct* (see Figure 3.3).

idiographic representation. Idiographic representation is a particular instance of *nomothetic span* in a given *domain*. Because idiographic representations are detailed and specific, they are the best way to study the more constant and general taxonomies of the *writing construct* (see Figure 3.2).

impact. The consequences of actions during the designated *strategic planning* period, impact analysis yields a sense of reflection in advance of programmatic action (see Figure 5.1 and Table 5.1).

ingredients. As a method of estimating costs, an ingredients framework facilitates identification of each element necessary to achieve a desired aim. The ingredients are then analyzed for their costs and benefits. While personnel, facilities, and equipment are among the most common elements of writing programs, full cost accounting may be accomplished by identifying the costs associated with the components of the Design for Assessment model (see Figure 5.1).

interpersonal domain. Along with *cognitive* and *intrapersonal domains*, the interpersonal domain is defined as those collaborative strategies used to accomplish a specific task (see Figure 3.1).

interpretation and use argument. As the argument used to advance the interpretation or use of scores from an assessment, the IUA argument allows *validation* to be viewed as an interpretative process with important *consequences* (see Figure 3.5).

intrapersonal domain. Along with *cognitive* and *interpersonal domains*, the intrapersonal domain is defined as those personality strategies of an individual used to accomplish a specific task (see Figure 3.1).

just-qualified student. The just-qualified student represents a category of learner for whom a specific curriculum is neither too easy nor too difficult. Determination of imagined success or failure is made by experts who examine actual student performance on a *construct model* to determine a course of action related to course placement, curricular advancement, and graduation.

mapping. Associated with *constructive alignment*, mapping allows a particular *domain* to be situated along with others. In program assessment, mapping allows the domain of the *writing construct* to be mapped to a given *construct sample*; as such, the *constructed-response task* used in that sample can then be used to link elicited student performance back to the taxonomy itself (see Tables 3.1 and 3.2).

mission. *Strategic planning* begins with the stated, general direction of the institution, serving to unify all stakeholders in a common pursuit. The mission is expressed in terms of core areas of expertise in instruction, research, and service. The writing program's mission, clearly defined and publicly accessible, demonstrates how it interprets instruction, research, and service to support its host institution. Writing program assessment focuses on the way a writing program fulfills its mission (see Table 5.1).

modeling. An identification of *variables* related to *construct modeling, relational modeling,* and *ecological modeling*, modeling is expressed as the visual representation of the *variables* of the *domain* of a given *construct* (see Figures 2.3, 2.4, 3.1, and 3.2).

nomothetic span. In general, nomothetic span is defined as the taxonomy of a given *domain*. Because such taxonomies tend to remain both constant and general, they are best expressed in the context of unique *idiographic representation* (see Figures 2.4 and 3.1).

null hypothesis. A form of heuristic reasoning, the null hypothesis is a statement that there will be no statistically significant difference in assessment results between or among groups. This process is designed to prevent confirmation bias—the human tendency to distort evidence in order to prove a study's hypothesis. To disprove the null hypothesis, a *validation argument* is required.

objective. As the aim of the *strategic priority*, an objective is expressed in very specific terms that will yield observable action. Precise, measureable objectives are at the center of *strategic planning* (see Table 5.2).

outcomes. Defined as the results of a curriculum for those students it was intended to serve, outcomes are expressed as statements of expected student performance at designated points in the curriculum. Articulating common *cognitive, interpersonal,* and *intrapersonal* domains, model outcome statements are found in the *WPA Outcomes Statement*, the *Framework for Success in Post-Secondary Writing*, and the STC Body of Knowledge Initiative.

Phase 2. Phase 2 *scoring* is a method of *ePortfolio* assessment that yields multiple scores based on *core competencies*. Key to Phase 2 scoring is the reflective statement that, combined with the requirement of *core competencies*, allows the ePortfolios to achieve a rhetorical sensitivity to audience, purpose, and setting—thus ensuring that the ePortfolio will not become a mere digital filing cabinet of student work (see Figure 2.3 and Tables 2.3, 3.3, 4.2, and 4.4).

process. As the varied actions that result in program success, the process of *validation* reinforces contemporary views of validity important to writing program assessment. Applying process and postprocess models of writing studies offers a view that stands in contrast to assessment as a mere stamp of approval (see Figure 5.1).

RAD research. Replicable, aggregable, and data-supported research allows writing programs to examine their local empirical measurements in comparison to state, regional, national, and international studies. As such, RAD research allows the body of knowledge of writing studies to advance (see Figure 4.1 and Tables 4.1, 4.2, 4.3, 4.4, 4.5, and 4.6).

relational modeling. Based on *construct modeling*, relational modeling is the study of associations between predictor *variables* (or *X*, the independent *variables*) as they contribute to a defined outcome (or *Y*, the dependent *variable*) (see Figure 2.3).

reliability. As a measure of consistency and precision across replications of an assessment, reliability establishes dependability. In certain kinds of assessment, reliability is a precondition to *validity*. Along with *fairness* and *validity*, reliability is an essential *aim* of assessment.

research. As the foundation for knowledge and decisions, research that accompanies writing program assessment is valuable to the institution and enhances the *body of knowledge* of writing studies (see Figure 5.1).

response processes. Response processes are studies of examinees and other stakeholders of the assessment as they engage the *writing construct* (see Figure 3.3).

responsible groups. Defined as those who will lead strategic priorities during a *strategic planning* period, group membership should be established across the institution. Such multidisciplinary membership assures that writing instruction and assessment become shared institutional responsibilities (Table 5.2).

sampling plan. As a method used to determine a representative part of a larger population, a sampling plan allows researchers to determine if the sample size captures a sufficiently robust population segment, determined by a *CI*, to achieve the research *aim* (see chapter 4, equations 1 and 2).

scoring. Part of the process of *validation* used to support *the validity argument*, scoring is defined as accuracy and consistency of observations leading to evidence of *reliability* (see Figure 3.3).

stakeholder. Advisory boards, administration, faculty and instructional staff, parents, professional organizations, students, and the public—each group is a key stakeholder of the writing program and its assessment (see Table 5.2).

standardization. With the *aim* of producing valid information, standardization is the use of uniform conditions to ensure that the results of the assessment are valid.

standpoint. As a theoretical framework, standpoint is based on two concepts: situated knowledge (location systematically influences our experiences) and epistemic advantage (standpoints of marginalized or oppressed groups allow distinctly valuable interpretations) (see Figure 5.1).

strategic planning. As the sum of activities associated with advancing the *mission* of the writing program, strategic planning is a collaborative *design* process that establishes a clear, longitudinal direction. Components of a strategic plan include the following: *strategic priorities, objectives,* those *responsible groups* who will advance the priorities, *targets, communication processes,* and anticipated *impact.* Strategic planning also includes *cost-effectiveness* analysis.

strategic priority. The major theme the writing program has decided to pursue for the designated *strategic planning* period, a strategic priority is expressed by a unique emphasis given to a general academic domain (Tables 5.1 and 5.2).

sustainability. Incorporating the fact that resources are allocated under conditions of scarcity, sustainability is the process of planning that focuses on past actions, present decisions, and future developments. Such focus allows key boundaries to be established so the writing program can fulfill its *mission* (see Figures 3.3 and 5.1).

targets. As aims for the designated *strategic planning* period, targets are expressed in measurable terms (see Figure 5.1 and Tables 5.1 and 5.2).

theorization. A process including the development, articulation, measurement, communication, and refinement of ideas concerning the *domain* of a given *construct,* theories may be developed through empirical studies, consensus models, historical and philosophical precedent, and a combination of such techniques and traditions (see Figure 5.1).

theory-based interpretation. Theory-based interpretation is driven by the process of *theorization.* A well-defined theory must be in place for any assessment; without such a firm theory, interpretation of empirical information is meaningless (see Figure 3.3).

trait. Synonymous with variable, a trait is a category that varies across time and circumstance. In a writing assessment episode using procedures such as Phase 2 scoring, trait scoring—producing multiple *scores*—yields information about the *writing construct* and how it is *modeled.*

transformation. A process of reconceptualization that emphasizes *ecological modeling,* transformation allows the *writing construct* to be re-imagined and re-interpreted as part of the *assessment* process (see Figures 3.3 and 5.1).

trope. With deeply philosophical associations of ontological essence, a trope is the unique turn of thought understood to reveal the essence of a belief system. In literature, a trope is understood as a recurring theme.

validation. A planned, predetermined method of identifying and investigating a *domain* as represented in a construct sample to assure that scores have meaning that supports the consequences of their use.

validation argument. As the persuasive position used to support the use of scores in a given assessment, the validity argument is advanced to stakeholders, who may then examine the argument to justify, question, or reject, the proposed *interpretation and use* and related *consequences* of an assessment (see Figure 3.5).

validity. As a deeply situated rhetorical statement used to explicate and interpret research, validity is defined as the extent to which evidence supports claims. Along with *fairness* and *reliability,* establishing validity is an essential *aim* of *assessment.*

validity evidence. Defined as a wide range of *documentation,* validity evidence is used to justify *interpretation and use* and related *consequences* of an assessment. This book identifies twelve sources of validity evidence to accompany writing program assessment: *aim, consequence, construct modeling, scoring, disaggregation, generalization, response processes, extrapolation, theory-based interpretation, cost effectiveness, sustainability, and transformation* (see Figure 3.3 and Table 3.3).

value dualism. Disjunctive pairs in which terms are seen as oppositional rather than complementary, value dualisms are often paired with value hierarchies—conceptualizations of diversity organized by metaphors associated with value.

variable(s). A broad category that varies across time and circumstance, variables are synonymous with traits and occur in both observed and latent forms. In terms of the *writing construct*, variables are those domains associated with defined communication environments; interactions within those environments; rhetorical expression; cognitive, interpersonal, and intrapersonal domains; and neurological, attention, and visual capacity (see Figure 3.1).

writing construct. As both the *nomothetic span* of writing and its *idiographic representation* in *construct samples*, the writing construct is that explanation of writing that informs a writing program and its assessment (see Figures 3.1 and 3.2).

writing program. Ranging from a defined *writing construct* to an articulated *research agenda*, a writing program is defined by a series of integrated activities *designed* to advance student learning. Under an *ecosystem model*, an institution's writing program is characterized by a constant and iterative process that results in improved instruction and student success throughout the curriculum.

writing program assessment. As a *documentation* effort, writing program assessment is the act *validating* that those *responsible* for the program have advanced its *mission*. Interpreted in this book as a planned, recurrent effort undertaken within a Design for Assessment perspective, writing program assessment should be undertaken at the local level of the institution and its students (see Figures 1.1, 3.6, 5.1 and Tables 3.3, 5.1, and 5.2).

writing theory. As a long-standing and critical practice in writing studies, the formulation of theory allows knowledge to be gathered in the following categories: typology, norms, modality, sequence, practice, reception, and cognition. Without a well-defined theory of writing, *theory-based interpretation* is not possible.

REFERENCES

Addison, Joanne, and Sharon James McGee. 2010. "Writing in High School/Writing in College: Research Trends and Future Directions." *College Composition and Communication* 62 (1): 147–79. http://dx.doi.org/10.2307/27917889.

Adler-Kassner, Linda. 2008. *The Activist WPA: Changing Stories about Writing and Writers.* Logan: Utah State University Press.

Adler-Kassner, Linda, and Heidi Estrem. 2009. "The Journey Is the Destination." In *Organic Writing Assessment: Dynamic Criteria Mapping in Action,* edited by Bob Broad, 1–13. Logan: Utah State University Press.

Adler-Kassner, Linda, and Peggy O'Neill. 2010. *Reframing Writing Assessment.* Logan: Utah State University Press.

Allee, Warder Clyde, Orlando Park, Alfred E. Emerson, Thomas Park, and Karl P. Schmidt. 1949. *Principles of Animal Ecology.* Philadelphia: W. B. Saunders.

Alvarez, Tara. 2014. Personal communication with authors, March 29.

American Academy of Arts and Sciences. 2013. *The Heart of the Matter: The Humanities and Social Sciences for a Vibrant, Competitive, Secure Nation.* Cambridge, MA: American Academy of Arts and Sciences.

American Association of University Professors. 2014. "Survey Report Tables." *Academe: Magazine of the American Association of University Professors* 100 (2): 22–38.

American Educational Research Association (AERA), American Psychological Association (APA), and National Council on Measurement in Education (NCME). 2014. *Standards for Educational and Psychological Testing.* Washington, DC: American Educational Research Association.

Anderson, Paul, Chris Anson, Bob Gonyea, and Charles Paine. 2009. "Summary: The Consortium for the Study of Writing in College (CSWC)." Web.

Anson, Chris, ed. 1989. *Writing and Response: Theory, Practice, and Research.* Urbana, IL: National Council of Teachers of English.

Anson, Chris. 2008. "The Intelligent Design of Writing Programs: Reliance on Belief." *WPA: Writing Program Administration* 32 (1): 11–36.

Arum, Richard, and Josipa Roksa. 2011. *Academically Adrift: Limited Learning on College Campuses.* Chicago: University of Chicago Press.

Astin, Alexander W., and Anthony Lising Antonio. 2012. *Assessment for Excellence: The Philosophy and Practice of Assessment and Evaluation in Higher Education.* 2nd ed. Lanham, MD: Rowman & Littlefield/American Council on Education.

Bachman, Lyle. 2013. "How Is Educational Measurement Supposed to Deal with Test Use?" *Measurement: Interdisciplinary Research and Perspectives* 11 (1–2): 19–23. http://dx.doi.org/10.1080/15366367.2013.784150.

Bamberg, Betty. 1982. "Multiple-Choice and Holistic Essay Scores: What Are They Measuring?" *College Composition and Communication* 33 (4): 404–6. http://dx.doi.org/10.2307/357953.

DOI: 10.7330/9780874219869.c006

Bateson, Gregory. 1987. *Steps to an Ecology of the Mind: Collected Essays in Anthropology, Psychiatry, Evolution, and Epistemology*. Chicago: University of Chicago Press.

Bazerman, Charles. 1999. "Introduction: Changing Regularities of Genre." Special issue, *IEEE Transactions on Professional Communication* 42 (1): 1–2. http://dx.doi.org/10.11 09/TPC.1999.749361.

Bazerman, Charles, Joseph Little, Lisa Bethel, Teri Chavkin, Danielle Fouquette, and Janet Garufis. 2005. *Reference Guide to Writing Across the Curriculum*. West Lafayette, IN: Parlor.

Beaufort, Anne. 2007. *College Writing and Beyond: A New Framework for University Writing Instruction*. Logan: Utah State University Press.

Behm, Nicholas N., Gregory R. Glau, Deborah H. Holdstein, Duane Roen, and Edward M. White. 2012. *The WPA Outcomes Statement: A Decade Later*. Anderson, SC: Parlor.

Beiser, Frederick. C. 2011. "Wilhelm Windelband and the Forces of History." In *The German Historicist Tradition*, edited by Frederick C. Beiser, 365–92. London, UK: Oxford University Press. http://dx.doi.org/10.1093/acprof:oso/9780199691555.003.0010.

Bejar, Isaac I. 2012. "Rater Cognition: Implications for Validity." *Educational Measurement: Issues and Practice* 31 (3): 2–9. http://dx.doi.org/10.1111/j.1745-3992.2012.00238.x.

Bennett, Randy Elliott. 1993. "On the Meanings of Constructed Response." In *Construction vs. Choice in Cognitive Measurement: Issues in Constructed Response, Performance Testing, and Portfolio Assessment*, edited by Randy Elliot Bennett and William. C. Ward, 1–27. Hillsdale, NJ: Erlbaum.

Berliner, David C., and Bruce J. Biddle. 1995. *The Manufactured Crisis: Myths, Fraud and the Attack on America's Public Schools*. Reading, MA: Addison-Wesley.

Bernard, H. Russell. 2013. *Social Research Methods: Qualitative and Quantitative Approaches*. 2nd ed. Los Angeles: Sage.

Berthoff, Ann E. 1990. "Killer Dichotomies: Reading In/Reading Out." In *Farther Along: Transforming Dichotomies in Rhetoric and Composition*, edited by Kate Ronald and Hephzibah Roskelly, 15–24. Portsmouth: Boynton/Cook.

Biggs, John, and Catherine Tang. 2011. *Teaching for Quality Learning at University*. 4th ed. New York: McGraw-Hill.

Bijker, Wiebe E. 2003. "The Need for Public Intellectuals: A Space for STS: Pre-Presidential Address." *Science, Technology and Human Values* 28 (4): 443–50.

Bitzer, Lloyd. 1968. "The Rhetorical Situation." *Philosophy and Rhetoric* 1 (1): 1–14.

Bleich, David. 2013. *The Materiality of Language: Gender, Politics, and the University*. Bloomington: Indiana University Press.

Bloom, Harold. 2011. *The Anatomy of Influence: Literature as a Way of Life*. New Haven, CT: Yale University Press.

Bok, Derek. 2004. *Universities in the Marketplace: The Commercialization of Higher Education*. Princeton, NJ: Princeton University Press.

Bourdieu, Pierre. 1991. "Symbolic Power." In *Language and Symbolic Power*, edited by J. B. Thompson 163–70. Cambridge, MA: Harvard University Press.

Borsboom, Denny. 2005. *Measuring the Mind: Conceptual Issues in Contemporary Psychometrics*. Cambridge: Cambridge University Press. http://dx.doi.org/10.1017/CBO97805114 90026.

Borsting, Eric, G. Lynn Mitchell, Marjean T. Kulp, Mitchell Schieman, Deborah Amster, Susan Cotter, and the CITT Study Group. 2012. "Improvement in Academic Behaviors after Successful Treatment of Convergence Insufficiency." *Optometry and Vision Science* 89 (1): 12–8. http://dx.doi.org/10.1097/OPX.0b013e318238ffc3.

Bowen, William G., Matthew M. Chingos, and Michael S. McPherson. 2009. *Crossing the Finish Line: Completing College at America's Public Universities*. Princeton, NJ: Princeton University Press.

Braddock, Richard Reed, Richard Lloyd-Jones, and Lowell Schoer. 1963. *Research in Written Composition*. Urbana, IL: National Council of Teachers of English.

Bradley, Andrew Cecil. 1949. *Shakespearean Tragedy: Lectures on Hamlet, Othello, King Lear, Macbeth*. New York: Macmillan.

Brady, Laura. 2004. "A Case for Writing Program Evaluation." *WPA: Writing Program Administration* 28 (1–2): 79–94.

Brady, M. Ann, and Joanna Schreiber. 2013. "Static to Dynamic: Professional Identity as Inventory, Invention, and Performance in Classrooms and Workplaces." *Technical Communication Quarterly* 22 (4): 343–62. http://dx.doi.org/10.1080/10572252.2013.794089.

Brennan, Robert L. 2006. "Perspectives on the Evolution and Future of Educational Measurement." In *Educational Measurement*, 4th ed., edited by Robert L. Brennan, 1–16. Westport, CT: American Council on Education/Praeger.

Broad, Bob. 2003. *What We Really Value: Beyond Rubrics in Teaching and Assessing Writing*. Logan: Utah State University Press.

Broad, Bob. 2012. "Mapping a Dialectic with Edward M. White (in Four Scenes)." In *Writing Assessment in the 21st Century: Essays in Honor of Edward M. White*, edited by Norbert Elliot and Les Perelman, 259–69. New York: Hampton Press.

Broad, Bob, Linda Adler-Kassner, Barry Alford, Jane Detweiler, Hedi Estrem, Susanmarie Harrington, Maureen McBride, Eric Stalions, and Scott Weden. 2009. *Organic Writing Assessment: Dynamic Criteria Mapping in Action*. Logan: Utah State University Press.

Broer, Marcus, Yong-Won Lee, Saba Rizavi, and Don Powers. 2005. *Ensuring the Fairness of GRE Writing Prompts: Assessing Differential Difficulty* (GRE Research Report No. 02–07R, ETS Research Report No. RR–05–11). Princeton, NJ: ETS. http://dx.doi.org/10.1002/j.2333-8504.2005.tb01988.x.

Broome, Edwin Cornelius. 1903. *A Historical and Critical Discussion of College Admission Requirements*. New York: Macmillan.

Brown, James Cooke. 2008. *Loglan 1: A Logical Language*. Ganesville, FL: The Loglan Institute. Web.

Bryson, John. 2011. *Strategic Planning for Public and Nonprofit Organizations: A Guide to Strengthening and Sustaining Organizational Achievement*. 4th ed. Hoboken, NJ: Wiley.

Burstein, Jill, and Norbert Elliot. 2014. "Disjuncture in School and Workplace Writing: A Study of Genre." Paper presented at the Annual Meeting of the National Council on Measurement in Education, Philadelphia, PA, April. Web.

Cambridge, Darren, Barbara Cambridge, and Kathleen Blake Yancey. 2009. *Electronic Portfolios 2.0: Emergent Research on Implementation and Impact*. Sterling, VA: Stylus.

Carroll, John B. 1993. *Human Cognitive Abilities: A Survey of Factor Analytic Studies*. Cambridge: Cambridge University Press.

Charney, David. 1996. "Empiricism Is Not a Four-Letter Word." *College Composition and Communication* 47 (4): 567–93. http://dx.doi.org/10.2307/358602.

Chen, Ai Hong, Willard Bleything, and Yee-Yin Lim. 2011. "Relating Vision Status to Academic Achievement among Year-2 School Children in Malaysia." *Optometry (St. Louis, Mo.)* 82 (5): 267–73. http://dx.doi.org/10.1016/j.optm.2011.02.004.

Chen, Huey T. 2015. *Practical Program Evaluation*. 2nd ed. Los Angeles: Sage Press.

Chernilo, Daniel. 2006. "Social Theory's Methodological Nationalism: Myth and Reality." *European Journal of Social Theory* 9 (1): 5–22. http://dx.doi.org/10.1177/1368431006060460.

Chomsky, Noam. 1957. *Syntactic Structures*. The Hague: Mouton.

Cizek, Gregory. J. 2008. "Assessing Educational Measurement: Ovations, Omissions, Opportunities." Review of *Educational Measurement*, 4th ed., by Robert L. Brennan. *Educational Researcher* 37 (2): 96–100. http://dx.doi.org/10.3102/0013189X08315727.

Cizek, Gregory. J., and Michael B. Bunch. 2007. *Standard Setting: A Guide to Establishing and Evaluating Performance Standards on Tests*. Thousand Oaks, CA: Sage Press.

Clauser, Brian E. 2000. "Recurrent Issues and Recent Advances in Scoring Performance Assessments." *Applied Psychological Measurement* 24 (4): 314–24. http://dx.doi.org/10.1177/01466210022031778.

Coetzee, J. M. 1980. *Waiting for the Barbarians*. New York: Penguin.

Cohen, Arthur M., and Carrie B. Kisker. 2010. *The Shaping of American Higher Education: Emergence and Growth of the Contemporary System*. San Francisco: Jossey-Bass.

Cohen, Jacob. 1992. "A Power Primer." *Psychological Bulletin* 112 (1): 155–59. http://dx.doi.org/10.1037/0033-2909.112.1.155.

Coles, Robert. 1998. *Doing Documentary Work*. New York: Oxford University Press.

College Board. 2013. *The 9th Annual AP® Report to the Nation*. New York: College Board. Web.

Collins, Regina, Norbert Elliot, Andrew Klobucar, and Fadi Deek. 2013. "Web-Based Portfolio Assessment: Validation of an Open Source Platform." *Journal of Interactive Learning Research* 24 (1): 5–32.

Condon, William. 2013. "Large-Scale Assessment, Locally-Developed Measures, and Automated Scoring of Essays: Fishing for Red Herrings?" *Assessing Writing* 18 (1): 100–8. http://dx.doi.org/10.1016/j.asw.2012.11.001.

Condon, William. 2014. Personal communication with authors, April 10.

Condon, William, and Carol Rutz. 2012. "A Taxonomy of Writing Across the Curriculum Programs: Evolving to Serve Broader Agendas." *College Composition and Communication* 64 (2): 357–82.

Conference on College Composition and Communication. 2007. *Principles and Practices in Electronic Portfolios*. Web.

Conference on College Composition and Communication. 2009. "Writing Assessment: A Position Statement." Web.

Connors, Robert. J. 1997. *Composition-Rhetoric: Backgrounds, Theory, and Pedagogy*. Pittsburgh: University of Pittsburgh Press.

Cooper, Charles R., and Lee Odell, eds. 1977. *Evaluating Writing: Describing, Measuring, Judging*. Urbana, IL: National Council of Teachers of English.

Cooper, Marilyn M. 1986. "The Ecology of Writing." *College English* 48 (4): 364–75. http://dx.doi.org/10.2307/377264.

Cooper, Peter L. 1984. *The Assessment of Writing Ability: A Review of Research* (ETS Research Report GREB 82-15R; ETS RR, 84-12). Princeton, NJ: Educational Testing Service.

Coppola, Nancy W. 2010. "The Technical Communication Body of Knowledge Initiative: An Academic-Practitioner Partnership." *Technical Communication* 57 (1): 11–25.

Coppola, Nancy, and Norbert Elliot. 2007. "A Technology Transfer Model for Program Assessment in Technical Communication." *Technical Communication* 54 (4): 459–74.

Coppola, Nancy W., and Norbert Elliot. 2010. "Assessment of Graduate Programs in Technical Communication." In *Assessment in Technical and Professional Communication*, edited by Margaret Hundleby and Jo Allen, 127–60. Amityville, NY: Baywood. http://dx.doi.org/10.2190/AITC9.

Coppola, Nancy W., and Norbert Elliot. 2013. "Conceptualizing the Technical Communication Body of Knowledge: Context, Metaphor, Direction." *Technical Communication* 60 (4): 267–78.

Corbett, Edward P. J. 1984. Introduction to *The Rhetoric and Poetics of Aristotle*, translated by W. Rys Roberts and Ingram Bywater, 5–26. New York: Modern Library.

CWPA. 2014. "WPA Outcomes Statement for First-Year Composition (Revisions adopted 17 July 2014)." *WPA: Writing Program Administration* 38 (1): 142–146.

CWPA, NCTE, and NWP. 2011. *Framework for Success in Postsecondary Writing*. Web.

Cronbach, Lee J. 1988. "Five Perspectives on Validity Argument." In *Test Validity*, edited by Howard Wainer and Henry I. Braun, 3–17. Hillsdale, NJ: Erlbaum.

Cronbach, Lee J. 1989. "Construct Validation after Thirty Years." In *Intelligence: Measurement, Theory, and Public Policy*, edited by Robert E. Linn, 147–71. Urbana: University of Illinois Press.

Cronbach, Lee J., and Paul E. Meehl. 1955. "Construct Validity in Psychological Tests." *Psychological Bulletin* 52 (4): 281–302. http://dx.doi.org/10.1037/h0040957.

Crusius, Timothy W. 1989. *Discourse: A Critique and Synthesis of Major Theories*. New York: Modern Language Association.

Das Bender, Gita. 2012. "Assessing Generation 1.5 Learners: The Revelations of Directed Self-Placement." In *Writing Assessment in the 21st Century: Essays in Honor of Edward M. White*, edited by Norbert Elliot and Les Perelman, 371–84. New York: Hampton.

De Raad, Boele. 2000. *The Big Five Personality Factors: The Psycholexical Approach to Personality*. Gottingen: Hogrefe and Huber.

Ding, Huiling, and Gerald Savage. 2013. "Guest Editors' Introduction: New Directions for Intercultural Professional Communication." *Technical Communication Quarterly* 22 (1): 1–9. http://dx.doi.org/10.1080/10572252.2013.735634.

DiPardo, Anne, Barbara A. Storms, and Makenzie Selland. 2011. "Seeing Voices: Assessing Writerly Stance in the NWP Analytic Continuum." *Assessing Writing* 16 (3): 170–88. http://dx.doi:10.1016/j.asw.2011.01.003.

Dryer, Dylan B. 2008. "The Persistence of Institutional Memory: Genre Uptake and Program Reform." *WPA: Writing Program Administration* 31 (3): 32–51.

Dryer, Dylan B., Darsie Bowden, Beth Brunk-Chavez, Susanmarie Harrington, Bump Halbritter, and Kathleen Blake Yancey. 2014. "Revising FYC Outcomes for a Multimodal, Digitally Composed World: The WPA Outcomes Statement for First-Year Composition (Version 3.0)." *WPA: Writing Program Administration* 38 (1): 127–41.

Edwards, Phillip, ed. 1985. *Hamlet, Prince of Denmark*, by William Shakespeare. Cambridge: Cambridge University Press.

Elbow, Peter. 2002. "Opinion: The Cultures of Literature and Composition: What Could Each Learn from the Other?" *College English* 64 (5): 533–46. http://dx.doi.org/10.2307/3250752.

Elbow, Peter. 2012. "Good Enough Evaluation: When Is It Feasible and When Is Evaluation Not Worth Having," In *Writing assessment in the 21st century: Essays in Honor of Edward M. White*, edited by Norbert Elliot and Les Perelman, 303–25. New York: Hampton.

Elbow, Peter, and Pat Belanoff. 1986. "Staffroom Interchange: Portfolios as a Substitute for Proficiency Examinations." *College Composition and Communication* 37 (3): 336–39. http://dx.doi.org/10.2307/358050.

Elliot, Norbert. 2005. *On a Scale: A Social History of Writing Assessment in America*. New York: Peter Lang.

Elliot, Norbert. 2014. *Henry Chauncey: An American Life*. New York: Peter Lang.

Elliot, Norbert. 2015. "Validation: The Pursuit." Review of *Standards for Educational and Psychological Testing*, American Educational Research Association, American Psychological Association, National Council on Measurement in Education. *College Composition and Communication* 66 (4): in press.

Elliot, Norbert, and Les Perelman, eds. 2012. *Writing Assessment in the 21st Century: Essays in Honor of Edward M. White*. New York: Hampton.

Elliot, Norbert, Perry Deess, Alex Rudniy, and Kamal Joshi. 2012. "Placement of Students into First-Year Writing Courses." *Research in the Teaching of English* 46 (3): 285–313.

Ellis, Paul D. 2010. *The Essential Guide to Effect Sizes: Statistical Power, Meta-analysis, and the Interpretation of Research Results*. Cambridge: Cambridge University Press.

Elman, Benjamin A. 2000. *A Cultural History of Civil Examinations in Late Imperial China*. Berkeley: University of California Press.

Elman, Benjamin A. 2009. "Civil Service Examinations." In *Berkshire Encyclopedia of China: Modern and Historic Views of the World's Newest and Oldest Global Power*, vol. 1, edited by Linsun Cheng, 405–10. Great Barrington, MA: Berkshire.

Embretson, S. 1983. "Construct Validity: Construct Representation versus Nomothetic Span." *Psychological Bulletin* 93 (1): 179–97. http://dx.doi.org/10.1037/0033-2909.93.1.179.

Englehard, George, and Stephanie A. Wind. 2013. "Educational Testing and Schooling: Unanticipated Consequences of Purposive Social Action." *Measurement* 11 (1–2): 30–35. http://dx.doi.org/10.1080/15366367.2013.784156.

Everett, Daniel L. 2012. *Language: The Cultural Tool.* New York: Vintage.

Feldman, Anne Merle. 2008. *Making Writing Matter: Composition in the Engaged University.* Albany: State University of New York Press.

Fish, Stanley. 1989. "Being Interdisciplinary Is So Very Hard to Do." *Profession* 89:15–22.

Fishman, Jenn. 2012. "Longitudinal Writing Research in (and for) the Twenty-First Century." In *Writing Studies Research and Practice: Methods and Methodologies,* edited by Lee Nickoson and Mary P. Sheridan, 171–82. Carbondale: Southern Illinois University Press.

Fleckenstein, Kristie S., Clay Spinuzzi, Rebecca J. Rickly, and Carole C. Papper. 2008. "The Importance of Harmony: An Ecological Metaphor for Writing Research." *College Composition and Communication* 60 (2): 388–419. http://dx.doi.org/10.2307/20457064.

Fleiss, Joseph L., and Jacob Cohen. 1973. "The Equivalence of Weighted Kappa and the Interclass Correlation Coefficient as Measures of Reliability." *Educational and Psychological Measurement* 33 (3): 613–19. http://dx.doi.org/10.1177/001316447303300309.

Flower, Linda, and John R. Hayes. 1981. "A Cognitive Process Theory of Writing." *College Composition and Communication* 32 (4): 365–87. http://dx.doi.org/10.2307/356600.

Foucault, Michel. 1979. *Discipline and Punish: The Birth of the Prison.* Translated by Alan Sheridan. New York: Vintage.

Fox, Rebecca, C. Stephan White, and Jie Tian. 2014. "Investigating Advanced Professional Learning of Early Career and Experienced Teachers through Portfolios." In *Reflectivity and Cultivating Student Learning: Critical Elements for Enhancing a Global Community of Learners and Educators,* edited by Edward G. Pultorak, 3–27. Lanham, MD: Rowman & Littlefield.

Fraiberg, Steven. 2010. "Composition 2.0: Toward a Multilingual and Multimodal Framework." *College Composition and Communication* 62 (1): 100–26. http://dx.doi.org/10.2307/27917886.

Fralix, Brandon, and Jill Gladstein. 2014. WPA listserv posting, January 6. Web.

Freeman, Melissa, Kathleen deMarrais, Judith Preissle, Kathryn Roulston, and Elizabeth A. St. Pierre. 2007. "Standards of Evidence in Qualitative Research: An Incitement to Discourse." *Educational Researcher* 36 (1): 25–32. http://dx.doi.org/10.3102/0013189X06298009.

Furness, Horace Howard, ed. 1877. "Hamlet." In *A New Variorum Edition of Shakespeare,* vols. 4. Philadelphia: J. B. Lippincott.

Gallagher, Chris. W. 2012. "The Trouble with Outcomes." *College English* 75 (1): 42–60.

George, Darren, and Paul Mallery. 2013. *IBM SPSS Statistics 21: Step by Step.* New York: Pearson.

Gere, Anne Ruggles. 1980. "Written Composition: Toward a Theory of Evaluation." *College English* 42 (1): 44–58. http://dx.doi.org/10.2307/376032.

Giles, Sandra L. 2010. "Reflective Writing and the Revision Process: What Were you Thinking?" In *Writing Spaces: Readings on Writing,* vol. 1, edited by Charles Lowe and Pavel Zemliansky, 191–204. Anderson, SC: Parlor.

Glaser, Barney G., and Anselm L. Strauss. 1967. *The Discovery of Grounded Theory: Strategies for Qualitative Research.* New Brunswick, NJ: Aldine Transactions.

Gold, David. 2008. *Rhetoric at the Margins: Revising the History of Writing Instruction in American Colleges, 1873–1947.* Carbondale: Southern Illinois University Press.

Gonyea, Robert M. 2014. Personal communication with authors, December 13.

Graham, Steve, and Dolores Perin. 2007. "A Meta-Analysis of Writing Instruction for Adolescent Students." *Journal of Educational Psychology* 99 (3): 445–76. http://dx.doi.org/10.1037/0022-0663.99.3.445.

Graham, Steve, and Karen Sandmel. 2011. "The Process Writing Approach: A Meta-Analysis." *Journal of Educational Research* 104 (6): 396–407. http://dx.doi:10.1080/00220671.2010.488703.

Haertel, Edward Henry. 2006. "Reliability." In *Educational Measurement,* 4th ed., edited by Robert L. Brennan, 65–110. Westport, CT: American Council on Education/Praeger.

Haertel, Edward Henry. 2013. "How Is Testing Supposed to Improve Schooling?" *Measurement: Interdisciplinary Research and Perspectives* 11 (1–2): 1–18. http://dx.doi.org/10.1080/15366367.2013.783752.

Hairston, Maxine. 1981. *Successful Writing: A Rhetoric for Advanced Composition.* New York: Norton.

Hamp-Lyons, Liz. 1986. "Testing Second Language Writing in Academic Settings." Unpublished PhD diss., University of Edinburgh, Edinburgh, UK.

Hamp-Lyons, Liz. 2012. "Linking Writing and Speaking in Assessing English as a Second Language Proficiency." In *Writing Assessment in the 21st Century: Essays in Honor of Edward M. White,* edited by Norbert Elliot and Les Perelman, 385–404. New York: Hampton.

Harcleroad, Fred F. 1980. "The Context of Academic Program Evaluation." In *Academic Program Evaluation,* edited by Eugene C. Craven, 1–20. San Francisco: Jossey-Bass.

Hardin, Garrett. 1968. "The Tragedy of the Commons." *Science* 162 (3859): 1243–48. http://dx.doi.org/10.1126/science.162.3859.1243.

Harrington, Susanmarie. 2013. "What Is Assessment?" In *A Rhetoric for Writing Program Administrators,* edited by Rita Malenczyk, 156–68. Anderson, SC: Parlor.

Harrington, Susanmarie, Keith Rhodes, Ruth Overman Fischer, and Rita Malenczyk, eds. 2005. *The WPA Outcomes Book: Debate and Consensus after the WPA Outcomes Statement.* Logan: Utah State University Press.

Harrington, Susanmarie, Rita Malencyzk, Irv Peckham, Keith Rhodes, and Kathleen Blake Yancey. 2001. "WPA Outcomes Statement for First-Year Composition." *College English* 63 (3): 321–25. http://dx.doi.org/10.2307/378996.

Harvey, David. 2010. *The Enigma of Capital and the Crises of Capitalism.* New York: Oxford University Press.

Haswell, Richard H. 2000. "Documenting Improvement in College Writing: A Longitudinal Approach." *Written Communication* 17 (3): 307–52. http://dx.doi.org/10.1177/0741088300017003001.

Haswell, Richard, ed. 2001. *Beyond Outcomes: Assessment and Instruction within a University Writing Program.* Westport, CT: Ablex.

Haswell, Richard. 2005. "NCTE/CCCC's Recent War on Scholarship." *Written Communication* 22 (2): 198–223. http://dx.doi.org/10.1177/0741088305275367.

Haswell, Richard. 2012a. "Fighting Number with Number." In *Writing Assessment in the 21st Century: Essays in Honor of Edward M. White,* edited by Norbert Elliot and Les Perelman, 413–23. New York: Hampton.

Haswell, Richard. 2012b. "Methodologically Adrift." Review of *Academically Adrift: Limited Learning on College Campuses* by Richard Arum and Josipa Roksa. *College Composition and Communication* 63 (3): 487–91.

Hayes, John R. 2012. "Modeling and Remodeling Writing." *Written Communication* 29 (3): 369–88. http://dx.doi.org/10.1177/0741088312451260.

Hayes, John R., and Linda S. Flower. 1980. "Identifying the Organization of Writing Processes." In *Cognitive Processes in Writing,* edited by Lee W. Gregg and Erwin Ray Steinberg, 3–30. Hillsdale, NJ: Erlbaum.

Herrington, Anne, and Charles Moran. 2005. *Genre Across the Curriculum.* Logan: Utah State University Press.

Hesse, Douglas. 2012. "Writing Program Research: Three Analytic Axes." In *Writing Studies Research and Practice: Methods and Methodologies,* edited by Lee Nickoson and Mary P. Sheridan, 140–57. Carbondale: Southern Illinois University Press.

Hillocks, George. 1986. *Research on Written Composition: New Directions for Teaching.* Urbana, IL: National Council of Teachers of English.

Holdstein, Deborah H. 2014. "Review: Theory, Practice, and the Disciplinary Cross-Narrative." Review of *Agents of Integration: Understanding Transfer as a Rhetorical Act, The Materiality of Language: Gender, Politics, and the University,* and *The Promise of Reason: Studies in The New Rhetoric. College Composition and Communication* 76 (5): 458–67.

Holland, Paul W. 1986. "Statistics and Causal Inference." *Journal of the American Statistical Association* 81 (396): 945–60. http://dx.doi.org/10.1080/01621459.1986.10478354.

Howe, Kenneth, and Margaret Eisenhart. 1990. "Standards for Qualitative (and Quantitative) Research: A Prolegomenon." *Educational Researcher* 19 (4): 2–9. http://dx.doi.org/10.3 102/0013189X019004002.

Hughes, Gail M. 1996. "The Need for Clear Purposes and New Approaches to the Evaluation of Writing-Across-the-Curriculum Programs." In *Writing Assessment: Politics, Policies, Practices*, edited by Edward M. White, William Lutz, and Sandra Kamusikiri, 158–73. New York: Modern Language Association.

Huot, Brian. 1996. "Towards a New Theory of Writing Assessment." *College Composition and Communication* 47 (4): 549–66. http://dx.doi.org/10.2307/358601.

Huot, Brian. 2002. *(Re)Articulating Writing Assessment for Teaching and Learning.* Logan: Utah State University Press.

Huot, Brian, Peggy O'Neill, and Cindy Moore. 2010. "A Usable Past for Writing Assessment." *College English* 72 (5): 495–517. http://dx.doi.org/10.2307/ 20749294.

Hussar, William J., and Tabitha M. Bailey. 2008. *Projections of Education Statistics to 2017.* 36th ed. Washington, DC: National Center for Education Statistics, Institute of Education Sciences, US Department of Education.

Inoue, Asao B. 2009. "The Technology of Writing Assessment and Racial Validity." In *Handbook of Research on Assessment Technologies, Method, and Applications in Higher Education*, edited by Christopher Schreiner, 97–120. Hershey: Information Science Reference.

Inoue, Asao B. 2014. "A Grade-Less Writing Course That Focuses on Labor and Assessing." In *First-Year Composition: From Theory to Practice*, edited by Deborah Coxwell-Teague and Ronald F. Lunsford, 71–110. Anderson, SC: Parlor Press.

Inoue, Asao B., and Mya Poe, eds. 2012. *Race and Writing Assessment.* New York: Peter Lang.

Inoue, Asao B., and Tyler Richmond. Forthcoming. "Theorizing the Reflection Practices of Hmong College Students: Is 'Reflection' a Racialized Discourse?" In *The Rhetoric of Reflection*, edited by Kathleen Blake Yancey. Logan: Utah State University Press.

Intemann, Kristen. 2010. "25 Years of Feminist Empiricism and Standpoint Theory: Where Are We Now?" *Hypatia* 25 (4): 778–96. http://dx.doi.org/10.1111/j.1527-2001.2010 .01138.x.

Isaacs, Emily J. 2014. "Writing Instruction, Support, and Administration of the State University: A Comparative Review and Report of 106 US Representative Institutions." Unpublished manuscript, Montclair State University, Montclair, NJ.

Isaacs, Emily, and Melinda Knight. 2012. "Assessing the Impact of the Outcomes Statement." In *The WPA Outcomes Statement: A Decade Later*, edited by Nicholas N. Behm, Gregory R. Glau, Deborah H. Holdstein, Duane Roen, and Edward M. White, 285–301. Anderson, SC: Parlor.

Johnson, Carol Siri, and Norbert Elliot. 2010. "Undergraduate Technical Writing Assessment." *Programmatic Perspectives* 2 (2): 110–51.

Jones, Joseph. 2001. "Recomposing the AP English Exam." *English Journal* 91 (1): 51–56. http://dx.doi.org/10.2307/821654.

Kagan, Shelly. 1989. *The Limits of Morality.* Oxford, UK: Oxford University Press.

Kagan, Shelly. 1998. *Normative Ethics.* Boulder, CO: Westview.

Kahneman, Daniel. 2011. *Thinking Fast and Slow.* New York: Farrar, Strauss, and Giroux.

Kane, Michael T. 2006. "Validation." In *Educational Measurement.* 4th ed., edited by Robert L. Brennan, 17-64. Westport, CT: American Council on Education/Praeger.

Kane, Michael T. 2013. "Validating the Interpretation and Uses of Test Scores." *Journal of Educational Measurement* 50 (1): 1–73. http://dx.doi.org/10.1111/jedm.12000.

Kaplan, Robert S., and David P. Norton. 2007. "Using the Balanced Scorecard as a Strategic Management System." *Harvard Business Review* 85 (7/8): 150–61.

Kaplan, Robert S., David P. Norton, and Bjarne Rugelsjoen. 2010. "Managing Alliances with the Balanced Scorecard." *Harvard Business Review* 88 (1): 114–20.

Keller, George. 1983. *Academic Strategy: The Management Revolution in American Higher Education.* Baltimore, MD: Johns Hopkins University Press.

Kelly-Riley, Diane, and Norbert Elliot. 2014. "The WPA Outcomes Statement, Validation, and the Pursuit of Localism." *Assessing Writing* 21 (3): 89–103. http://dx.doi.org/10.1016/j.asw.2014.03.004.

Kerlinger, Fred N., and Howard B. Lee. 1999. *Foundations of Behavioral Research.* Mason, OH: Cengage Learning.

Kidder, William C., and Jay Rosner. 2002. "How the SAT Creates Built-in-Headwinds: An Educational and Legal Analysis of Disparate Impact." *Santa Clara Law Review* 43 (1): 131–211.

Kinneavy, James L. 1971. *A Theory of Discourse: The Aims of Discourse.* New York: Prentice-Hall.

Kitzhaber, Albert R. 1963. *Themes, Theories, and Therapy: The Teaching of Writing in College.* New York: McGraw-Hill.

Klobucar, Andrew, Norbert Elliot, Perry Deess, Oleksandr Rudniy, and Kamal Joshi. 2013. "Automated Scoring in Context: Rapid Assessment for Placed Students." *Assessing Writing* 18 (1): 62–84. http://dx.doi.org/10.1016/j.asw.2012.10.001.

Lagemann, Ellen Condiffe. 2000. *An Elusive Science: The Troubling History of Educational Research.* Chicago: University of Chicago Press.

Lakoff, George. 2004. *Don't Think of an Elephant! Know Your Values and Frame the Debate.* White River Junction, VT: Chelsea Green.

Lakoff, George, and Mark Johnson. 1980. *Metaphors We Live By.* Chicago: University of Chicago Press.

Langer, Susanne K. 1942. *Philosophy in a New Key: A Study in the Symbolism of Reason, Rite, and Art.* Cambridge, MA: Harvard University Press.

Latour, Bruno, and Steve Woolgar. 1979/1986. *Laboratory Life: The Construction of Scientific Facts.* Princeton, NJ: Princeton University Press.

Lauer, Janice M., and J. William Asher. 1988. *Composition Research: Empirical Designs.* New York: Oxford University Press.

Leary, David E. 1990. *Metaphors in the History of Psychology.* Cambridge: Cambridge University Press.

Lee, Carol D. 2010. "Soaring above the Clouds, Delving the Ocean's Depths: Understanding the Ecologies of Human Learning and the Challenge for Education Science." *Educational Researcher* 39 (9): 643–55. http://dx.doi.org/10.3102/0013189X10392139.

Levin, Henry M., and Patrick J. McEwan. 2001. *Cost-Effectiveness Analysis: Methods and Applications,* 2nd ed. Thousand Oaks, CA: Sage.

Levin, Jack A., James Alan Fox, and David R. Forde. 2014. *Elementary Statistics in Social Research.* Boston: Pearson.

Lewis, John. 2013. "Union College Commencement Speech," June 16.

Lindemann, Erika. 1993. "Freshman Composition: No Place for Literature." *College English* 55 (3): 311–16. http://dx.doi.org/10.2307/378743.

Lindemann, Erika. 2001. *A Rhetoric for Writing Teachers.* 4th ed. New York: Oxford University Press.

Linkon, Sherry Lee, Irvin Peckham, and Benjamin G. Lanier-Nabors, eds. 2004. "Struggling with Class in English Studies." Special issue, *College English* 67 (2): 149–230. http://dx.doi.org/10.2307/4140714.

Little, David. 2007. "The Common European Framework of Reference for Languages: Perspectives on the Making of Supranational Language Education Policy." *Modern Language Journal* 91 (4): 645–55. http://dx.doi.org/10.1111/j.1540-4781.2007.00627_2.x.

Litvin, Margaret. 2011. *Hamlet's Arab Journey: Shakespeare's Prince and Nasser's Ghost.* Princeton, NJ: Princeton University Press.

Lloyd, Geoffrey E. R. 2009. *Disciplines in the Making.* London: Oxford University Press. http://dx.doi.org/10.1093/acprof:oso/9780199567874.001.0001.

Lockhart, Robert S. 1998. *Introduction to Statistics and Data Analysis for the Behavioral Sciences.* New York: W. H. Freeman.

Lynne, Patricia. 2004. *Coming to Terms: A Theory of Writing Assessment.* Logan: Utah State University Press.

MacMillan, Stuart. 2012. "The Promise of Ecological Inquiry in Writing Research." *Technical Communication Quarterly* 21 (4): 346–61. http://dx.doi.org/10.1080/10572252.2012.674 873.

Maki, Peggy L. 2010. *Assessing for Learning: Building a Sustainable Commitment.* 2nd ed. Sterling, VA: Stylus.

Malenczyk, Rita, ed. 2013. *A Rhetoric for Writing Program Administrators.* Anderson, SC: Parlor.

Markus, Keith A., and Denny Borsboom. 2013. *Frontiers of Test Validity Theory: Measurement, Causation, and Meaning.* New York: Routledge.

Maxwell, Scott E. 2000. "Sample Size and Multiple Regression Analysis." *Psychological Methods* 5 (4): 434–58. http://dx.doi: IO.I037//I082-989X.5.4.434.

Maylath, Bruce, and Jeffrey Grabill. 2009. "The Council for Programs in Technical and Scientific Communication at 35 Years: A Sequel and Perspective." *Programmatic Perspectives* 1 (1): 29–44.

McGinn, Robert E. 1990. *Science, Technology, and Society.* New York: Pearson.

McGuire, William J., and Demetrios Papageorgis. 1961. "The Relative Efficacy of Various Types of Prior Belief-Defense in Producing Immunity against Persuasion." *Journal of Abnormal Psychology* 62 (2): 327–37. http://dx.doi.org/10.1037/h0042026.

McKee, Heidi. 2003. "Changing the Process of Institutional Review Board Compliance." *College Composition and Communication* 54 (3): 488–93. http://dx.doi.org/10.2307/3594176.

McMillan, John A., Alan Shepard, and Gary Tate, eds. 1998. *Coming to Class: Pedagogy and the Social Class of Teachers.* Portsmouth, NJ: Boynton/Cook.

Melzer, Dan. 2014. *Assignments across the Curriculum: A National Study of College Writing.* Logan: Utah State University Press.

Messick, Samuel. 1979. "Potential Uses of Noncognitive Measurement in Education." *Journal of Educational Psychology* 71 (3): 281–92. http://dx.doi.org/10.1037/0022-0663.71.3 .281.

Messick, Samuel. 1989. "Validity." In *Educational Measurement,* 3rd ed., edited by Robert L. Linn, 13–103. New York: American Council on Education and Macmillan.

Micciche, Laura R. 2002. "More Than a Feeling: Disappointment and WPA Work." *College English* 64 (4): 432–58. http://dx.doi.org/10.2307/3250746.

Middaugh, Michael F. 2010. *Planning and Assessment in Higher Education: Demonstrating Institutional Effectiveness.* San Francisco: Jossey-Bass.

Middle States Commission on Higher Education. 2014. *Standards for Accreditation and Requirements of Affiliation.* 13th ed. Philadelphia: Middle States Commission on Higher Education.

Miller, Benjamin. 2014. "Mapping the Methods of Composition/Rhetoric Dissertations: A Landscape Plotted and Pieced." *College Composition and Communication* 61 (1): 145–76.

Miller, Carolyn 1984. "Genre as Social Action." *Quarterly Journal of Speech* 70 (2): 151–67. http://dx.doi.org/10.1080/00335638409383686.

Mills, C. Wright. 1956/2000. *The Power Elite.* Cambridge, MA: Oxford University Press.

Mislevy, Robert. J. 2007. "Validity by Design." *Educational Researcher* 36 (8): 463–69. http://dx.doi.org/10.3102/0013189X07311660.

Mislevy, Robert J., Linda S. Steinberg, and Russell G. Almond. 2002. "Design and Analysis in Task-Based Language Assessment." *Language Testing* 19 (4): 477–96. http://dx.doi.org /10.1191/0265532202lt241oa.

Mislevy, Robert J., Russell G. Almond, and Janice F. Lukas. 2004. *A Brief Introduction to Evidence-Centered Design* (ETS Research Report–03–16). Princeton, NJ: Educational Testing Service. Web.

Mitchell, Joni. 1974. *Court and Spark*. Elektra/Asylum.

Morison, Samuel Eliot. 1936. *The Puritan Pronaos: Studies in the Intellectual Life of New England in the Seventeenth Century*. New York: New York University Press.

Moss, Pamela A. 1994. "Can There Be Validity without Reliability?" *Educational Researcher* 23 (2): 5–12. http://dx.doi.org/10.3102/0013189X023002005.

Mueller, Derek. 2012. "Grasping Rhetoric and Composition by Its Long Tail: What Graphs Can Tell Us about the Field's Changing Shape." *College Composition and Communication* 65 (1): 195–223.

Murray, Jody. 2009. *Non-Discursive Rhetoric: Image and Affect in Multimodal Composition*. Albany: State University of New York Press.

National Association of Student Financial Aid Administrators. 2014. *Peers in PIRS: Challenges and Considerations for Rating Groups of Postsecondary Institutions*. Washington, DC: National Association of Student Financial Aid Administrators.

National Center for Education Statistics. 2012. *Digest of Education Statistics*. Web.

National Governors Association. 2014. *Common Core State Standards Initiative*. Washington, DC: National Governors Association. Web.

National Survey of Student Engagement. 2013. "NSSE 2013 Frequencies and Statistical Comparisons: Interpreting Your Report." Bloomington: Indiana University. Web.

NCTE and CWPA. 2008. *NCTE-WPA White Paper on Writing Assessment in Colleges and Universities*. Web.

Neal, Michael. R. 2011. *Writing Assessment and the Revolution in Digital Texts and Technologies*. New York: Teacher's College Press.

Neff, Joyce Magnotto, and Carl Whithaus. 2008. *Writing across Distances and Disciplines: Research and Pedagogy in Distributed Learning*. New York: Earlbaum.

Nichols, Paul D., and Natasha Williams. 2009. "Consequence of Test Score Use as Validity Evidence: Roles and Responsibilities." *Educational Measurement: Issues and Practice* 28 (1): 3–9. http://dx.doi.org/10.1111/j.1745-3992.2009.01132.x.

Nickoson, Lee, and Mary P. Sheridan, eds. 2012. *Writing Studies Research and Practice: Methods and Methodologies*. Carbondale: Southern Illinois University Press.

North, Steven M. 1987. *The Making of Knowledge in Composition: Portrait of an Emerging Field*. Portsmouth, NH: Heinemann.

O'Connor, Melissa C., and Sampo V. Paunonen. 2007. "Big Five Personality Predictors of Post-Secondary Academic Performance." *Personality and Individual Differences* 43 (5): 971–90. http://dx.doi.org/10.1016/j.paid.2007.03.017.

Odell, Lee. 1983. "Introduction." In *Evaluating College Writing Programs*, edited by Stephen P. Witte and Lester Faigley, ix–xi. Carbondale: Southern Illinois University Press.

Odendahl, Nora Vivian. 2011. *Testwise: Understanding Educational Assessment*. Vol. 1. Lanham, MD: Rowman and Littlefield.

O'Neill, Peggy, Cindy Moore, and Brian Huot. 2009. *A Guide to College Writing Assessment*. Logan: Utah State University Press.

O'Neill, Peggy, Linda Adler-Kassner, Cathy Fleischer, and Anne-Marie Hall. 2012. "Symposium: On the *Framework for Success in Postsecondary Writing*." *College English* 74 (6): 520–53.

Ong, Walter. 1982. *Orality and Literacy: The Technologizing of the Word*. London, UK: Methuen. http://dx.doi.org/10.4324/9780203328064.

Ostheimer, Martha, and Edward M. White. 2005. "Portfolio Assessment in an American Engineering College." *Assessing Writing* 10 (1): 61–73. http://dx.doi.org/10.1016/j.asw.2005.02.003.

Outcomes Group. 1999. "The WPA Outcomes Statement for First-Year Composition." *WPA: Writing Program Administration* 23 (1–2): 59–69.

Pagano, Neil, Stephan A. Bernhardt, Dudley Reynolds, Mark Williams, and Matthew Kilian McCurrie. 2008. "An Inter-Institutional Model for College Writing Assessment." *College Composition and Communication* 60 (2): 285–320. http://dx.doi.org/10.2307/20457061.

Paine, Charles, Robert M. Gonyea, Chris M. Anson, and Paul V. Anderson. 2013. "What Is NSSE?" In *A Rhetoric for Writing Program Administrators*, edited by Rita Malenczyk, 265–75. Anderson, SC: Parlor.

Parsons, Michael D. 1997. *Power and Politics: Federal Higher Education Policymaking in the 1990s*. Albany: State University of New York Press.

Peckham, Irvin. 1987. "Statewide Direct Writing Assessment." *English Journal* 76 (8): 30–33.

Peckham, Irvin. 1999. "Whispers from the Margin: A Class-Based Interpretation of the Conflict between High School and College Writing Teachers." In *History, Reflection and Narrative: The Professionalization of Composition, 1963–1983*, edited by Mary Rosner, Beth Boehm, and Debra Journet, 253–69. Norwood, NJ: Ablex.

Peckham, Irvin. 2009. "Online Placement in First-Year Writing." *College Composition and Communication* 60 (3): 517–40. http://dx.doi.org/10.2307/ 20457080.

Peckham, Irvin. 2010a. *Going North Thinking West: The Intersections of Social Class, Critical Thinking, and Politicized Writing Instruction*. Logan: Utah State University Press.

Peckham, Irvin. 2010b. "Online Challenge versus Offline ACT." *College Composition and Communication* 62 (4): 718–45. http://dx.doi.org/10.2307/ 27917870.

Pellegrino, James W., and Margaret L. Hilton, eds. 2012. *Education for Life and Work: Developing Transferable Knowledge and Skills in the 21st Century*. Washington, DC: National Academies Press.

Perelman, Les. 2014. Personal communication with authors, May 10.

Persky, Hillary. 2012. "Writing Assessment in the Context of the National Assessment of Educational Progress." In *Writing Assessment in the 21st Century: Essays in Honor of Edward M. White*, edited by Norbert Elliot and Les Perelman, 69–86. New York: Hampton.

Phelps, Louise Wetherbee, and John M. Ackerman. 2010. "Making the Case for Disciplinarity in Rhetoric, Composition, and Writing Studies: The Visibility Project." *College Composition and Communication* 62 (1): 180–215. http://dx.doi.org/10.2307/ 27917 890.

Piketty, Thomas. 2014. *Capital in the Twenty-First Century*. Translated by Arthur Goldhammer. Cambridge, MA: Harvard University Press.

Poe, Mya. 2014. "The Consequences of Writing Assessment." *Research in the Teaching of English* 48 (3): 271–5.

Poe, Mya, Norbert Elliot, John Aloysius Cogan, and Tito G. Nurudeen. 2014. "The Legal and the Local: Using Disparate Impact Analysis to Understand the Consequences of Writing Assessment." *College Composition and Communication* 65 (4): 588–611.

Poe, Mya, Neal Lerner, and Jennifer Craig. 2010. *Learning to Communicate in Science and Engineering: Case Studies from MIT*. Cambridge, MA: Massachusetts Institute of Technology Press.

Price, Margaret, Berry O'Donovan, Chris Rust, and Jude Carrol. 2008. "Assessment Standards: A Manifesto for Change." *Brookes eJournal of Learning and Teaching* 2 (3). Web.

Purves, Alan C. 1995. "Apologia Not Accepted." *College Composition and Communication* 46 (4): 549–50. http://dx.doi.org/10.2307/358328.

Quinn, James B. 1980. *Strategies for Change: Logical Incrementalism*. Homewood, IL: Richard D. Irwin.

Rawls, John. 1971/1999. *A Theory of Justice*. Rev. ed. Cambridge, MA: Harvard University Press.

Rockström, Johan, Will Steffen, Kevin Noone, Asa Persson, F. Stuart Chapin, Eric F. Lambin, Timothy M. Lenton, Marten Scheffer, Carl Folke, Hans Joachim Schellnhuber, Björn Nykvist, Cynthia A. DeWit, Terry Hughes, Sander van der Leeuw, Henning Rodhe, Sverker Sörlin, Peter K. Snyder, Robert Costanza, Uno Svedin, Malin Falkenmark, Louise Karlberg, Robert W. Corell, Victoria J. Fabry, James Hansen, Brian Walker, Diana Liverman, Katherine Richardson, Paul Krutzen, and Johathan A. Foley. 2009. "A Safe Operating Space for Humanity." *Nature* 461 (7263): 472–75. http://dx.doi.org /10.1038/461472a.

Roozen, Kevin., and Karen J. Lunsford. 2011. "'One Story of Many to Be Told:' Following Empirical Studies of College and Adult Writing Through 100 Years of NCTE Journals." *Research in the Teaching of English* 46 (2): 193–209.

Rorty, Richard. 1989. *Contingency, Irony, and Solidarity.* Cambridge: Cambridge University Press. http://dx.doi.org/10.1017/CBO9780511804397.

Rose, Shirley. 2012. "The WPA Within: WPA Identities and Implications for Graduate Education in Rhetoric and Composition." Review of *The Activist WPA: Changing Stories about Writing and Writers*, by Linda Adler-Kassner, *The Managerial Unconscious in the History of Composition Studies*, by Donna Strickland, and *GenAdmin: Theorizing SPA Identities in the Twenty-First Century*, by Colin Charlton, Jonikka Charlton, Tarez Samra Graban, Kathleen J. Ryan, and Amy Ferinandt Stolley. *College Composition and Communication* 75 (2): 218–30.

Rose, Shirley, and Irwin Weiser, eds. 1999. *The Writing Program Administrator as Researcher: Inquiry in Action and Reflection.* Portsmouth, NH: Boynton/Cook.

Rose, Shirley, and Irwin Weiser. 2002. *Writing Program Administrator as Theorist: Making Knowledge Work.* Portsmouth, NH: Boynton/Cook.

Rouse, Michael, Eric Borsting, G. Lynn Mitchell, Marjean Taylor Kulp, Mitchell Scheiman, Deborah Amster, Rachael Coulter, Gregory Fecho, and Michael Gallaway. 2009. "Academic Behaviors in Children with Convergence Insufficiency with and without Parent-Reported ADHD." *Optometry and Vision Science* 86 (10): 1169–77. http://dx.doi.org /10.1097/OPX.0b013e3181baad13.

Royer, Daniel J., and Roger Gilles. 1998. "Directed Self Placement: An Attitude of Orientation." *College Composition and Communication* 50 (1): 54–70. http://dx.doi.org/10.2307 /358352.

Ruiz de Mendoza Ibanez, Francisco José, and Lorena Perez Hernandez. 2011. "The Contemporary Theory of Metaphor: Myths, Developments and Challenges." *Metaphor and Symbol* 26 (3): 161–85. http://dx.doi.org/10.1080/10926488.2011.583189.

Ruth, Leo, and Sandra Murphy. 1988. *Designing Writing Tasks for the Assessment of Writing.* Norwood, NJ: Ablex.

Rutz, Carol, and Jacqulyn Lauer-Glebov. 2005. "Assessment and Innovation: One Darn Thing Leads to Another." *Assessing Writing* 10 (2): 80–99. http://dx.doi.org/10.1016/j.asw.20 05.03.001.

Ryan, Kathleen J. 2012. "Thinking Ecologically: Rhetorical Ecological Feminist Agency and Writing Program Administration." *WPA: Writing Program Administration* 36 (1): 74–94.

Sánchez, Raul. 2012. "Outside the Text: Retheorizing Empiricism and Identity." *College English* 74 (3): 234–46.

Sapir, Edward. 1963. "The Status of Linguistics as a Science." In *Selected Writings in Language, Culture and Personality*, edited by David G. Mandelbaum, 160–66. Berkeley: University of California Press.

Schendel, Ellen, and William J. Macauley. 2012. *Building Writing Center Assessments That Matter.* Logan: Utah State University Press.

Schneider, Barbara, Martin Carnoy, Jeremy Kilpatrick, William H. Schmidt, and Richard J. Shavelson. 2007. *Estimating Causal Effects Using Experimental and Observational Designs.* Washington, DC: American Educational Research Association.

Schwartz, Daniel L., John D. Bransford, and David Sears. 2005. "Efficiency and Innovation in Transfer." In *Transfer of Learning from a Modern Multidisciplinary Perspective*, edited by Jose P. Mestre, 1–51. Greenwich, CT: Information Age.

Scott, Tony, and Lil Brannon. 2013. "Democracy, Struggle, and the Praxis of Assessment." *College Composition and Communication* 65 (2): 273–98.

Scriven, Michael. 1981. *Evaluating the Bay Area Writing Project: The Scriven Report.* San Francisco: University of San Francisco. Web.

Shapiro, Shawna. 2011. "Stuck in the Remedial Rut: Confronting Resistance to ESL Curriculum Reform." *Journal of Basic Writing* 30 (2): 24–52.

Shepard, Lorrie A. 2006. "Classroom Assessment." In *Educational Measurement*, 4th ed., edited by Robert. L. Brennan, 623–46. Westport, CT: American Council on Education/Praeger.

Shepard, Lorrie A. 2013. "Why Lessons Learned from the Past Require Haertel's Expanded Scope for Test Validation." *Measurement: Interdisciplinary Research and Perspectives* 11 (1–2): 50–54. http://dx.doi.org/10.1080/15366367.2013.784164.

Slomp, David H., Julie A. Corrigan, and Tamiko Sugimoto. 2014. "A Framework for Using Consequential Validity Evidence in Evaluating Large-Scale Writing Assessments: A Canadian Study." *Research in the Teaching of English* 48 (3): 276–302.

Smagorinsky, Peter. 2006. "Overview." In *Research on Composition: Multiple Perspectives on Two Decades of Change*, edited by Peter Smagorinsky, 1–14. New York: Teachers College Press.

Smith, Dean O. 2011. *Managing the Research University*. Oxford, UK: Oxford University Press. http://dx.doi.org/10.1093/acprof:oso/9780199793259.001.0001.

Smith, Jane Bowman, and Kathleen Blake Yancey, eds. 2000. *Self-Assessment and Development in Writing: A Collaborative Inquiry*. Cresskill, NJ: Hampton.

Sommers, Nancy. 2005. *Across the Drafts: Responding to Student Writing—A Longitudinal Perspective*. Featured Session. Fifty-Sixth Annual Convention Program Book. San Francisco, March 17.

Sparks, Jesse R., Yi Song, Wyman Brantley, and Ou Lydia Lou. 2014. *Assessing Written Communication in Higher Education: Review and Recommendations for Next-Generation Assessment*. ETS Research Report No. RR-14-37. Princeton, NJ: ETS. Web. http://dx.doi.org/10.1002/ets2.12035.

Spinuzzi, Clay. 2003. *Tracing Genres through Organizations*. Cambridge: Massachusetts Institute of Technology Press.

Stake, Robert E. 2006. *Multiple Case Study Analysis*. New York: Guilford.

Stemler, Steven E. 2004. "A Comparison of Consensus, Consistency, and Measurement Approaches to Estimating Interrater Reliability." *Practical Assessment, Research and Evaluation* 9 (4). Web.

Sternberg, Robert J. 2010. *College Admissions for the 21st Century*. Cambridge, MA: Harvard University Press.

Sternglass, Marilyn. 1997. *Time to Know Them: A Longitudinal Study of Writing and Learning at the College Level*. Mahwah, NJ: Erlbaum.

Stiggins, Richard J. 1982. "A Comparison of Direct and Indirect Writing Assessment Methods." *Research in the Teaching of English* 16 (2): 101–4. http://dx.doi.org/10.2307/40170937.

Straub, Eileen, and Ronald Lunsford, eds. 2006. *Key Works on Teacher Response: An Anthology*. Portsmouth, NH: Boynton/Cook.

Tate, Gary. 1993. "A Place for Literature in Freshman Composition." *College English* 55 (3): 317–21. http://dx.doi.org/10.2307/378744.

Tate, Gary, Amy Rupiper Taggart, Kurt Schick, and H. Brooke Hessler. 2013. *A Guide to Composition Pedagogies*. 2nd ed. New York: Oxford University Press.

Tedesco, Barbara L. 1999. "The Impact of Environmental Issues and Stakeholder Expectations on US Institutional and Programmatic Accreditation." Unpublished PhD diss., Seton Hall University, South Orange, NJ.

Tough, Paul. 2014. "Who Gets to Graduate?" *New York Times Magazine*, May 18, 26–33, 41–42, 54.

Toulmin, Stephen E. 1958/2003. *The Uses of Argument*. Cambridge: Cambridge University Press. http://dx.doi.org/10.1017/CBO9780511840005.

Trimbur, John. 2011. *Solidarity of Service: Essays on US College Composition*. Portsmouth, NJ: Boynton/Cook.

Trochim, William M. K., and James P. Donnelly. 2008. *The Research Methods Knowledge Base*. 3rd ed. Mason, OH: Cengage Learning.

Tufte, Edward R. 2001. *The Visual Display of Quantitative Information*. 2nd ed. Cheshire, CT: Graphics Press.

United States Census Bureau. 2013. "Census Bureau Estimates Nearly Half of Children under Age 5 Are Minorities." US Census Bureau. US Dept. of Commerce. Accessed May 2009. Web.

United States Department of Education. 2013. *The Database of Accredited Postsecondary Institutions and Programs.* Web.

Unruh, Vicky, ed. 2012. "Special Topic: Work." Special issue, *Publications of the Modern Language Association* 127 (4): 731–911.

Wardle, Elizabeth. 2013. "What Is Transfer?" In *A Rhetoric for Writing Program Administrators,* edited by Rita Malenczyk, 143–55. Anderson, SC: Parlor.

Wardle, Elizabeth, and Kevin Roozen. 2012. "Addressing the Complexity of Writing Development: Toward an Ecological Model of Assessment." *Assessing Writing* 17 (2): 106–19. http://dx.doi.org/10.1016/j.asw.2012.01.001.

Warren, Karen J. 1990. "The Power and the Promise of Ecological Feminism." *Environmental Ethics* 12 (2): 125–46. http://dx.doi.org/10.5840/enviroethics1990122 21.

Weir, Cyril J. 2005. "Limitations of the Common European Framework for Developing Comparable Examinations and Tests." *Language Testing* 22 (3): 281–300. http://dx.doi.org/10.1191/0265532205lt309oa.

Weiss, Carol H. 1998. *Evaluation.* 2nd ed. Upper Saddle River, NJ: Prentice Hall.

White, Edward M. 1985. *Teaching and Assessing Writing: Understanding, Evaluating and Improving Student Performance.* San Francisco: Jossey-Bass.

White, Edward M. 1989. *Developing Successful College Writing Programs.* San Francisco: Jossey-Bass.

White, Edward M. 1990. "Language and Reality in Writing Assessment." *College Composition and Communication* 41 (2): 187–200. http://dx.doi.org/10.2307/358159.

White, Edward M. 2001. "The Opening of the Modern Era of Writing Assessment: A Narrative." *College English* 63 (3): 306–20. http://dx.doi.org/10.2307/378995.

White, Edward M. 2005. "The Scoring of Writing Portfolios: Phase 2." *College Composition and Communication* 56 (4): 581–600. http://dx.doi.org/10.2307/ 30037887.

White, Edward M., and Linda G. Polin. 1986. *Research in Effective Teaching of Writing: Final Report on Phase I* (NIE-G-81-0011; NIE-G-82-0024; ERIC 239 292, 239 293, and 275 007). Washington, DC: National Institute of Education.

White, Edward M., and Cassie A. Wright. 2015. *Assigning, Responding, Evaluating: A Writing Teachers' Guide.* 5th ed. New York: Bedford/St. Martin's.

Whitehead, Alfred North. 1925. *Science and the Modern World.* New York: Macmillan.

White House. 2013. *Fact Sheet on the President's Plan to Make College More Affordable: A Better Bargain for the Middle Class.* Washington, DC: White House. Web.

Whorf, Benjamin Lee. 1956. "Science and Linguistics." In *Language, Thought, and Reality: Selected Writings,* edited by John B. Carroll, 207–79. Cambridge, MA: Massachusetts Institute of Technology Press.

Williams, Donald C. 1953. "On the Elements of Being." *Review of Metaphysics* 7 (1): 3–18, 171–92.

Williams, Julia M. 2010. "Evaluating What Students Know: Using the RosE Portfolio System for Institutional and Program Outcomes Assessment." *IEEE Transactions on Professional Communication* 53 (1): 46–57. http://dx.doi.org/10.1109/TPC.2009.20387 37.

Williamson, David M., Xiaoming Xi, and F. Jay Breyer. 2012. "A Framework for Evaluation and Use of Automated Scoring." *Educational Measurement: Issues and Practice* 31 (1): 2–13. http://dx.doi.org/10.1111/j.1745-3992.2011.00223.x.

Willingham, Warren. W. 1974. *College Placement and Exemption.* New York: College Board.

Willingham, Warren W., Judith M. Pollack, and Charles Lewis. 2002. "Grades and Test Scores: Accounting for Observed Differences." *Journal of Educational Measurement* 39 (1): 1–37. http://dx.doi.org/10.1111/j.1745-3984.2002.tb01133.x.

Wills, Katherine V., and Rich Rice, eds. 2013. *ePortfolio Performance Support Systems: Constructing, Presenting, and Assessing Portfolios.* Perspectives on Writing. Fort Collins, CO: WAC Clearinghouse and Parlor.

Windelband, Wilhelm. 1894/1980. "Rectorial Address, Strasburg, 1894." *History and Theory* 19 (2): 169–85. http://dx.doi.org/10.2307/2504798.

Witte, Stephen P. 1987. "Review of the *Research on Written Communication: New Directions for Teaching*, by George Hillocks." *College Composition and Communication* 38 (2): 202–7. http://dx.doi.org/10.2307/357721.

Witte, Stephen P., and Lester Faigley. 1983. *Evaluating College Writing Programs.* Carbondale: Southern Illinois University Press.

Wood, Tara, Margaret Price, and Chelsea Johnson. 2012. *Disability Studies* (WPA-CompPile Research Bibliographies, No. 19). Web.

Wooldridge, Adrian. 1994. *Measuring the Mind: Education and Psychology in England, c.1860–c.1990.* Cambridge: Cambridge University Press. http://dx.doi.org/10.1017/CBO978 0511659997.

World Commission on Environment and Development. 1987. *Our Common Future.* New York: United Nations. Web.

Yancey, Kathleen Blake. 1998. *Reflection in the Writing Classroom.* Logan: Utah State University Press.

Yancey, Kathleen Blake. 1999. "Looking Back as We Look Forward: Historicizing Writing Assessment." *College Composition and Communication* 50 (3): 483–503. http://dx.doi.org /10.2307/358862.

Yancey, Kathleen Blake. 2012. "The Rhetorical Situation of Writing Assessment: Exigence, Location, and the Making of Knowledge." In *Writing Assessment in the 21st Century: Essays in Honor of Edward M. White,* edited by Norbert Elliot and Les Perelman, 475–92. New York: Hampton Press.

Yancey, Kathleen Blake, and Brian Huot. 1997. *Assessing Writing across the Curriculum: Diverse Approaches and Practices.* Greenwich, CT: Ablex.

Yancey, Kathleen Blake, Liane Robertson, and Kara Taczak. 2014. *Writing across Contexts: Transfer, Composition, and Sites of Writing.* Logan: Utah State University Press.

Yancey, Kathleen Blake, Stephen J. McElroy, and Elizabeth Powers. 2013. "Composing, Networks, and Electronic Portfolios: Notes toward a Theory of Assessing ePortfolios." In *Digital Writing Assessment and Evaluation,* edited by Heidi A. McKee and Dànielle Nicole DeVoss. Logan: Computers and Composition Digital Press/Utah State University Press. Web.

Yarbrough, Donald B., Lyn M. Shulha, Rodney K. Hopson, and Flora A. Caruthers. 2011. *The Program Evaluation Standards: A Guide for Evaluators and Evaluation Users.* 3rd ed. Los Angeles: Sage.

Yeager, David S., and Gregory M. Walton. 2011. "Social-Psychological Interventions in Education: They're Not Magic." *Review of Educational Research* 81 (2): 267–301. http:// dx.doi.org/10.3102/0034654311405999.

Yin, Robert K. 2014. *Case Study Research: Design and Methods.* 4th ed. Los Angeles: Sage.

Young, Richard E., Alton L. Becker, and Kenneth L. Pike. 1970. *Rhetoric: Discovery and Change.* New York: Harcourt.

Zak, Frances, ed. 1998. *The Theory and Practice of Grading Writing.* Albany: State University of New York Press.

ABOUT THE AUTHORS

EDWARD M. WHITE is a visiting scholar in English at the University of Arizona and Professor Emeritus of English at California State University, San Bernardino, where he served prolonged periods as English department chair and coordinator of the upper-division university writing program. He has been coordinator of the state-wide CSU Writing Skills Improvement Program and for over a decade was director of the English Equivalency Examination. On the national scene, he directed the consultant-evaluator service of WPA for fifteen years and in 1993 was elected to a second term on the executive committee of CCCC. His *Teaching and Assessing Writing* (1985) has been called "required reading" for the profession; a new edition in 1994 received an MLA Mina Shaughnessy award "for outstanding research." He is author of more than one hundred articles and book chapters on literature and the teaching of writing, and has coauthored five English composition textbooks, most recently *Inquiry* (2004) and *The Promise of America* (2006). His *Developing Successful College Writing Programs* was published in 1989, and *Assigning, Responding, Evaluating: A Writing Teacher's Guide* was published in a 5th edition in 2015. He is also coeditor of three essay collections for the MLA and SIU presses. His work has recently been recognized by the publication of *Writing Assessment in the 21st Century: Essays in Honor of Edward M. White* (2012) and by the 2011 Exemplar Award from the CCCC.

NORBERT ELLIOT is Professor Emeritus of English at New Jersey Institute of Technology. Winner of the Outstanding Book Award from the Conference on College Composition and Communication for *On a Scale: A Social History of Writing Assessment in America*, his current empirical research has been published in *Assessing Writing, College Composition and Communication*, and *Research in the Teaching of English*. He is author, most recently, of *Henry Chauncey: An American Life*.

IRVIN PECKHAM is currently the director of the First-Year Writing Program at Drexel University. He was the director of the required writing program for ten years at Louisiana State and for four years at the University of Nebraska, Omaha. His research interests are writing assessment, the intersections of social class and writing instruction, and the use of personal writing in academic settings. He is the author of *Going North Thinking West: The Intersections of Social Class, Critical Thinking, and Politicized Writing Instruction* and articles in several edited collections and in *WPA: Writing Program Administration, Composition Studies, Pedagogy, Computers and Composition, English Journal,* and *College Composition and Communication.* He also coedited with Sherry Lee Linkon and Benjamin G. Lanier-Nabors a special issue of *College English* (67.2, 2004) focusing on social class and writing instruction.

INDEX

ABET. *See* Accreditation Board for
    Engineering and Technology
accountability, 4, 5, 8, 9, 15, 17, 19, 38, 59,
    65, 109, 133, 143, 146, 152, 154, 159,
    163, 168–71
accreditation, 6, 9, 14–15, 17, 24–27, 33,
    36, 39, 48, 54, 65, 89, 166, 170
Accreditation Board for Engineering and
    Technology (ABET), 9, 26
Ackerman, John M., 6
Addison, Joanne, 129
Adler-Kassner, Linda, 38, 65, 69, 160
Advanced Placement (AP) Program in
    English and Composition, 12, 23, 71,
    94, 149
AERA. *See* American Educational Research
    Association
aim, 65, 86, 88, 98–99, 110, 126, 135, 149,
    152–53, 170–75
Allee, Warder Clyde: *Principles of Animal
    Ecology*, 31
Almond, Russell G., 21, 69, 153, 166. *See
    also* evidence-centered design (ECD)
Alvarez, Tara, 76
American Academy of Arts and Sciences,
    113
American Association of University
    Professors, 4, 18, 69
American Educational Research
    Association (AERA), 19, 21, 32, 61, 82,
    84, 88
American Psychological Association
    (APA), 19, 21, 61, 82, 84, 88, 118, 165
Anderson, Paul, 129
Antonio, Anthony Lising, 15
AP. *See* Advanced Placement
APA. *See* American Psychological
    Association
Arum, Richard, 141
Asher, J. William, 138–39, 169
assessment, 13, 19, 24–28, 70–72, 135–37,
    153–65, 170, 176
Astin, Alexander W., 15
axiology, 151, 170, 184

Bachman, Lyle, 155
Bailey, Tabitha M., 12

balanced scorecard approaches, 159–60
Bamberg, Betty, 40–44
Bateson, Gregory, 31
Bay Area Writing Project, 13, 42
Bazerman, Charles, 14, 50, 55, 64
Beaufort, Anne, 23
Becker, Alton, 103
Behm, Nicholas N., 15
Beiser, Frederick C., 80
Bejar, Isaac I., 87
Belanoff, Pat, 42
Bennett, Randy Elliot, 77
Berliner, David C., 144
Bernard, H. Russell, 29, 114, 139
Berthoff, Ann E., 80
bias, 87, 113, 145, 170, 172–73. *See also*
    consequence; fairness
Biddle, Bruce J., 144
Biggs, John, 36, 54, 70, 110, 162. *See also*
    constructive alignment; Tang, Catherine
Bijker, Wiebe E., 51
Bitzer, Lloyd, 39. *See also* exigence
Bleich, David, 74
Bloom, Harold, 2
body of knowledge, 20, 28, 60–61, 68, 71,
    74, 109, 133, 136, 143, 169–70, 173–74
Bok, Derek, 65
Borsboom, Denny, 22, 154, 158, 166
Borsting, Eric, 76
Bourdieu, Pierre, 51
Bowen, William G., 44
Braddock, Richard, 13
Bradley, Andrew Cecil, 1
Brady, Laura, 23
Brannon, Lil, 166–67
Bransford, John D., 76, 110
Brennan, Robert L., 23, 81
Breyer, F. Jay, 122
Broad, Bob, 38, 42, 133, 141, 159. *See also*
    Dynamic Criteria Mapping (DCM)
Broer, Marcus, 23
Broome, Edwin Cornelius, 14
Brown, James Cooke, 31
Brundtland Commission, 160
Bryson, John, 19
Bunch, Michael B., 42
Burstein, Jill, 23

California Assessment Project, 42
Cambridge, Barbara, 97. *See also* National
  Coalition for Electronic Portfolio
  Research
Cambridge, Darren, 97. *See also* National
  Coalition for Electronic Portfolio
  Research
Carroll, John B., 67
CASO. *See* Commission on the Assessment
  of Student Outcomes
causal inference, 128–29, 136, 170
Charney, Davida, 137–38
Chen, Ai Hong, 76
Chen, Huey T., 21, 69
Chernilo, Daniel, 157
Chingos, Matthew G., 44
Chomsky, Noam, 31
CI. *See* confidence interval
CIP. *See* Classification of Instructional
  Programs
Cizek, Gregory J., 42, 144
Classification of Instructional Programs
  (CIP), 5–7, 24, 112–13, 138, 147, 151,
  168
Clauser, Brian E., 87
Coetzee, J.M., 147
cognitive domain, 16, 74, 94–95, 170. *See
  also* domain; interpersonal domain;
  intrapersonal domain; noncognitive
  domain
Cohen, Arthur M., 20
Cohen, Jacob, 122, 130, 132, 141
Coleridge, Samuel Taylor, 1
Coles, Robert, 64, 158–59
College Board, 12
Collins, Regina, 41, 97, 120
Comer, Denise, 98
Commission on the Assessment of Student
  Outcomes (CASO), 93–97
Common Core State Standards, 71
communication, 5, 9, 31, 51, 54, 59, 65,
  67, 74, 91, 95, 109–11, 144, 148, 149,
  150, 161, 168, 170–71, 175–76
comparative studies, 136
Condon, William, 22, 50, 74, 87
Conference on College Composition and
  Communication (CCCC), 4, 20, 158
confidence interval (CI), 59, 118–20, 150,
  170, 174
Connors, Robert J., 138
consensus models, 170, 175
consequence, 9, 21–22, 38–39, 43, 48–49,
  63–64, 68, 82–84, 86–87, 89, 98, 141,
  149, 152, 154–56, 159, 162, 166–67,
  170–71, 175. *See also* bias; fairness

Consortium for the Study of Writing in
  College (CSWC), 129–31
Consortium of Doctoral Programs in
  Rhetoric and Composition, 5–6, 114
construct, 5, 7–9, 13, 16–18, 21, 22, 28–33,
  35, 37, 40–45, 49–53, 55, 57–62, 64,
  66–68, 70–79, 81–90, 92–95, 98, 100,
  102–4, 106–10, 118, 123–24, 126–27,
  129, 132–34, 136, 139–40, 151–54,
  156–59, 161–62, 164, 168, 170–76
construct articulation, 90
construct coverage, 72, 82, 85, 88
construct definition, 152
construct domain, 77, 118
construct interpretation, 84
construct irrelevance, 40, 171
construct mapping, 76
construct modeling, 8, 28–30, 35, 37, 50,
  53, 57, 60, 68, 76, 84, 87–88, 98, 136,
  152, 171–75
construct representation, 22, 30, 32,
  40–41, 44, 72, 76–77, 84–86, 90, 123,
  126, 128, 132–33, 156, 171–72
construct sample, 22, 77–78, 85–89, 109,
  129, 156, 159, 170–73, 175–76
construct span, 8, 55, 61–62, 72–74
construct underrepresentation, 118, 171
construct validity, 41, 44, 171
constructed response, 76–79, 90, 97, 103,
  123, 126, 134, 151, 171, 173
constructive alignment, 36, 54, 70, 72,
  110, 162, 171, 173. *See also* Biggs, John;
  Tang, Catherine
Consultant Evaluator Service, 23
contextual justification, 157
Cooper, Charles, 42
Cooper, Marilyn, "Ecology of Writing," 31
Coppola, Nancy, 10, 20, 60–61, 90
Corbett, Edward P.J., 74
core competencies, 51–52, 59–60, 65, 68,
  90–92, 97–98, 101–3, 106–8, 171–74
correlation analysis, 113, 123–24, 152
Corrigan, Julie A., 22, 68
cost effectiveness, 89, 152, 159–60, 171,
  175
Coughlin, Elizabeth, 41
Council of Writing Program
  Administrators (CWPA), 4, 13, 16, 35,
  61, 71–74, 87, 112
Coursera, 98
Craig, Jennifer, 14, 55
criterion measure, 115, 152, 171
criterion variable, 124, 136, 163
criterion variable identification, 136
Cronbach, Lee J., 28, 81, 83, 88–89